OP

YALE HISTORICAL PUBLICATIONS

David Horne, Editor

MISCELLANY 64

Published under the direction of
the Department of History from the income of
the Frederick John Kingsbury Memorial Fund

Dakota Territory
1861–1889

A STUDY OF FRONTIER POLITICS

BY HOWARD ROBERTS LAMAR

NEW HAVEN

YALE UNIVERSITY PRESS

To LUCIA HOWARD LAMAR
and JANE HUDSPETH ROBERTS

Preface

THE AMERICAN FRONTIERSMAN reached the Mississippi Valley in large numbers only fifty years after he had crossed the Appalachians. His advance into this rich river valley represented one of the most rapid adjustments to a new environment that the world had ever seen. After 150 years of trial and error east of the Appalachians, the pioneer had perfected a technique of conquest which had subdued both nature and the Indian on a vast front. But what had been merely a technique of survival during a temporary pioneer phase often had lasting effects: the means sometimes became the end, and the pioneer spoke in glowing terms of his enforced self-sufficiency, his lack of neighbors, and his political and economic independence. Pioneering had become a way of life with highly desirable moral, social, and political qualities.

Yet the Mississippi Valley settler was an expert operating in too restricted a field, for his whole store of knowledge—whether of trail-blazing, Indian fighting, or pioneer farming—dealt with a forest environment; and when he came to the "oak openings" of the Illinois prairie or the Black Belt plains of Alabama and Mississippi, he bypassed them for twenty years because he did not realize their agricultural value. Similarly, when he came to the Great Plains west of the Mississippi River, he chose to ignore the whole region and pushed on to Texas, California, and Oregon.

The Mexican War, gold discoveries in California, the Mormon experiment in Utah, and the expansionist spirit of the country—the latter dignified by a rationale about manifest destiny—focused new attention on the possibilities of settlement in the entire trans-Mississippi West. Even the Great Plains began to look more inviting. By 1850 explorations had proved that Major Long's Great American Desert was more legendary than real; successful farming of the Illinois and Iowa prairie sections had changed prevailing opinions about the agricultural potentialities of the lands west of Iowa, Missouri, and Minnesota. Rumors of transcontinental railroads and irrigation canals threading the Plains region helped to convert many a skeptical farmer to the belief that the Plains could

vii

be farmed, and in the mid-fifties speculators in the boom town of St. Paul, Minnesota, began taking up lands in the Red River Valley of the North and along the Big Sioux River in anticipation that settlers would appear there in the near future. Merchants and speculators of St. Louis and Dubuque, Iowa, laid claims to town-sites on the Missouri above Sioux City, just as others were doing on a much vaster scale in the Kansas region west of Missouri. On a thousand-mile Plains frontier, then, stretching from southern Kansas to the Canadian border, a huge settlement boom was in progress.

To populate this new frontier, however, the forest man had to develop a new set of techniques. Would this new method of conquest, like the former, come to represent a way of life? And if it did, what would be the characteristics of the new plains society? Would it produce a new degree of individualism, a new level of aggressive self-confidence that would find expression in a dozen Davy Crocketts? Would the new frontier foster or prevent slavery? In the political field would there be a fresh crop of Jeffersonian and Jacksonian democrats, or would the traditions of American democracy be modified by this new environment? These were questions which a contemporary historian of the period would have had to ask and a present-day student of the period must answer.

The first major attack on the Plains wilderness was made in Kansas and Nebraska, but the momentous question of slavery made the political situation there a particularly abnormal one. The second attempt was made in Dakota Territory where, during the Civil War, a few hardy settlers braved Indians, drought, and grasshopper plagues to take up homesteads under the law of 1862. There in Dakota, as in Kansas and Nebraska, a new technique of conquering nature and controlling the Indian was worked out between 1861 and 1889. It has been with the idea of treating a territory whose history fell within this last neglected period, that I have undertaken a study of politics in Dakota. This very large unit—at the time of its organization it included North and South Dakota and parts of Wyoming and Montana—contained no less than three distinct types of frontier settlements within its borders. In the southeast, along the Missouri River, a diversified agricultural frontier developed, while northern Dakota possessed an intensively commercialized agricultural frontier characterized by bonanza farming. In the Black Hills to the southwest a mining frontier appeared. The settlement and political development of these three regions took place under conditions so different from those of earlier frontiers that the settler's traditional views of government and politics were considerably altered.

It is one of the themes of this study that government, both federal and local, was a highly important factor in making the settlement of Dakota possible; therefore, to understand the nature and history of this last agricultural and mining frontier, the settler's concept and use of government must be closely examined. The distinction should be made, too, that it was the settler's use of government on the spot, and not necessarily a government policy, which was the key factor in settlement, and for that reason this study concentrates upon Dakota politics and confines a discussion of the territorial policy of the federal government to the Introduction.

The approach from a political point of view has been selected for a second reason. The farmer of the Great Plains, in which the Dakotas lie, has been called the instigator of many of the radical political movements that occurred in this country after 1865. The basic provocation for his actions was the severe economic maladjustment in agriculture, caused in part by overexpansion, in part by the new system of large-scale capitalism which came to dominate the American economy after the Civil War. In attempting to fight the "interests," the term he used to designate the new capitalism, the western farmer employed almost every new political idea and plan of governmental reform in vogue at the time. This effort to solve an economic and social problem by political means has been termed by some reactionary—that is to say, the farmer wished to return to a past golden age of agriculture when he ruled the country. Others have called the farmer's actions radical, since he tried to make use of combinations, just as the new capitalism had done, and went even further by suggesting state control or ownership of railroads.

What is suggested here is that the Dakota settler and farmer had developed political precedents during the territorial period which made a political approach to an economic problem neither reactionary nor radical, but logically dictated by these precedents in combination with his new environment. The patterns which were developed by the Alliance Movement, the Populist party, and later the Non-Partisan League had been designed in no small part by frontier experiences unknown to the forest man. Such patterns are still adhered to in North Dakota today, where state-owned warehouses, state-owned grain elevators, and farm insurance companies are operated by a semisocialistic state government. One of the chief concerns of this study will be the origins of these significant patterns.

Originally prepared as a doctoral dissertation at Yale University, where it was awarded the George Washington Egleston Prize, my study has benefited immeasurably from the wise counsel and pertinent criticisms of Ralph H. Gabriel. James T. Babb, Archibald Hanna, and the staff of the Yale University Library made the newly acquired manuscripts and newspapers of the William Robertson Coe Collection of Western Americana available even before they were catalogued. Similarly, the officials of the National Archives in Washington were unstinting in their efforts to unearth for me the many and often obscure materials relevant to this study. I will always be indebted to the hospitable people of the two Dakotas who made my research visits in those states so pleasant and profitable in 1948. Among them I must mention Will Robinson and Mrs. Mabelle Patrick of the South Dakota State Historical Society at Pierre; Russell Reid and Mrs. Florence Davis of the State Department of History of North Dakota at Bismarck; and Mr. and Mrs. Frank Martz, formerly of Carrington, North Dakota. Mrs. Fred V. Cahill, Jr., has done more than yeoman service in preparing the final manuscript. Finally, I am indebted to the Morse Fellowship Committee of Yale University and to the Yale University Department of History for a research grant and a year's leave of absence, which allowed me to revise and complete the manuscript, and for assistance in its publication.

H. R. L.

Silliman College
Yale University
September 1956

Contents

Illustrations

Maps

Introduction. Territorial Policy of the

United States: 1789–1889

> Our colonial system did not begin with the Spanish War; the United
> States has had a colonial history and policy from the beginning of the
> Republic; but they have been hidden under the phraseology of "inter-
> state migration" and "territorial organization."
>
> *Frederick Jackson Turner*

ONE OF THE supposedly unique accomplishments of the American
federal system has been its solution of the age-old "colonial problem" through the adoption of the Northwest Ordinance of 1787.
This famous document embodied a plan by which western land
areas not possessing the rank of states but politically subordinate
to the federal government could become full-fledged states in the
American union after certain conditions of settlement had been
met. By guaranteeing that colonial or territorial status would be
temporary, and by providing an escape hatch to statehood, the
authors of the Ordinance of 1787 hoped to prevent the rise of
separatist political sentiment in the American West.

The success of their plan of prevention has been adequately
demonstrated by the results. For 125 years the territorial system
remained the American pattern of government and administration
for its unsettled land possessions. In reviewing the first hundred
years of the system, Lord Bryce justly wrote that "the American
scheme of Territorial government, though it suffers from the occasional incompetence of the Governor, and is inconsistent with
democratic theory, has in practice worked well, and gives little
ground for discontent even to the inhabitants of the Territories
themselves." [1]

Bryce's modest but kindly verdict contrasts strongly with the
fulsome praise heaped upon this document by scholars and politicians since 1787. Judge Timothy Walker declared on its fiftieth

1. James, Lord Bryce, *The American Commonwealth* (New York, 1889), p. 560.

1

anniversary that "it approaches as nearly to absolute perfection as anything to be found in the legislation of mankind, for after the experience of fifty years it would perhaps be impossible to alter without marring it," and in a splendid burst of Middle Period oratory added, "it is one of those matchless specimens of sagacious forecast, which even the reckless spirit of innovation would not venture to assail." [2] A hundred years later Theodore Pease was to tell the Mississippi Valley Historical Association that "the devil's advocate may be allowed to say everything that can be said in its disfavor, and when he has done his worst, its sanctity will still prevail beyond all doubt." [3] When the six states carved from the Old Northwest celebrated the Ordinance's one hundred and fiftieth birthday in 1937, no criticisms passed the lips of the many speakers who eulogized the document. Most American history texts have provided a more sober yet sympathetic echo to these praises by simply noting that a successful territorial system established by the Ordinances of 1784 and 1787 quietly functioned until 1912, when the last of the inland territories, Arizona and New Mexico, entered the Union as states.

In the midst of such ringing filiopietistic honor, similar to that reserved for the Declaration of Independence and the Constitution, one is tempted to ask what precisely *was* the Ordinance of 1787, and *did* it function as successfully as the praise of it indicates? [4]

By the law of 1787, a territory could achieve political equality by going through three stages. In the first, a governor, a secretary, and three judges—all appointed by Congress—were to have almost arbitrary governing powers over federal territories, since only Congress was to exercise a veto curb over their decisions. The governor and the judges could write a code of laws by borrowing piecemeal from the laws of the older states. Thus the executive and the judiciary combined to constitute the legislative branch in this first stage.

The second period of political apprenticeship could be achieved

2. Timothy Walker, "Annual Discourse," *Transactions of the Historical and Philosophical Society of Ohio, 1*, Pt. 2 (1839), 189.

3. Theodore C. Pease, "The Ordinance of 1787," *Mississippi Valley Historical Review*, 25 (1938), 168.

4. For the text of the Ordinance see Francis N. Thorpe, *The Federal and State Constitutions* (Washington, 1909), 2, 957–62; see also pp. 963–4 for the provisions of its reenactment by the new Congress of 1789.

as soon as the territory—or a district therein—could boast of a population of five thousand inhabitants. Then a bicameral assembly elected by the landowners of the district could be convened as the law-making body of the region and a nonvoting delegate could be elected by this assembly to represent the territory in Congress. Even so, the assembly had very limited powers, since Congress had to approve the members of the upper house or council in much the same way that the old colonial councils were approved by the king, and the assembly laws could be vetoed both by the territorial governor and by Congress.

When the population of a district had reached sixty thousand, however, the free citizens could write a constitution, form a state government, and apply for entrance into the Union with all the rights and privileges of the original thirteen states. This bright promise of eventual equality, it was hoped, would exorcise the specter of a second American revolution in the West.

This admirable political scheme of future territorial equality represents only one facet of the Ordinance, however, for the Congress which formulated it was a very different body from the one which had passed Jefferson's unusually liberal Ordinance of 1784. In the election of 1786 more conservative members had been returned, and to them—and their colleagues who were to write the Constitution—must go the credit for instituting the American Thermidor. Composed of good men of property, this last Confederation Congress regretted that "banditti" had illegally homesteaded on rich Ohio lands, and they feared the precedent it seemed to establish. These same conservatives had shuddered at the news that Captain Daniel Shays and an army of debtors were marching on Boston in 1786. To protect their investments and holdings in future periods of unrest, they included in the Ordinance adequate legal protection for private property; they clarified the method of its conveyance from one to another; and they declared the sanctity of private contract in a clause which was deemed so important that it was copied into the Constitution by the convention meeting in Philadelphia that same summer.[5] The conservative tenor of these clauses, and in-

5. Part 1 of the Ordinance concerns the law of descent and conveyance of estates, while Part 3, Article II deals with private property and contracts. Thorpe, *Federal and State Constitutions*, 2, 957–62.

deed, of the whole document, was clearly demonstrated by Richard Henry Lee's remarks to George Washington in a letter concerning the Ordinance. "It seemed necessary," he wrote, "for the security of property among uninformed, and perhaps licentious people, as the greater part of them who go there are, that a strong toned government should exist, and the rights of property be clearly defined." [6]

If one were to judge the new system merely by its form and by Lee's interpretation of its purpose, it would look as though Congress had revived the old British colonial order of weak legislatures and appointed governors and nonvoting agents. If one were to look to the clauses on property and voting qualifications, it would appear that the conservative large landowner might gain both economic and political control of the Northwest. But the authors, like Jefferson in 1784, also remembered the lessons of the Revolution and the nature of frontier settlements and so included a Lockean compact of perpetual union between the Northwest and the states, as well as a bill of rights allowing for freedom of religion, writ of *habeas corpus*, right of bail, the observance of just fines and imprisonments, trial by jury, proportionate representation in the assembly, and the preservation of liberty and property. What is more, a mixture of New England conscience and revolutionary sentiment was to be found in clauses prohibiting slavery in the Northwest, encouraging all means of education, and providing for just dealing with the Indians. As a final sop to the politically minded frontiersman, the Ordinance promised that not one but from three to five states might be carved out of the new territory.[7]

As Congress rushed the Ordinance into law in July 1787 another body some sixty miles away in Philadelphia was drafting the Constitution. Some twelve years after the Revolution had begun, the nation's leaders simultaneously found what were to be satisfactory answers to a double riddle: how to institute national

6. Richard Henry Lee to George Washington, July 15, 1787, in James C. Ballagh, ed., *The Letters of Richard Henry Lee* (New York, 1914), 2, 425.
7. For full discussions of the Ordinance see Jay A. Barrett, *Evolution of the Ordinance of 1787* (New York, 1891); John M. Merriam, "The Legislative History of the Ordinance of 1787," *Proceedings of the American Antiquarian Society*, new ser., 5 (1889), 303–47; Pease, "The Ordinance of 1787."

self-government and how to run an empire. Fortunately, the Ordinance and the Constitution not only proved compatible but also reconciled liberty with order to a degree of success never before achieved in government.

Between 1789 and 1889 American territorial policy evolved through three stages. The first, lasting until after the War of 1812, was one of uneasy experiment in which the precedents for future policy had to be safely established. The second period, ending with the outbreak of the Civil War, was characterized by an increasing uniformity and strength of the system despite occasional collapses, as in Utah in 1857 and in Kansas between 1854 and 1857. With the triumph of the Republicans in 1860, however, an era of absolute control was initiated. From then until 1912 the government ran the territories as they would a passive group of colonial mandates, taking the protests and demands of the western citizens with a casualness that would have provoked serious rebellion in the Old Northwest.[8]

The experimental period began when Governor Arthur St. Clair proclaimed the establishment of the first government in the Northwest Territory in the small town of Marietta, Ohio, in July 1788. The new governor was an important man. An extremely capable if somewhat crochety Scot, he had served with distinction under Washington and had advanced to the rank of major general by the close of the Revolution. Always a conservative, he had been elected to the last Confederation Congress and had been its president for a time.[9]

St. Clair's fellow appointees, Secretary Winthrop Sargent and Judges James Mitchell Varnum, Samuel Holden Parsons, and John Cleves Symmes, while not so prominent politically were such large property holders in the Northwest that the first government was actually an oligarchy. As good Federalists they were more

8. Max Farrand in his excellent *The Legislation of Congress for the Government of the Organized Territories of the United States, 1789–1895* (Newark, 1896), pp. 34 ff., 45 ff., argues that legislatively only two periods existed. The first ended in 1836 with the passage of the Wisconsin Act, a detailed law in which all the previous experience was included and in which many of the principles of 1787 were changed. The second period was one of absolute control characterized by standardized organic acts and congressional legislation applicable to all the territories simultaneously.

9. William H. Smith, ed., *The St. Clair Papers* (Cincinnati, 1882), *1*, 1–256, contains a useful summary of St. Clair's life.

interested in the preservation of property than of liberty, though as governing officers they were called upon to settle as many disputes of one type as the other, and during their tenure encountered every major problem that faced administrators of all territories established subsequently. While St. Clair's long and stormy administration—it lasted from 1788 to 1802—set many important precedents and patterns, its everyday workings do not concern us here. Certain key problems—indeed weaknesses—did crop up, however, which reflected in a revealing manner some basic conflicts common to all facets of American political history; since they virtually determined territorial policy, these problems are worthy of note.

Before St. Clair had been in Ohio a year, the Constitution was ratified, Washington had become president, and Congress had reenacted the 1787 Ordinance as a part of the new federal system. Under the new government St. Clair saw himself in a position roughly parallel to that of President Washington. As his old commander's trusted friend, he was to be the chief executive for the West. In that capacity he felt it his duty to build up executive powers and thus to strengthen the federal government's shaky hold on its inland empire. Consequently, St. Clair was content to rule by proclamation and decree as much as possible and to enact a code of laws selected from the laws of the older states by the judges and himself. The first convening of a territorial assembly he viewed with both regret and terror. When after much agitation the second stage was achieved in 1799 and a legislature did meet, St. Clair, in a mournful post mortem of their actions, wrote:

> A multitude of indigent and ignorant people are ill quali-
> fied to form a constitution and a government for them-
> selves; but that is not the greatest evil to be feared from
> it. They are too far removed from the seat of government
> to be impressed with the power of the United States. Their
> connection with any of them is very slender—many of
> them having left nothing but creditors behind them. . . .
> Fixed political principles they have none, and though at
> present they seem attached to the General Government,
> it is in fact but a passing sentiment, easily changed or

even removed, and certainly not strong enough to be counted upon as a principle of action; and there are a good many who hold sentiments in direct opposition to its principles, and who, though quiet at present, would then take the lead. Their government would most probably be democratic in its form and oligarchic in its execution, and more troublesome and more opposed to the measures of the United States than even Kentucky.[10]

St. Clair's pessimistic views could have been those of an English colonial governor writing in 1763; and they were bound to be anathema to any frontier community; yet the issues which brought the Assembly of 1799 as well as succeeding legislatures into conflict with the governor were the products of a larger condition: the peculiar relation of geography and expanding settlements to political power in the American governmental system. For all his prejudices St. Clair was touching upon the same condition in the above letter.

The first of these conflicts to appear in the Northwest arose from the evolutionary nature of settlement and the economic speculation upon its probable form of development. For example, there was tremendous interest in the location of the infant territorial capital. Wherever it was placed, land values would be enhanced, important people would locate, trade would increase, and a sizable town develop. The conservative St. Clair naturally placed the Ohio capital at Cincinnati, then a stronghold of settlers from the northern and middle states who were sympathetic to his views. His decision was vigorously opposed by a southern faction living on the Virginia Military Reserve lands. They wanted the capital at Chillicothe, which was in the very heart of the Reserve. What was a local politico-economic struggle immediately took on the broader characteristics of a sectional fight between Federalists and Republicans. To some degree it was even a social war between two ways of life, for the Virginians, though they owned relatively few slaves, defended the institution of slavery and throughout the history of the Old Northwest used it to arouse emotion in order to gain practical political ends.

Another manifestation of local sectionalism occurred when

10. St. Clair to James Ross, December 1799, *St. Clair Papers*, 2, 482.

the Assembly disputed St. Clair's authority to create new counties
by executive decree. If St. Clair formed a county, its appointed
officers and its Assemblymen would be, perforce, Federalists; if
the Assembly created the unit, they would appoint Republicans.
This situation was vastly complicated by the fear on the part of
the older eastern counties that they would lose strength in the
Assembly to the newer counties (just as the older states feared
the new western ones in Congress). But this form of sectionalism
led to still another: the desire of the most western of settlements
to break away from the distant and supposedly inaccessible
government at Cincinnati, to form their own territory! Almost
before St. Clair was well in office, demands began to stream in
from Michigan, Indiana, and Illinois for separate governments.
As if this were not enough to complicate the confused political
picture, there was the most appealing of all sectional demands
to be reckoned with: the cry for "home rule" in the form of statehood. To demand the end of territorial status, to promise popularly elected officials, and to achieve the removal of hated federal
appointees whose loyalty was only to the distant central government was a magic formula which ambitious politicians of Ohio
and all succeeding territories could not resist using.

In this complex hierarchy of sectional issues the symbol of
absentee control was St. Clair and the judges, and the symbols
of autonomy and self-rule were the Assembly and the delegate to
Congress, who was elected by the Assembly. What took place in
Ohio between the meeting of the first Assembly in 1799 and
Ohio's accession to statehood in 1803 was nothing less than a
bloodless repetition of the American Revolution. St. Clair, the
"colonial governor" with his absolute veto power, was driven
from office by a popular legislature and delegate. The analogy
might even apply to details, for his opponents, the Virginians,
under the leadership of Charles Willing Byrd and Thomas Worth-
ington, even formed Committees of Correspondence, as in the
pre-revolutionary period, to keep hot the flame of popular discontent.[11] So great was the desire of the "out group" for home

11. Beverly W. Bond, Jr., "Some Political Ideas of the Colonial Period as They
Were Realized in the Old Northwest," *Essays in Colonial History Presented to
Charles McLean Andrews by His Students* (New Haven, 1931), pp. 309, 314.

rule that the Virginians in the Old Northwest pushed for statehood long before the population numbered sixty thousand; and
despite the illegality of their actions a friendly Congress, controlled by Jeffersonian Republicans, passed an enabling act in
1802 and joyfully welcomed a new and predominantly Republican
state into the Union.

The Northwest Ordinance had produced results unforeseen
by its authors. Richard Henry Lee's "strong-toned government"
had created an opposition party whose catchwords were local
autonomy, legislative supremacy, and democracy. With these
magic phrases the party succeeded in capturing Ohio and em-
bodying its wishes in the state constitution. That document,
democratic in tone, enhanced the powers of the Assembly, limited
the executive authority—particularly the governor's veto power
—and curbed the judiciary. Finally, by allying themselves with
the dominant party in Congress and ignoring the population requirements of the Ordinance, the Ohio Republicans entered the
Union in time to help reelect Jefferson in 1804. A pattern of
action, to be repeated many times by the party in power, had
been established.

Proponents of the Turner theory that the frontier experience
breeds a democratic outlook might note with interest this significant relation between democratic demands and territorial authority. The triumph of local autonomy in Ohio was the result of a
highly sophisticated campaign in which a set of professional
politicians deliberately played on a whole scale of sectional
feelings. Theirs might be called a frontier victory or further evidence of the spreading of Jeffersonian democracy, but it was no
less a partisan success achieved by the use of time-tested political
tactics familiar to Americans for a hundred years.

From the tempestuous history of the Old Northwest the federal
government drew several lessons. The first was to appoint governors who were popular as well as capable men, residents of the
West and experienced in Indian relations and frontier warfare
as well as in administration. Thus Washington, upon the creation
of the "Territory South of the Ohio River" (1794), chose a
Tennessee pioneer and political leader, William Blount, to be its

first governor. Blount's prominence in the region was second only
to that of John Sevier's, and within the region the appointment
was widely approved. For the same reasons John Adams asked
William Henry Harrison, the vigorous and shrewd delegate from
the Northwest Territory, to become the first governor of Indiana
Territory when it was created in 1800. Although Adams could
not be sure that Harrison was a Federalist, the new governor
seemed impressively qualified for the position: he had fought
with Anthony Wayne at Fallen Timbers and thus had something
of a military reputation; he had served as Secretary of the Northwest Territory and had been elected delegate to Congress, where
he had pushed a liberalized land law through Congress in 1800.
This law alone virtually guaranteed Harrison a future political
career in the West, because it allowed the settler to buy land
in 320-acre lots outright from the government and to pay for it in
easy installments.[12]

Harrison proved to be the ideal territorial governor.[13] Unlike
St. Clair, he had a remarkable talent for shifting with the political
winds. In 1800 he became an ardent Jeffersonian and thus remained in office when the Republicans came to power. When
Indiana in its early years seemed to have a majority of proslavery
settlers, Harrison allowed an indenture act to pass the Assembly.
Five years later, when Indiana had become antislavery, Harrison
willingly approved the repeal of the law that had virtually permitted slavery! [14] When more Indian lands were needed, Harrison pressed for cessions with a ruthlessness that forced Tecumseh
and the Prophet into rebellion; whereupon the intrepid governor
defeated the Indians at Tippecanoe and proceeded to win more
territory by treaty.[15] For all his political flexibility, however,
Harrison could not remove the stigma attached to federal officers,
and it is not surprising to find that statehood for Indiana was
achieved, as in Ohio, by an antigubernatorial faction led by the
popular delegate Jonathan Jennings.[16]

12. A good summary of Harrison's career as a territorial governor is Homer J.
Webster's "William Henry Harrison's Administration of Indiana Territory," *Publications of the Indiana Historical Society*, 4 (1907), 177–297.

13. R. Carlyle Buley, *The Old Northwest* (Bloomington, Indiana, 1951), *1*, 60.

14. Webster, pp. 203 ff., 211, 225–7.

15. Ibid., pp. 246 ff.

16. Buley, pp. 61–5.

Both Jefferson and Madison continued the policy of appointing popular and able westerners to territorial office. William C. C. Claiborne, a Virginian with courtly manners, winning honesty, and valuable experience as a judge in frontier Tennessee served as a successful governor of Mississippi Territory and later as governor of Orleans Territory.[17] For Louisiana Territory (renamed Missouri Territory in 1812) Jefferson selected Amos Stoddard, a learned and scholarly Revolutionary patriot who moved with such great tact that he persuaded the hostile citizens of St. Louis to accept American rule without complaint during the crucial first year.[18] Although Jefferson failed to find successful officers for Michigan Territory, which was created in 1805, Madison chose Lewis Cass, long a resident of frontier Ohio and skilled in frontier defense, to bring some semblance of government to the peninsula region.[19] Similarly, Ninian Edwards, a Kentucky judge with some military abilities, was to succeed as governor of Illinois Territory in 1809, and William Clark, an expert in Indian relations and a national hero because of his expedition with Meriwether Lewis to the Pacific, served as the governor of Missouri between 1809 and 1819.[20]

While Jefferson and his successors sought to rule the West with the most competent officials in the whole of American territorial history, Congress was hesitantly changing the Ordinance to fit the needs of experience. Until the end of the War of 1812 their policy was largely one of adjustment by passing two types of laws: (1) those meeting the westerner's demands for a more democratic system, and (2) those recognizing that special laws were needed to deal with unique conditions to be found in a particular territory.

The liberalization process began as early as 1794, when Congress allowed the Southwest Territory (Tennessee) to ignore the first stage, convene a legislature, and elect a delegate immediately.[21] A few years later Congress gave the citizens of Indiana and Mississippi permission to elect a legislature whenever they

17. See "William C. C. Claiborne" in *Dictionary of American Biography* (*DAB*).
18. See "Amos Stoddard" in *DAB*.
19. See "Lewis Cass" in *DAB*.
20. See "William Clark" in *DAB*.
21. Farrand, *The Legislation of Congress*, p. 17.

desired, regardless of the Ordinance's population requirements.[22] In 1808 Congress went even further when it began to make the delegate and the council members elective by the people instead of by the Assembly.[23] At the same time property and residence requirements for voters were successively reduced until universal male suffrage had been achieved, or voting qualifications were left up to the various assemblies.[24] Finally, the popular demands for statehood were usually heeded by Congress in this first period despite the lack of a population of sixty thousand in the territories.

Special legislation to deal with peculiar circumstances was pushed through Congress throughout the period of experiment. Congress refused to interfere with slavery in the southern territories, although the original ordinance seemed to establish the principle that it should be forbidden in all territories. Again in 1803 the acquisition of Louisiana forced Congress to give the American governor of Orleans extraordinary powers and a completely appointed council of thirteen. Congress felt that the French residents of Louisiana, though numerous enough to qualify the region for statehood, were so unused to governing themselves that a fairly arbitrary system somewhat resembling the late Spanish administration must be instituted. And to protect the property of these new citizens, American land laws were suspended and the complicated grants and titles made under French and Spanish regimes were allowed to continue in force. Even in Orleans, however, the democratic tendencies appearing in all territories soon had their effect on government. Aided, abetted, and angered by the rough pioneer Americans who flooded into Orleans after 1803, the French creoles discovered their rights as American citizens in an extremely short time; they were able to secure an elective assembly in 1805 and statehood in 1812.[25]

Another unusual problem of administration arose when Congress acquired Florida in 1819. Its citizens, like those of Orleans, were thought not to be ready for self-government. Moreover, the Seminoles and Creeks of Florida were so rebellious that Con-

22. Ibid., p. 19.
23. Ibid., pp. 25–6.
24. Ibid., p. 34.
25. Ibid., pp. 21–4.

gress appointed a military governor, Andrew Jackson, who would work in conjunction with an appointive council.[26] Unlike Orleans, it was to take Florida more than two decades to gain local autonomy through statehood.

Still a third set of unique conditions prevailed in Michigan, where the fur-trapping, partly French inhabitants remained so indifferent to the political rights to be achieved under territorial government that they remained in the first stage for more than ten years, and as late as 1818 voted down a request for an Assembly, although they were eligible for it. In such a situation Congress decided that a strong governor, supported by a completely appointive council of nine, could best administer the region.[27]

The period of uneasy experiment ended with the Anglo-American War in 1815 and the purchase of Florida in 1819. The removal of major foreign powers along the American frontier and the emergence of a genuine nationalism in the 1820's and 1830's meant that Congress and the pioneer could now concentrate on internal political and economic problems and Indian affairs without fear of interruption. In a remarkably short time the difficulties of communication with the West were solved by an orgy of turnpike, canal, and railroad building; simultaneously, the Black Hawk and Florida Indian wars and the Jacksonian policy of forced removal of the Cherokees, Creeks, Chickasaws, and other tribes ended the Indian problem east of the Mississippi. Despite gradually mounting southern protests, public lands were made steadily more available in smaller parcels and at lower prices. By 1820 the citizen could buy an eighty-acre plot for only one hundred dollars, and after a decade of special laws had set the precedent, the Preemption Act of 1841 allowed him to squat on the public domain and pay for the land only after it had been surveyed. Then, in 1854, Thomas Hart Benton's pet "graduation scheme" became law. It provided that public lands which had remained unsold for a certain number of years should be successively reduced in price until they could eventually be purchased at twelve and one-half cents an acre!

26. Ibid., p. 30.
27. Ibid., pp. 32, 34.

Such acts represented the government's complete conversion to a social land policy. But beneficent as these laws were, they stimulated unsound speculation, caused an overissue of paper money, and contributed heavily to a series of "boom and bust" cycles in the national economy. The interrelation of the issue of public land with banking, tariff, and slavery expansion questions does not concern us here, however; what does concern us is the fact that the new social policy set a whole nation on the march and brought eleven new territories into existence between 1819 and 1854: Arkansas (1819), Florida (1822), Wisconsin (1836), Iowa (1838), Oregon (1848), Minnesota (1849), Utah and New Mexico (1850), Washington (1853), and Kansas and Nebraska (1854). As cheap as land was, government receipts were so great that they more than paid for the expensive business of Indian removal and left the government with an embarrassing surplus in the 1830's.

The earlier trends toward a more democratic territorial system continued in the new regions. By 1850, territories elected their delegates, both houses of their assemblies, and most of their county officials, while Congress continued to limit and define the powers of federal officials to a surprising degree.[28] Yet a paradox existed, for Congress also exercised a constantly increasing control over the territories by standardizing their different governments and by enumerating in lengthy acts with minute detail the duties and rights of the governor, judges, and assembly. Max Farrand notes that with the Wisconsin Organic Act of 1836, the territorial system had been so perfected that all succeeding acts were but a repetition of the Wisconsin one.[29]

This close national scrutiny, undreamed of in St. Clair's time, had several unexpected and perhaps unfortunate effects:

1. It ended the necessity of appointing to territorial office high-caliber men capable of true leadership. Now that the frontier was unquestionably loyal, office seekers and party hacks, and not future presidents and national heroes, were chosen to carry out the detailed instructions of Congress. After 1830 the party in power used the system to satisfy patronage demands and as a

28. Ibid., p. 34.
29. Ibid., pp. 38–9.

means of succoring an infant branch of the party on the frontier.

2. The very perfecting and standardizing of the system also brought to the fore the deep-set sectional quarrel over slavery and the constitution of the Union. When the crisis over Missouri's admission as a slave state occurred in 1819, every citizen realized that with a Senate balanced equally between North and South, the type of institutions a territory happened to possess could virtually determine which part or which section would control the federal government. This gave Missouri—and indeed all future territories—a peculiar importance it should not have had, and it supplied the frontier politician with the golden prospect of national political interest and backing for his local ambitions. What was more tragic, it meant that the winning of a local battle over capital location, or the choice of delegates to a state constitutional convention, had national repercussions. On such petty issues the fate of the Union was to hinge between 1820 and 1860.

3. On still another count the increasing Congressional rule of territories aggravated the long standing fight between southern states-righters and northern unionists over the make-up of the Union itself. The former, fearing that the North was luring the West into the orbit of free states, argued that the national domain belonged to the states in common and not to the federal government, so that regardless of the wishes of the local frontier population or of congressional acts, the South must have an equal share of the West and must retain the right to take slaves there. When this argument failed to produce the wanted results and the Mexican War did not give the South the slave empire it had expected, southern leaders eagerly grasped the Douglas doctrine of "popular sovereignty" implicit in the Compromises of 1850 and blatantly stated in the Kansas and Nebraska Acts of 1854.

On the local level popular sovereignty represented Congress' ultimate concession in the democratization of the territorial system, but on the national level it reversed not only the wise sixty-year-old policy of ever broadening federal control but also the basic principle of the Northwest Ordinance: that a frontier territory was unfit for self-government until certain qualifications had been filled. Just as land policy was now "possession by preemption," territorial policy was reduced to "government by pre-emption." This reversal alone was folly, but to place the future of the nation itself in the hands of border ruffians, townsite speculators, and irresponsible slavery and antislavery factions roaming the Kansas prairies, and to appoint party hacks to deal with this explosive situation in 1854, was to court national disaster and go against the clear lessons of the past. Back in the 1790's Chillicothe and Cincinnati had seemed to be merely amusing symbols of sectional difference, but they had carried an undertone of warning. LeCompton and Topeka were tragic examples that the warning had been unheeded; there followed "Bleeding Kansas," the Dred Scott decision, John Brown's raid, secession, and civil war.

To say that unfortunate changes in territorial policy and the breaking of historic compromises in the 1850's were two major causes of the Civil War is but to state the obvious; the point here, however, is that the nature of the American territorial system itself aggravated sectional issues. Its unsettled evolutionary nature bred factions enamored of future office, profits, and fame. It made the use of national symbols, sectional institutions, and party labels mere weapons in the petty fights of locality against locality. For these very reasons Washington, Adams, and Jefferson had chosen strong governors to curb and channel the passions of the frontier, and for these reasons Washington had ordered Harmar to drive the "banditti" from Ohio, Jefferson had summarily arrested Aaron Burr, and Jackson had been made the military governor of Florida. Ironically, President Buchanan, who felt helpless in the face of the Kansas imbroglio, did not hesitate to use these time-honored tactics when he sent an army against the fractious Mormons in 1857, after they had driven some gentile officials from Utah and had hurled defiance at the federal government. Had such a policy been followed in Kansas, the results might have been considerably different.

Before the Civil War the nature of the territory had been a major issue of national debate, since it brought into prominence constitutional questions arising out of problems created by sectional issues, public land disposal, and Indian relations. When the Lincoln administration assumed office in March 1861, however, the American territorial system entered its third period, a less controversial but nevertheless important phase in which the territory was made to serve as an instrument to forward the nationalist policy of the Republican party. Even before Buchanan left office the Republican Congress took the time to organize the remainder of the trans-Mississippi West into territories. While the immediate purpose of this organization was to conciliate the seceding South by omitting any reference to slavery in the organic acts, at the same time the Republicans were establishing a loyal system of government to operate over the West in case of war. In a sense Republican colonial policy marked a return to the principles of 1787.

Republican advocacy of a homestead law also made it necessary to organize new territories, so that the public domain of the West could be settled by free, independent farmers whose votes would undoubtedly be cast for the right party in coming elections. It was no accident that the most ardent sponsor of the organic acts of 1861 was Congressman Galusha A. Grow, who has been called the father of the Homestead Act.

The new territories created in 1861—Colorado, Dakota, and Nevada—were related to still another feature of the nationalist program. The transcontinental railroad land grants, provided by later Congresses, necessitated the organization of the regions through which the roads were to run, for unless these lands could be purchased from the Indians, surveyed, sectioned, and sold to migrating settlers, they would be of little use to the railroads as a source of income.

Finally, the organization of the remaining western regions offered the prospect of new sources of patronage in the form of federal territorial offices, new land and post offices, army camps, and Indian agencies. Anticipation of patronage undoubtedly accounted for much of the pressure put on the Republican Congress to create these new political units at the very moment the Union was being dissolved.[30] The patronage aspect, more than anything else, in fact determined the relationship of territory and federal government between 1861 and 1890. During this time

30. See below, pp. 39 ff., 49-54.

most of the territorial governments were largely dependent upon federal funds for their very existence, and since statehood was not imminent, the territorial government assumed a permanency and importance which it had never had before 1860. The citizens of New Mexico, Arizona, Utah, Colorado, Washington, Idaho, Wyoming, Montana, and Dakota found that they had to tolerate broken-down hack politicians who were sent out as federal officers.[31] They also discovered that a majority of these officials were so inept or corrupt, or both, that territorial government was usually of a poor quality. Under these mediocre officials the western territories experienced a period of economic exploitation and administrative neglect for three decades.[32]

The State Department—which was in charge of territories until 1873—and its successor, the Interior Department, gave territorial problems only the most perfunctory attention in this third period. A clerk handled the complaints and problems that at one time occupied the full attentions of Washington and Jefferson. It seemed almost unbelievable that only a few years before, internal events in any territory could have rocked the nation.

The Justice Department also allowed the territorial judicial systems so much freedom that courts were often completely corrupt. One consequence of this lack of interest and absence of policy was that the individual congressman, with an eye on patronage, often exercised more control over these western regions and their officials than the Interior or the Justice Departments. Most officials had secured their appointments through a congressman, in fact, so that their loyalty was not to a department or to the party but to a single politician. The result was complete decentralization if not disorganization of territorial administration in the very period when it promised to be most permanent.[33]

Lack of administration policy did not mean that the territories had the freedom to follow a course of their own choosing, how-

31. Earl S. Pomeroy, "Carpet-baggers in the Territories, 1861–1890," *The Historian, 2* (1939), 53–64.

32. The administrative history of the territories for this third period is covered in an excellent study by Earl S. Pomeroy, *The Territories and the United States, 1861–1890,* Philadelphia, 1947.

33. Ibid., pp. 6–27, 51–79.

ever, for another major characteristic of federal-territorial relations between 1861 and 1890 was the absolute control which
Congress now exercised. Ever since the Wisconsin Act of 1836
Congress had passed more stringent and uniform laws, but in the
post-War decades the territories were so standardized that general
laws could be passed applying to all territories.[34]

As congressional rule grew more thorough and arbitrary, it
became more difficult for a territory to achieve statehood. Only
one state, Colorado, was admitted to the Union between 1867
and 1889, while in the territories of Dakota, Montana, Utah,
New Mexico, and Washington an entire generation grew up
under territorial rule. Although the United States never developed
a "colonial policy" for these regions, there could not fail to
develop in the regions themselves new ideas concerning local
and national government and politics. Thirty years of appointive
officers responsible only to individual congressmen inevitably
meant that territorial politics would exhibit some unusual characteristics.

Congress' exercise of control and at the same time its lack of
concern should not suggest that western problems had been
solved. On the local level, community still fought against community for the privilege of housing the territorial capital, delegates intrigued to have unpopular governors recalled, and dis-
satisfied citizens from time to time petitioned Congress to organize new territories. While these older local issues persisted,
in many sectors the existing national policies of government, land
disposal, and Indian relations broke down between 1865 and
1890. The continuing discoveries of gold and silver after 1848
in various parts of the West, for example, caused such a swift
influx of people into the mining regions that Congress could
never move fast enough to organize a territorial government.
When Governor Caleb Lyon arrived in the Idaho gold camps
to take up his duties in November 1864, he found that most of
the federal appointees had never been there. Indeed, he could
find only one judge in residence. Six months later the situation
was even worse, for the territorial secretary, C. De Witt Smith,

34. Farránd, *The Legislation of Congress*, pp. 38–9.

reported to Seward that the governor himself was absent, the secretary being the only federal officer on duty in the whole of Idaho! [35]

Lack of on-the-scene officials was just one of the many problems in the gold and silver regions, for with an agriculturally oriented colonial system and with almost no tradition of mining law, neither officials nor Congress proved competent to handle the unique legal and police problems arising in a mining community. In the anarchy that ensued the miners themselves were forced—as they had been in California in 1849—to borrow from Spanish mining law, from the meager precedents set by lead mining in Missouri and Iowa, and from the principles practiced in the agricultural claim associations that had been set up in the midwest during the 1840's.[36] Out of these customs they fabricated a highly colorful, temporarily practical, code of local laws concerning claims, water rights, and police measures. Some of them proved to be so wise that Congress later made them a part of federal mining law, but more often than not both laws and police failed so miserably that the westerners resorted to vigilante action. The old territorial structure was too rigid to deal effectively with the highly concentrated, mobile population of the various Deadwoods and Cripple Creeks of the inland West.

The miner put a strain on the governmental framework of the West, and he and the transcontinental railroads ruined the old Indian policy. When they pierced this final retreat, the time had come for the ultimate fate of the Indian to be decided. But now the problem was more difficult than ever, for the Indian no longer had any place to go. With the exception of the Pueblos and the Five Civilized Tribes, he was even less inclined to agriculture than his eastern counterpart had been. Moreover, the western Indian was under less restraint from the whites, and in many cases they were effective, even formidable fighters. The Plains Sioux, mounted on their swift ponies, could strike and disappear so quickly that few lumbering United States cavalry units could ever catch them. As late as 1864 General John Pope,

35. Caleb Lyon to William H. Seward, Lewiston, Idaho Territory, August 10, 1864; in U.S. Dept. of State Territorial Papers, Idaho Letterbook, *1*, National Archives. C. De Witt Smith to Seward, Boise City, April 15, 1865, ibid.
36. See below, Chap. 5.

an army officer with much frontier experience, predicted that the Plains tribes would never be conquered.[37] Finally, the tribes now west of the Mississippi represented the most extreme gradations of cultural difference. While the Civilized Tribes of Oklahoma were painfully but successfully imitating their American masters, but a few hundred miles to the southwest wild Comanches and Apaches rode unchecked, raiding and killing both Indians and whites. In turn, the Pueblo and Navajo were extremely different from the warlike Sioux and Cheyenne of Dakota, Wyoming, and western Nebraska; and the latter Indians, proud and powerful and constantly at war, contrasted strangely with the pitiable Diggers of Utah and the salmon fishing tribes of the Far Northwest. It was no wonder that the government had difficulty in discovering a new and workable Indian policy.

As disparate as they were in abilities and cultures, the forest, plains, and desert Indians alike reacted with fury to the last white invasion. For nearly thirty years there was a constant series of Indian skirmishes and outbreaks which kept the American army busy until at the feeble battle of Wounded Knee in December 1890 the Indian finally surrendered to the white man.

This general hostility of the tribes after 1865 forced Congress to work out some satisfactory destiny for its unhappy "domestic dependents." But it was to be a slow and painful process lasting until the passage of the Dawes Act in 1887, for the debate over policy was as embittered and complicated as the Indian question itself. Certain reform and humanitarian groups in the East demanded a humane peace policy which envisaged the education and eventual civilization of the Indian. The public at large remained skeptical of the Indian's capacity for civilized life, while at the same time it hesitated to demand extermination. Westerners, on the other hand, in their passionate hatred for the Indian were more intent on absolute control (and stern retributive measures should the Indian refuse to obey) than they were on discovering proper civilizing methods. Yet even they did not condone the complete destruction of the race. Thus the West

37. General John Pope to E. M. Stanton, Milwaukee, February 6, 1864, in U.S. Dept. of Interior Indian Division, Letters Received from War Department, National Archives.

wanted the Army to take charge of Indian affairs but did not agree with certain Army extremists who urged that tribes be treated as a sovereign, foreign, warring enemy who should be annihilated. The Indian Bureau held still another view. It fought vigorously against its transfer to the War Department and resisted the demands of both the eastern and western reformers. The tragic result was that in such a many-sided fight no single policy ever gained complete acceptance.[38]

Fortunately for the Indian the first round of debate was won by the humanitarians. A Congressional committee had reported in 1865 that most Indian wars were caused by outrageous acts committed by frontiersmen against the tribes; moreover, a star-studded Indian Commission, created in 1867 and including Generals Sheridan, Terry, and Harney, urged in its report that a series of useful reforms, new laws, and periodic inspections be enacted and that more competent agents be found. Congress shied away from many of these healthy steps, but it did accept a proposal to concentrate the Indians on two large reservations and to keep them away from the main channels of white migration. One reserve was to be located in the existing Indian Territory (Oklahoma) and the other west of the Missouri River and north of Nebraska and Colorado.[39] Shortly thereafter, President Grant, under pressure from influential Quakers and tractarians, adopted a so-called "peace policy" when he entered office in 1869. This new program gave religious groups the power to appoint honest agents for the various reservations and created a Board of Indian Commissioners consisting of philanthropists and reformers whose purpose was to survey the Bureau's activities and particularly to oversee the purchase and disbursement of Indian supplies. It was hoped that under the eyes of such a commission the Indians could at last be justly treated.[40]

38. Loring Benson Priest, in his *Uncle Sam's Stepchildren: the Reformation of United States Indian Policy, 1865–1887* (New Brunswick, 1942), pp. 23 ff., has found that the debate over transferral of the bureau to the War Department was so bitter that it held up reform measures for a decade.

39. Laurence F. Schmeckebier, *The Office of Indian Affairs, Its History, Activities and Organization* (Baltimore, 1927), pp. 53–4, has a convenient summary of their recommendations. For the full report see the Commissioner of Indian Affairs, *Annual Report, 1868*, Washington, 1869.

40. For a very good summary of Indian policy see Priest, *Uncle Sam's Stepchildren.*

From the outset the "peace policy" was a failure. The clergy-men or their appointees often proved to be poor agents; the westerners became enraged at the sentimental paternalism which seemed to characterize the policy. In many cases the church agents had to be replaced with army officers in order to restore discipline on the reservations. As raids and small wars continued, the government, while refusing to subject the Indian to exclu-sive military control, did begin to break up the large reservations, for the smaller the agency, the easier it was to watch the tribe. Finally, the government initiated a program frequently suggested but never before tried. The new theory was that in order "to save the individual Indian, the race must be destroyed." [41] The first step came when, in 1871, Congress dropped the unrealistic practice of treaty-making with the Indians, and with it went the concept that the tribe was a "domestic dependent nation." Like the territory, the Indian was now to be under the complete domination of the federal government.[42] Between 1871 and 1887, barring the intermittent wars, he was segregated on small reserva-tions, given food and clothing, and curbed in an ever-increasing number of ways by agents and by the presence of army detach-ments.

The final evolution of policy occurred when the government began to bring certain Indians into the sphere of white society. Indian education, which had been a farce until 1871, became an important plank in the new program after that year. Then in 1875 Congress allowed certain Indians to homestead if they so wished, and eight years later it created a Court of Indian Offenses to try red men who broke the rules of the Indian Office. Three years after the creation of this special court, they were made to answer in regular courts for certain criminal acts.[43] The move to place the hand of authority on the shoulder of the individual Indian culminated in the most significant development in Indian-white relations for three hundred years: the dissolution of the tribal unit by allotting the Indian land in severalty. This act served a multiple purpose: it made the Indian responsible for his

41. Ibid., p. 145.
42. Schmeckebier, pp. 58 ff.
43. Ibid., pp. 70–8.

own livelihood and it forced him to earn it by agriculture. This type of subsistence supposedly made him an independent yeoman, just as the Homestead Law supposedly perpetuated Jefferson's ideal of a free, self-sufficient citizen who was the backbone of the Republic. The severalty policy, its advocates hoped, would also civilize and christianize him and bring him into white contact. The new approach, embodied in the Dawes Act of 1887, was hailed as the final answer after three centuries of questioning. The Indian, decimated by disease and war, was, in the eleventh hour of his destiny, to be preserved by his masters.

As one can easily surmise, Indian policy—unlike territorial policy—throughout this final period was heavily debated by reformers, politicians, army men, newspapers, and private citizens. The brutal Comanche raids in Texas, Red Cloud's War in Wyoming, Custer's last stand, and Chief Joseph's remarkable anabasis in 1877 all dramatically placed the Indian question on the front page, while the continual revelations of corruption and Indian rings in the Indian Bureau, the failure of the peace policy, the appearance of Mrs. Jackson's eloquent *A Century of Dishonor* (1881), and the Indian Rights Association kept at least a part of the public stirred up for either a humanitarian or an extermination program.

Yet perhaps the most effective determinants of policy were the western settlers and the Indians themselves. The latter could not resist the urge to rebel as they saw the buffalo deliberately slaughtered, their land occupied, and the tribesmen debauched by liquor. Their rebellion inevitably led to defeat; their defeat to more control, and to the conclusion—since genocide would never be condoned—that the Indian was a ward of the nation. The western citizens, on the other hand, exerted pressure on local federal officials, or worked through their congressmen or delegates so effectively that they shared a large responsibility for the policy eventually carried out between 1865 and 1890. Barring periodic investigations and reforms, the Indian relations of a particular region were determined by the views of the local politicians and citizens. The Mormons, for example, practiced a peace policy toward the Utah tribes long before the national policy began in 1869. The local officials of New Mexico, while wishing to kill every Apache, considered the Pueblos as peaceful semicitizens. A large number of Coloradans so violently condemned Chivington's heartless massacre of Indian women and children at Sand Creek in 1864 that their position became a political issue in Colorado elections for several years. While it was true that they hated the Indian with an abiding passion, they sometimes disagreed with General Sherman that the good Indian was a dead one, for he was, after all, a major market for the western farmer and rancher, whose grain and cattle the government purchased to feed the treaty Indians. Further, the presence of the Indians in such large numbers meant the presence of large cash annuities and of soldiers to keep order. Pursuing a course that smacked of the diabolic, the West alternated between screams for army protection and demands for the restoration of peaceful relations.[44] It is not surprising, therefore, to find westerners, particularly in Dakota and New Mexico, united in their dislike of the Indian but at the same time willing to tolerate both the peace policy and the Dawes Act. The latter proved popular, since it not only preserved the Indian but also cut down the size of existing reservations, thus throwing open millions of acres of new lands to white settlement.[45]

It was with this problem of the disposal of the last free lands that the government experienced its third set of colonial difficulties. Here as elsewhere, new conditions rendered the knowledge of the past largely useless. The Homestead Act of 1862, passed as the ultimate concession to the pioneer's constant cry for free land, was of limited value in the semi-arid West, where it often took a thousand instead of one-hundred-sixty acres to

44. General William T. Sherman, on a tour of the West in 1866, sent several members of the Cabinet a graphic description of the reasons why the westerners wanted military protection. Sherman cited one "Captain Craig" as a typical example of the pioneers settling in the Huerfano River Valley. Craig had proved that he could produce grain but could find no market for it. "The miners of Colorado, two hundred miles distant will take some, but the cost of hauling is enormous. The few travellers and stage companies will buy a little, but he and all situated like him look to our military for a market, and that is the real pressure for garrisons and an Indian war. The Utes are harmless and peaceable, and the Cheyennes and Arapahoes are off after the Buffalo. God only knows where, and I don't see how we can make a decent excuse for an Indian war." Sherman to U. S. Grant, W. R. Stanton, and O. H. Browning, Ft. Lyon, Colorado Territory, in U.S. Dept. of Interior Indian Division, Colorado Indian Affairs.

45. Priest, *Uncle Sam's Stepchildren*, pp. 192–3.

farm or ranch successfully. Moreover, a lack of timber, water, and other resources, forced the western farmer to depend heavily upon eastern goods and supplies. He needed to be a small capitalist, and often a specialist as well, to live profitably on the lands of Dakota, Wyoming, or New Mexico.[46] At the very moment the dream of the self-sufficient farm had been enacted into law, the western environment rendered it void, and developments in communication and industry made for a truly national, interdependent economy. As a result, the western settlers of the plains and highland parks had to devise new laws governing water and range rights, purchase expensive machinery, and farm on a scale that would have shocked the farmers of a generation before. They also began to take interest in fantastic irrigation projects and to listen to Major John Wesley Powell's theories on water rights and correct land use. They persuaded Congress to enact new laws, such as the Timber Culture Act of 1873, the Desert Land Law of 1877, and a Minerals Land Act in 1878. While many of these laws cloaked large-scale land speculation schemes, they also represented the westerner's crying need for a more intelligent land system.

Forced to improvise mining laws, exercise the harsh prerogatives of vigilante justice, preempt lands illegally, revolutionize farming techniques, and shape a confused, unrealistic Indian policy to serve their own ends, the territorial pioneers after 1860 sought answers in locally conceived social, economic, and political policies of their own, and in statehood movements that stemmed from a time-honored desire for local autonomy.

The third territorial period and the frontier itself closed when the last pioneers achieved this final wish. By 1888 the territorial West had become so fully settled and had so completely met the requirements for statehood that neither Congress nor either major party could any longer ignore western demands. Accordingly that body passed the Omnibus Bill of 1889, allowing North and South Dakota, Washington, and Montana to enter the Union. Some echoes of the old sectionalism were heard when various senators argued that their joint entrance would not upset the existing balance of power in Congress, for Washington and

46. Walter Prescott Webb, *The Great Plains* (New York, 1931), chaps. 8, 9.

Montana were Democratic and the Dakotas were Republican in their politics. A year later Idaho and Wyoming gained entrance, to be followed by a recently virtuous and monogamous Utah in 1896. The old American empire was being liquidated just as the agitation for an overseas one was to find expression in the Spanish-American War. In 1907 Oklahoma, once the heart of Indian country, became a state; five years thereafter President Taft rounded out the Union by declaring New Mexico and Arizona Territories to be the forty-seventh and forty-eighth states. There was real cause for celebration: the first American colonial system, though constantly amended, abused, and ignored, had somehow been a success.

Chapter 1. Background to Political Organization: 1855–61

> The West is a rich museum of political forms and experimentations
> that will reward study.   *Frederick Jackson Turner, 1897*

> The history of the Northwest presents examples of all the forms of early
> extra-legal organizations for government so characteristic of the frontier.
>   *Joseph R. Star, 1928*

THE MISSOURI RIVER was to 19th-century Americans what the Mississippi had been to their forefathers in the 18th century: a crooked, muddy avenue to exotic adventure, profits, and empire. An Indian legend reported by La Harpe and Du Tisné in 1719 said that the Missouri led to the Pacific, and for nearly a hundred years thereafter French and British explorers, among them Vérendrye, swarmed along its sprawling course in efforts to prove the legend or to find new sources of furs. Its mystery interested Jefferson in projects for its exploration for a decade before he saw his wish fulfilled in the Lewis and Clark Expedition. And the reports of these two men started a new era in the fur trade. Between 1806 and 1850 Spaniards from St. Louis, Frenchmen from Quebec, Scots and Britons from Hudson's Bay and Montreal, and Americans working either as "free traders" or *engagés* for a dozen fur companies sailed, rowed, keeled, or steamed their way up the Missouri. In less than fifty years they were to strip the "shining mountains" and the plains of their animal wealth and to pave the way for the farmer and the miner.

Sometimes these trappers were accompanied by army topographical engineers who tried to chart the course of this erratic stream which meandered diagonally across the Dakota plains. Sometimes Indian agents, armed with a trunkful of medallion likenesses of the incumbent president and a sheaf of blank treaties of friendship and trade, shared the journey upstream. Often an intrepid naturalist like William Bradbury joined a trapping expedition to seek out new species of flora. Scores of adventurers, hunters, traders, and writers found their way up

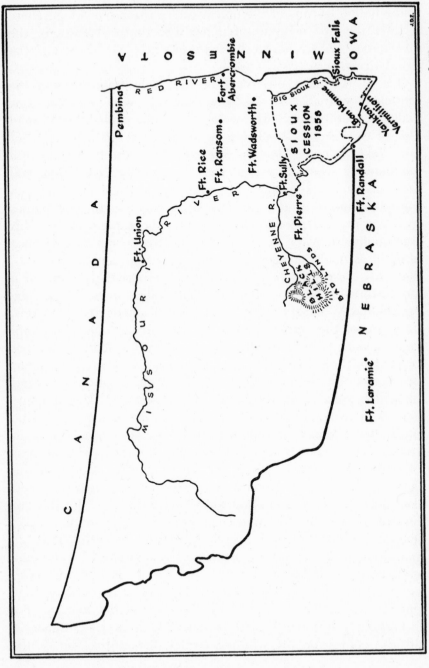

Dakota Territory at the time of its organization in 1861. It included parts of the future territories of Montana and Wyoming.

and down the Missouri during these years. From their reports the young nation learned of the northwestern reaches of its purchase of 1803; the citizen became familiar with the warlike Sioux, the treacherous Arikara, those shrewd traders the Mandans, and the proud Crow.

One of the most observant of the early travelers was the gentleman-journalist H. M. Brackenridge, who joined a fur-trading expedition in 1811 which was commanded by Manuel Lisa of St. Louis. (Brackenridge wisely took along a copy of Lisa's favorite book, *Don Quixote*, to read to the temperamental commandant when he was angry.) The trip to Fort Union and back was for Brackenridge a fascinating experience. From his pen poured accounts of the ruthless wars between fur companies operating in the Upper Missouri country; he wrote frankly of his disappointment when he found the Indians, whom he had once admired as noble savages, to be filthy, bestial, and treacherous. With just the right touch of mystery he reported the ruins of a "pre-historic fort" at Bon Homme Island and commented upon the legend that Welsh-speaking Indians lived among the Mandans. He spoke of the curious prairie dog whom he found "insignificantly fierce"; he was awed by the fact that the scarcity of trees forced field lark, blackbird, thrush, marten, and wren to crowd together into the branches of the willows, elms, cottonwood, and ash which grew along the banks of the Missouri. The antelope seemed so swift and beautiful in its "man-like flight" across the prairie that it reminded him of the African gazelle mentioned in Arabian poetry. But Brackenridge saved his most lyrical passages for the scenery itself. Along the lower part of the river the black earth seemed enormously fertile. To him the uplands looked like "old fields" and the bottoms like "rich meadows." Further up the stream he found the prairie grass "short and close, of a deep blue, and intermixed with a great variety of beautiful flowers." And although most travelers were greatly depressed by the barren look of the plains, Brackenridge, with a rare lack of prejudice, wrote in his journal one evening: "The sky is as clear as that represented in a Chinese painting. The face of the country (is) enchanting. The flowery mead, the swelling ground, the romantic hill, the bold river, the winding rivulet, the groves, the shrubberies, all disposed and arranged in the most exquisite manner." [1]

Brackenridge's account was followed by a score of others. Major Long's explorations were published; the discoveries of new routes to the Pacific by mountain men and traders were eagerly printed in Missouri newspapers; distinguished travelers such as Prince Maximilian of Wied wrote heavy volumes about their experiences in western America; Miller, Bodmer, Catlin, and other artists sketched the country and Indians—adding just enough of the Hudson River School atmosphere to guarantee a certain popularity. Still others brought back geographic facts, scientific observations, anthropological data about the Indians, and legends and tales as well.

By 1850, then, the Missouri had become a vast cornucopia pouring forth an abundance of information about itself and about the plateau through which it flowed. As varied as the information was, through it ran three constant themes: all observers were convinced that this was a land extremely different from that east of the Mississippi; they felt, too, that it would perhaps always be inhabited by the Indians, and they doubted that a white population of any size would ever settle this dry, high plateau.

In September 1855 Major Alfred Vaughan, an Indian agent on the Upper Missouri, took up the second theme in his annual report on the Indian tribes with which he dealt. Most of the report was gloomy; measles and whooping cough were taking their toll among the Indians; the majority of the tribes—some of the Mandans, Arikaras, and Assiniboines excepted—refused to farm or do work of any sort; and Vaughan predicted that all of the tribes would soon be wiped out by starvation. Already their destitute condition had caused them to resort to murder and depredation. [2]

What Major Vaughan was describing was the end of the first period of white influence on the Upper Missouri. In the fifty years after the Lewis and Clark Expedition the entire region had been invaded by trappers and traders, and by 1855 the Missouri River banks north of Sioux City, Iowa, were dotted with trading posts,

1. H. M. Brackenridge, *Journal of a Voyage Up the River Missouri* (Baltimore, 1815), p. 103; see also pp. 43, 91 ff.
2. "Alfred Vaughan's Upper Missouri Journal," 1855, MS in W. R. Coe Collection of Western Americana of the Yale University Library.

temporary picket forts erected by various army expeditions, and woodyards which furnished fuel for steamboats plying the river to Fort Union at the mouth of the Yellowstone River.[3]

The influence of these trappers and traders on the lives of the Indians of the Missouri Plateau was striking. The trappers' constant presence for a half century and their introduction of new weapons and materials caused fundamental changes in Sioux life and customs.[4] In spite of all these changes, however, the Upper Missouri Sioux tribes did not become "blanket" or "treaty" Indians who looked to a beneficent White Father for food and supplies.[5] The Indians of the Sioux Country had become partially adjusted by 1855 to the presence of the white trappers and traders. Moreover, the whites—most of them of French or French-Canadian origin—frequently married Indian women and settled down to become squaw men. By 1855 they and their half-breed offspring had become so numerous that they constituted a considerable and often very articulate faction within the tribes.[6] The presence and untiring activity of French Jesuit missionaries, who had converted hundreds of Sioux to a nominal Christianity in the 1830's and the 1840's, also contributed to the adjustment of the Indian to this new element in his society.[7] When General Phillippe de Trobiand, a French literary critic who joined the American Army during the Civil War and rose to the rank of major general, was stationed in Dakota Territory in 1867, he expressed the belief that the Indian of the Upper Missouri had achieved a sort of natural and permanent rapport with the white of French blood—a rapport

3. Hiram M. Chittenden, *The History of Early Steamboat Navigation on the Missouri River* (New York, 1905), *1*, chaps. 10, 18. See also Everett Dick, *Vanguards of the Frontier* (New York, 1941), pp. 162–75.

4. Webb, *The Great Plains*, pp. 52–68; see especially chap. 3.

5. Lucy E. Textor, *Official Relations between the United States and the Sioux Indians* (Palo Alto, 1896), pp. 70–2. Miss Textor (pp. 71–2) describes the Missouri Sioux as being still independent in 1851 and "still in possession of broad hunting grounds and, as yet, not demoralized by the pernicious system of annuities."

6. See M. K. Armstrong, *History of Resources of Dakota, Montana, and Idaho* (Yankton, Dakota Territory, 1866), p. 34; also Armstrong in the *Dakota Herald* (Yankton, D.T.), July 2, 1872, which mentions half-breeds who dealt with the whites; see also Milo M. Quaife, ed., *Army Life in Dakota, 1867–1869*, by Phillippe Regis Denis de K. de Trobiand (Chicago, 1941), pp. xxiv–xxvi.

7. Gilbert J. Garraghan, *The Jesuits of the Middle United States* (New York, 1938), *2*, 446 ff., describes the activities of Father de Smet and other missionaries among the Missouri tribes. For a good summary of the role of the missionary on the plains frontier see Everett Dick, *The Story of the Frontier* (New York, 1941), chap. 5.

which he felt the English-speaking Americans could never understand.[8]

But even this colorful trapper-trader-Indian society had begun to disintegrate by 1855. Some of the tribes had been decimated by the white man's diseases, and the introduction of whiskey had had its usual effects on the Indian.[9] There was also a noticeable decline in the amount of game available for food and for furs. Father Point, a Catholic missionary, observed that as early as the 1840's the "buffalo was gradually disappearing and the number of hunters was increasing in direct proportion to the disappearance of the animal." [10]

Paradoxically, then, the Indian of the Upper Missouri Plateau was much more sophisticated with regard to the ways and inventions of the white man in 1855, and at the same time was much worse off because of the white man's contributions to and effects on Indian life and society.[11] The same situation had occurred on earlier Indian-white frontiers, and the Indian had either been moved to a new region or eliminated. But the Sioux of the Missouri were faced by a totally new problem: by 1855 the land to the West was already scarce or occupied by the hostile Blackfeet and Cheyenne. At the same time it was popularly believed that the Upper Missouri region was unfit for cultivation, so that the Indian would be unable to turn to farming as an escape from inevitable starvation when the game should give out. This belief also raised the question which the white pioneer thought was of much more importance than the fate of the Indian: could the white man himself successfully settle the Upper Missouri? To Major Vaughan, long a resident of the Sioux Country, the answer seemed to be no. In describing the physical nature of the region to the Indian Commissioner, he wrote in his 1855 report:

> If the value of a portion of the country depends in any respect on the value of the whole, then this country for a white man is worthless. It is true a few fertile spots are seen

8. Quaife, *Army Life*, pp. 70–1, 261.

9. Garraghan, *Jesuits*, 2, 458–9. See also the "Journal of Granville Stuart," MS in the W. R. Coe Collection of the Yale University Library, for a description of the condition of the Indians around Fort Union in 1861.

10. Garraghan, 2, 451–2.

11. See Webb, *The Great Plains*, 52–68, for an account of the Plains Indian's degree of sophistication in the midnineteenth century.

in the bottoms, but they are . . . subject to be overflowed by the rise in the River [Missouri, which] renders their occupation very precarious. The fertile spots in this country are like the Oasis in the desert; around [them] is desolation and gloom. I am well aware that most new countries have been evilly reported upon from the time of Moses, when he sent the twelve messengers to spy out the promised land; they returned, ten out of the twelve gave an evil report of the country, for which we are told they were punished by detention in the wilderness for forty years, they having reported there was no soil, no timber, no water. This country fully answers their report, and in fact it will apply to the greater part of the Upper Missouri, or that portion of it inhabited by the eight bands of Sioux embraced in this report.[12]

Other observers fully agreed with Vaughan's estimate. Lieutenant G. K. Warren of the United States Topographical Engineers concluded, after exploring the "Dacota Country" with General Harney's Expedition in 1855, that land west of the ninety-seventh meridian was not fit for agricultural settlement.[13] Warren bluntly stated that "agricultural settlements have now nearly reached their western limits on our great plains; the tracts beyond must ever be occupied by a pastoral people, whether civilized or savage." [14]

Ironically enough, Warren and Vaughan were not only repeating the role of the ten Mosaic spies but reapplying Major Stephen H. Long's famous "Great American Desert" legend to the future Territory of Dakota. Warren and Vaughan's opinions, expert though they might be, left a few observers unconvinced, however, for the publicity which accompanied the organization of the Kansas and Nebraska Territories awakened new agricultural and speculative interest in the entire plains frontier. The increasingly popular ideas of a transcontinental railroad led the

12. "Vaughan's Journal," p. 12. The "eight bands of Sioux" totaled 16,000 population, Vaughan estimated. This was roughly one-half of the Indian population of the future territory of Dakota.
13. Lieutenant G. K. Warren, *Explorations in the Dacota Country in the Year 1855*, Senate Executive Document No. 76, 34th Cong., 1st sess. (1856), pp. 21–2.
14. Ibid., pp. 17–18.

negotiators of the Indian Treaty of Laramie (1851) to include
a clause which would allow a railroad to cross part of the Sioux
Country.[15] Two years later Governor I. I. Stevens, of Washington
Territory, together with a group of engineers explored the northern part of the Sioux Country between the forty-seventh and the
forty-ninth parallels to find a suitable route for a railroad line
which would run from St. Paul to the Columbia River.[16] Explorations for practicable railroad routes along the forty-first
parallel also took place.[17]

These explorations naturally aroused interest in the regions
through which the railroad was to pass. The members of the
Minnesota Territorial Assembly became so excited by the prospects of wealth which railroads and settlement would bring to
the area between St. Paul and the Upper Missouri River that they
did little after 1855 but grant charters to railroad and land companies and create paper counties and towns.[18] In commenting
upon the huge speculative schemes afoot in 1857, a Minnesota
citizen facetiously urged "that a small portion of the land be
reserved for agriculture and not all be laid out in town lots." [19]

Meanwhile the agricultural frontier was creeping slowly up
the banks of the Missouri despite the Warren and Vaughan predictions. Everett Dick has found that even in the middle 1850's
settlers hovered impatiently on the eastern fringe of the future
Territory of Dakota while waiting for the Indian lands to be
ceded. In much the same way settlers had waited on the Kansas-
Nebraska border in 1853–54.[20]

Thus by 1855 a new attitude toward the value of the Upper

15. Dick, The Story of the Frontier, p. 111.
16. I. I. Stevens, Report of Exploration of a Route for the Pacific Railroad, Near
the Forty-Seventh and Forty-Ninth Parallels from St. Paul to Puget Sound, United
States War Department Report on Pacific Railroad Explorations (Washington,
1855), Vol. 1. Stevens' enthusiastic reports interested Stephen A. Douglas as much
as the central Nebraska route reports did, Allan Nevins asserts in his Ordeal of the
Union (New York, 1947), 2, 85 ff.; see also 104–5.
17. E. G. Beckwith, Report of Exploration for the Pacific Railroad on the Line of
the Forty-First Parallel, United States War Department Report on Pacific Railroad
Explorations (Washington, 1855), Vol. 2.
18. R. J. Forrest, "Mythical Cities of Southwestern Minnesota," Minnesota History, 14 (1933), 243–62.
19. James H. Barker, "Lives of the Governors of Minnesota," Collections of the
Minnesota Historical Society, 13 (1908), 70.
20. Everett Dick, The Sod-House Frontier, 1854–1890 (New York, 1937), p. 20.

Missouri Plains Region was developing, an attitude due not so much to the actual pressure of agricultural settlers or to the decline of the fur trade as to the pressure and the interest of the land speculators and the railroad expansionist. These two latter groups were the ones who were first responsible for persuading the prospective pioneer that the future Territory of Dakota was not an inhospitable grassy plain which suffered from extremes in weather but a prairie paradise of rich farming land, healthy climate, and untold opportunities.

The glowing prospect of speculation in the Sioux Country prompted Captain John Blair Smith Todd, an army officer stationed at Fort Randall on the Missouri, to resign his commission in 1856 and form a trading company which would operate along the Upper Missouri.[21] Todd, a West Point graduate and a member of a prominent Kentucky family, had served on various Indian frontiers for twenty years, and he knew the signs of coming settlement. Indeed, this shrewd, distinguished-looking officer was so well aware of the evolutionary stages a new region passed through in the process of settlement that he made a financial profit on every new stage. He was, in fact, a classic example of the small-time "phase capitalist" who played such an important economic and political role on all American frontiers.

Although Todd had become an acquaintance of Lieutenant Warren's when both men were members of the Harney Expedition in 1855, he seems to have been little affected by Warren's adverse account of the Dakota and Sioux Country.[22] Far from agreeing with Warren or the Indian agent Vaughan, Todd became the leading advocate for the settlement of the Upper Missouri region by a white farming population. To Todd new settlements meant

21. For biographical accounts of Todd (1814–72) see *General Cullum's Biographical Register of the Officers and Graduates of the United States Military Academy* (New York, 1868–79), *1*, No. 929; C. A. Lounsberry, *Early History of North Dakota* (Washington, 1919), pp. 263 ff.; George W. Kingsbury, *History of Dakota Territory* (Chicago, 1915), *1*, 115–16; and *2*, 493–513; W. A. Goodspeed, ed., *The Province and the States* (Madison, 1904), *6*, 204, 217.

22. E. G. Taylor, *Gouverneur Kemble Warren, the Life and Letters of an American Soldier, 1830–1882* (New York, 1932), p. 25. Warren wrote in his journal that he served in Todd's company at the Indian battle of Blue Water Creek, which took place Sept. 5, 1855.

an increase not only in the demand for supplies along the Missouri but also in the number of army units which must be stationed on the frontier to protect the firstcomers from the Indians. He decided to profit from this latter development by securing the post sutlership at Fort Randall the same year that he formed his trading firm.[23]

Todd's business partner in the trading company was Colonel Daniel Marsh Frost, a wealthy St. Louis merchant, soldier, and politician who later became notorious for his attempt to seize the city of St. Louis for the Confederacy in the spring of 1861.[24] Todd and Frost had probably met at Jefferson Barracks, Missouri, in 1848 when both men were stationed there.[25] The ostensible purpose of the Frost-Todd company was to engage in the fur and store trade, but before the firm was a year old, both partners turned their interest to that second major source of wealth on the frontier: land and townsite speculation.[26]

In 1857 Todd learned that the federal government had entered into negotiations with the Yankton Sioux for the cession of a large tract of land lying between the Big Sioux and Missouri Rivers. At that time this area constituted the southwestern part of the Territory of Minnesota, but it was obvious that Minnesota would soon be admitted as a state and that this unceded portion would be excluded from the new state and made a part of a new territory. Thus if the treaty of cession were successfully concluded, there was every likelihood that the entire Sioux Country would

23. Goodspeed, *The Province and the States*, 6, 204.

24. For biographical accounts of Frost (1814–1900) see Howard L. Conard, ed., *Encyclopedia of the History of Missouri* (St. Louis, 1901), 2, 528–9; *Cullum's Biographical Register*, 2, No. 1209; Lounsberry, *Early History of North Dakota*, pp. 263 ff.; *National Cyclopaedia*, 5; J. T. Scharf, *History of St. Louis City and County* (Philadelphia, 1883), 1, 501–4; Edward Conrad Smith, *The Borderland in the Civil War* (New York, 1927), pp. 127, 151, 233, 234, 237. See also the biographical references to Todd, above, n. 21.

25. *Cullum's Biographical Register*, 1, 2. It is possible that Frost and Todd met during the Mexican War, for both men participated in the battle of Cerro Gordo and the siege of Vera Cruz.

26. Elliott Coues, ed., *Forty Years a Fur Trader on the Upper Missouri; the Personal Narrative of Charles Larpenteur, 1833–1872* (New York, 1898), 2, 306. Larpenteur implies that the Frost-Todd company seriously went into the fur trade but that it was forced to abandon several forts or posts because of a lack of furs. See also Harold E. Briggs, *Frontiers of the Northwest* (New York, 1940), p. 357.

be given separate territorial status and that settlers would pour in.[27] Frost and Todd, with the history of the recent townsite booms in Iowa, Kansas, and Nebraska fresh in their minds and with the Minnesota boom at its height in 1857, naturally became ardent sponsors of the treaty of cession. When the first treaty negotiations failed in 1857, the Department of the Interior requested Todd to take over the discussions.[28]

By enlisting the aid of Charles F. Picotte, a Yankton half-breed of considerable ability, and Theophile Bruguière, a French-Canadian "squaw man" greatly respected by the Yanktons, Todd was able to persuade the Yanktons to sign a treaty in February 1858. By this the Yanktons agreed to relinquish some fourteen million acres of land at the price of twelve cents an acre. In return the government promised annuities, the establishment of reservations and Indian schools, and all the mills and tools necessary for farming.[29]

While negotiations were still in progress, Todd, Picotte, Bruguière, Frost, and a number of frontier speculators interested in the Yankton lands formed the Upper Missouri Land Company to speculate in townsites.[30] The activities of this company were so interrelated with those of the Frost-Todd Trading Company that the new firm seems to have been only a special branch of the original Frost-Todd concern.[31] In any event the two companies worked in close cooperation. Since the Frost-Todd agents held licenses which permitted them to trade with the Indians and establish trading posts along the Missouri, the agents conveniently located these posts wherever the Upper Missouri Land Company thought a suitable townsite existed. In this way, writes Harold Briggs, the Upper Missouri Land Company "would be able to select desirable townsite locations while the region was still Indian country and not open to settlement." [32]

27. Minnesota had already fulfilled most of the qualifications for statehood in 1857. A constitution was written and the state officers were elected in that year. The territory became a state in May 1858.

28. Goodspeed, 6, 208–9.

29. For a discussion of this treaty see Textor, *United States and Sioux Relations*, pp. 141–3. For the treaty itself see *United States Statutes at Large*, 11, 743–9.

30. Moses K. Armstrong in the *Dakota Herald*, July 2, 1872. Armstrong was one of the earliest settlers of Yankton.

31. Briggs, *Frontiers of the Northwest*, p. 357.

32. Ibid.

When Congress ratified the Yankton treaty of cession in April 1858, the Frost-Todd agents had already occupied some eight townsites.[33] The company also hoped that one of its trading posts —Yankton—would be selected as the territorial capital.[34] The day that news of ratification came, in fact, company men floated logs across the Missouri River from the Nebraska side to Yankton and spent all night laying the foundations of twelve log cabins and marking off town lots.[35]

Both Frost and Todd spent the winter of 1858–59 in Washington as lobbyists for the creation of a new territory, which by common consent was already called Dakota. Minnesota had become a state in 1858, and the entire region lying within the Big Sioux, Red, and Missouri Rivers—an area as large as the state of Illinois —was left without any government. With settlers pouring in and with a dozen townsite companies other than the Upper Missouri Land Company anxious for a territorial government to legalize their actions, some sort of territorial organization was imperative. The stakes were so large by 1859, an observer reported, that unclaimed land was already difficult to find along the Missouri.[36] The Upper Missouri Land Company found itself unable to control its members with so much speculation in the air; its directors met in Yankton in the fall of 1859 and dissolved the firm. It was immediately succeeded by a new firm, the Yankton Land and Town Company, which like the other was dominated by Todd and Frost.[37]

Meanwhile the Frost-Todd settlers had resorted to the old Iowa expedient of establishing a "claim club" at Yankton to protect their holdings in the absence of any local law. Members of the club took an oath to uphold the constitution and by-laws of the organization, and in March 1860 the club exercised its judicial powers by rendering a formal decision in a claim contest.[38]

The important political aspect of the Frost-Todd company and its settlers was not the rudimentary claim-club form of govern-

33. Ibid., pp. 357–8.
34. See map, p. 29.
35. Goodspeed, 6, 210.
36. Dick, *Sod-House Frontier*, p. 33.
37. *Dakota Herald*, July 9, 1872.
38. Ibid. See Kingsbury, *History of Dakota Territory*, 1, 426–7, for discussion of "claim club" techniques which were used around Sioux City, Iowa.

ment which they organized, or the use of political pressure in
Washington to insure the success of economic ventures in land
and townsite speculation. The political significance of the company's actions lay in the realization by its leaders that the third
major source of wealth on a relatively unsettled frontier was
political office and patronage. The company and the settlers were
well aware, for example, that the treaty of cession of 1858 provided $65,000 in the form of supplies and annuities alone for the
neighboring Yankton Indians. At least part of the supplies could
be furnished by settlers if they could secure government contracts. They also knew that if Yankton were made the capital
of the new territory, the benefits of local, territorial, and federal
office would come to some of them. The fact that Congress paid
the expenses of territorial administration was still another economic attraction to politically minded settlers and speculators.
There is every evidence that the expectation of political office
brought many of the earliest and most able settlers to Yankton
and to the other settlements on the Missouri River. A comparison
of names reveals, for example, that almost every member of the
Yankton Town and Land Company secured office under the new
Territory of Dakota and that for several years they controlled
the territorial Assembly.[39] Such evidence suggests that a large
number of Dakota frontiersmen thought of the federal government not only as a paternalistic provider of land and governmental organization but also as a subsidizing agency which furnished needed development funds in the form of offices, Indian
and army supply orders, and post and land office positions. In
short, many frontiersmen joined the vanguard of settlement to
profit from the "business of government," and for that reason they
thought of economic security in political terms.

While there is no record of the detailed activities of Frost and
Todd in Washington, it is apparent that Todd, at least, was interested in the political office and preferment that the creation
of Dakota Territory would bring. In the winter of 1858–59 the
two men actually used their influence in Washington to postpone
the organization of the territory, for they feared that Sioux Falls,

39. See below, pp. 81 ff.

a townsite owned by a rival company, had a better chance of becoming the capital than Yankton.[40] A year later, however, when the number of Yankton settlers more than equaled that of Sioux Falls, they brought pressure for the immediate organization of the territory. In the fall of 1859 Todd and Frost returned to the Sioux Country and persuaded the Yankton settlers and others along the Missouri to petition Congress for a territorial organization. It is interesting to find that the settlers included within the petition the suggestion that Todd be made the first governor of Dakota.[41] Todd himself presented the petition to Congress in December 1859, but Congress took no action, since every mention of a new territory revived the slavery issue. Consequently all bills for the organization of Dakota remained in committee.[42]

While the Frost-Todd forces built log cabins and sod huts in Dakota and buttonholed Congressmen in Washington, they heard disquieting rumors about the large-scale activities of some speculators calling themselves the Dakota Land Company who had laid claim to a series of townships at or near the falls on the Big Sioux River, some sixty miles northeast of Yankton. Not content with claiming large parcels of land, they had also formed an extra-legal government complete with elections, governor, assembly, and laws.[43] This disturbing outburst of popular sovereignty at Sioux Falls seemed even more menacing to the Yankton settlers when they learned that the Dakota Land Company and its government was backed by the full support of the Minnesota Democratic party. Minnesota politicians, in turn, were urging Congress to bless the extralegal organization at Sioux Falls by making it the authorized government of the new territory.

The primary political importance of the Dakota Land Company's "squatter government" is difficult to exaggerate, but writers have so consistently mistaken the attempt for another "noble

40. Goodspeed, 6, 215.

41. M. K. Armstrong, *Dakota Herald,* July 9, 1872; see also Armstrong, *History of Southeastern Dakota* (Sioux City, 1881), p. 18.

42. Lounsberry, *Early History of North Dakota,* p. 263; see also Kingsbury, *History of Dakota Territory, 1,* 166.

43. Goodspeed, 6, 218 ff.

frontier experiment" in true democracy and so loosely compared it to the State of Franklin in Tennessee that a closer scrutiny of the Company's methods and aims is desirable for a clearer conception of its true nature.[44]

The Minnesota Territorial Assembly chartered the Dakota Land Company of St. Paul in the winter of 1856–57, along with dozens of other land companies.[45] By the charter the Dakota firm had the right to issue 2,000 shares of stock at one hundred dollars each, but because of various setbacks, such as the Panic of 1857, the company had sold only 900 shares by 1859.[46] From its very beginning the company was virtually a financial venture of the Minnesota Democratic party. Governor S. A. Medary of Minnesota Territory was a director of the company and many of its stockholders were in the Territorial Assembly.[47]

The company's first interest was to secure land in areas where a railroad might run—whether in Minnesota or in Dakota. During 1857 company officials induced the Minnesota Assembly to create four new counties in southwestern Minnesota where the company held townsite claims in the hope that they would become not only county seats but railroad towns as well.[48] Company supporters usually became county officials and located the county seats where they pleased. Although it was obvious that these counties were actually unpopulated, as political units they had a right to seats in the Minnesota Assembly and the privilege of sending delegates to the territorial Democratic convention.[49]

The Company's alliance with the fur trade element—or the

44. For two accounts of the Sioux Falls' government see "The Settlement at Sioux Falls," *Collections of the State Historical Society of South Dakota*, 6 (1912), 133–80; also Samuel J. Albright, "The First Organized Government of Dakota," *Collections of the Minnesota Historical Society*, 8 (1896), 129–47. Both accounts support the idea that the Sioux Falls government was a true democracy and was like that of Franklin.

45. *Session Laws of the Territory of Minnesota* (1857), p. 191; see also Briggs, *Frontiers of the Northwest*, pp. 350–6, for a very good résumé of the Dakota Company's settlement activities.

46. Annual report of the company quoted in "The Settlement at Sioux Falls," p. 179.

47. Goodspeed, *6*, 206.

48. R. J. Forrest, "Mythical Cities of Southwestern Minnesota," pp. 243–4. See map, above.

49. Ibid., pp. 249–50. Forrest refers (p. 245) to the St. Paul *Pioneer and Democrat* of September 16, 1857, which complained that three Dakota Land Company men were seated in the 1857 Territorial Democratic Convention without credentials.

"Moccasin Democrats" as they were derisively called—further strengthened its political position in the party. Since many of these roving frontiersmen already depended upon political dispensation in the form of licenses in order to trade with the Indians, they did not object to the new source of income to be gained from land and townsite sales and political office. R. J. Forrest has found, in fact, that in the territorial period the fur traders of Minnesota ran the local Democratic party. In the Minnesota statehood elections of 1857, for example, the Democratic candidate, General H. H. Sibley, depended heavily upon the votes of the Moccasin Democrats, and these hardy citizens obliged with so many votes from the unpopulated counties and the "mythical" towns of the Dakota Land Company that most of the ballots had to be thrown out.[50]

When it became evident that Minnesota would enter the Union, the Dakota Land Company extended its interests beyond the proposed borders of the new state. The company hoped to capture no less than the future territorial government of Dakota.[51] In the summer of 1857 the directors of the firm sent a claim party to Sioux Falls on the Big Sioux River to establish a townsite which they hoped would be the new capital of Dakota.[52] Upon their arrival, however, they found that agents of the Western Town Company of Dubuque, Iowa, had preceded them to the Sioux Falls site. The Western Town Company was a smaller and perhaps more typical boomtown firm, but its officials and agents were men of tremendous energy who were determined that Sioux Falls should not be just another paper city. At first there was friction between the two groups, and both firms established rival townsites, but later both organizations decided that the stakes involved were so large that they should pool their efforts to make Sioux Falls the capital.[53]

The Dakota Company also established townsite claims west of the Big Sioux River in what is today eastern South Dakota. So

50. Ibid., pp. 245–50.
51. Briggs, p. 351.
52. Sioux Falls had the advantage over other townsites because of its tremendous water-power potential, a large amount of timber, and rich soil.
53. Goodspeed, 6, 205–10; also Albright, "The First Organized Government of Dakota," pp. 135–6; and Dana R. Bailey, *History of Minnehaha County* (Sioux Falls, 1899), pp. 10–24.

ambitious were their plans, in fact, that Everett Dick aptly described the company's activities as a new development in town booming, since its officials had a "chain store" conception of establishing towns. The company's alleged aim was to seize "every valuable townsite that could be found on the James, Vermillion, and Wanari Rivers, and on the Missouri from the mouth of the Sioux to old Fort Lookout." [54]

In the fall of 1857 the Dakota Company persuaded the Minnesota Legislature to create Big Sioux County around its Sioux Falls townsite. Governor Medary appointed county officials, all of whom were either members of the Dakota or the Western Town Company, but there is no record of their ever having functioned.[55] The Dakota Company officials seem to have expected that if county organization could be established at the time of the creation of the new territory, this county would have the advantage of a political head start. In any event it was the company's influence that caused the Minnesota Assembly to place Big Sioux County outside the new state of Minnesota.[56]

Settlers began to appear at Sioux Falls and Yankton in the spring of 1858, but an Indian raid on a Dakota Company settlement made the settlers in the Big Sioux Valley aware that they had no protection. This situation, plus the Company's natural interest in politics, led to the organization of a "squatter government" at Sioux Falls in the fall of 1858. Of this experiment, Judge Charles E. Flandrau, who was a member of the Dakota Company, wrote, "it presents the only actual attempt to form a government on the principle of 'squatter sovereignty' pure and simple that has ever occurred in this country." [57] Actually the Sioux Falls "government" was not so unique as Flandrau claimed, nor so extensive or ambitious as that carried on by the State of Franklin. Frederick L. Paxson has noted that "there are many incidents in the history of statehood movements in which settlement has rushed forward more rapidly than legal institutions, with results

---

54. Dick, *Sod-House Frontier*, p. 43; Briggs, p. 351.
55. *Session Laws of the Territory of Minnesota* (1857), pp. 67–9; Bailey, *History of Minnehaha County*, p. 13; Goodspeed, 6, 208.
56. Goodspeed, 6, 212.
57. Flandrau, "The Settlement at Sioux Falls" (above, n. 44), p. 133.

in the erection of illegitimate provisional governments." [58] Not only were there examples of extralegal governments in Michigan, Oregon, and California before statehood, but at the very time when the squatter government was in power in Dakota, the miners of Denver, Colorado, were meeting to create the "Territory of Jefferson." The miners adopted a constitution, elected all necessary territorial officials, convened an assembly, and passed comprehensive laws "for the regulation of titles in lands, water, and mines." [59] Of the two squatter experiments the government of Jefferson was by far the more serious and extensive.

Between the two governments, however, there was a more fundamental difference than that of size and scope, namely their purpose. The miners of Colorado, some 30,000 in number by 1859, genuinely needed and desired a government regardless of who might originate it, while the few hundred speculators of Dakota were primarily interested in securing key properties through the medium of political organization and in presenting a false impression of the future territory to the prospective settler. Both experiments arose partly out of the traditions of the American frontier for political self-sufficiency and partly from the popular sovereignty ideas of Stephen A. Douglas, but their aims were diverse.

It should be said that the company decided to erect its own provisional government only after it had dispatched A. G. Fuller, a member of the company, to Washington in the spring of 1858 to urge the immediate organization of the territory. Through influence Fuller secured admittance to the floor of the House of Representatives, where he sat as a sort of quasi-delegate. But he was unsuccessful in obtaining an organic act for Dakota.[60] When he returned west to report his failure, the agents and settlers at Sioux Falls issued a call for a mass convention on September 18, 1858. The convention ordered the election of a legislature, and

58. "The Territory of Colorado," *University of Colorado Studies*, 4 (1907), 71; and "The Territory of Jefferson: a Spontaneous Commonwealth," ibid., 3, 15–18.
59. Paxson, "The Territory of Colorado," pp. 68–71. The Jefferson government fell in December 1860, on the issue of the power of an extralegal government to tax.
60. Albright, "The First Organized Government of Dakota," p. 142; Briggs, *Frontiers of the Northwest*, p. 352.

on October 4, fifty of the citizens of Sioux Falls split into parties
of three or four and traveled over the countryside near the settlement.[61] Every few miles each party would halt, take a drink of
whiskey, establish a voting precinct, and then proceed to vote
several times themselves by putting the names of all their relatives or friends on the ballots. After a reasonable number of
fictitious voters had cast their ballots, the party would travel to
the next polling place and repeat the process. That they even
troubled to go through the formality of voting is surprising, but
the result was that the vote for territorial legislators ran into the
hundreds.[62] This jovial but by no means original travesty of the
right of suffrage was the first election in Dakota Territory.[63]

The "squatter assembly" elected on October 4 met in November
at Sioux Falls. The rival companies divided the honors of office by
allowing Samuel J. Albright, a Dakota Company director and
editor of the Sioux Falls *Democrat*, to be made speaker of the
house, while Henry Masters of the Western Town firm became
president of the council. Later the Assembly elected Masters
provisional governor "of that portion of Minnesota without the
state limits now called Dakota." [64]

There are many indications that despite the youthful age of
most of the squatter legislators, they took their work seriously.
One authority has stated that this first session, while short, was
a very dignified one. The president of the council, Henry Masters,
a follower of Swedenborg and reputedly a poet, probably dignified
the proceedings by his presence, for he appears to have had great
prestige among the pioneer solons. One of his contemporaries
described him as a "sort of unofficial magistrate in the Sioux
Valley, to whom the citizen turned for counsel and arbitration in
matters of controversy." [65]

61. Bailey, *History of Minnehaha County*, p. 18.
62. Ibid., p. 19; Goodspeed, 6, 214.
63. Nevins, *Ordeal of the Union*, 2, 88, tells of an illegal delegate election in
Kansas. See, too, Avery Craven's *The Coming of the Civil War* (New York, 1942),
p. 359, for an account of Nebraska census padding for the purpose of influencing
the location of the capital.
64. Quotation from a Sioux Falls document cited in "The Settlement at Sioux
Falls," p. 147.
65. Albright, p. 144; Goodspeed, 6, 116–17; 214–15. Some parts of Albright's account of the Sioux Falls government are to be questioned, as Bailey has pointed out

The Assembly of 1858 took little action except to make Masters the provisional governor and to reconfirm A. G. Fuller as the territorial delegate to Washington. When Fuller failed to secure recognition a second time, however, the citizens of Sioux Falls held another mass political convention in the summer of 1859 and assigned authority to a second legislature to enact laws which would be valid until the region received a legal government. The convention, after deciding that all territorial officers should be elected, chose Masters as its candidate for governor, and Jefferson P. Kidder, a Vermont politician who had once been lieutenant governor of his native state, as delegate to Congress. At the time Kidder was a member of the Dakota Land Company.[66]

There is some dispute as to whether the settlers along the Missouri took part in the second squatter election held in October 1859, but this time the half-breeds and settlers of the Red River Valley some four hundred miles north participated, and returned the Sioux Falls candidates by an overwhelming majority.[67] With Red River support of their candidates the Dakota Company doubtless expected that their case could be argued more strongly before Congress.[68]

Before the second Assembly met in November, the Dakota Land Company stockholders assembled in St. Paul for their third annual meeting. The secretary reported that the company's funds were low because of the Panic of 1857 and the Indian scare, but that the future was bright. The company had 2640 "acres of

in his *History of Minnehaha County*, pp. 19–20, but Albright's description of Masters appears to be correct.

66. Albright, p. 144.

67. Albright, the editor of the Sioux Falls *Democrat* in 1859, has stated that Yankton and the Missouri towns voted against Kidder and for Todd for the delegateship in 1859 and that as a result the race was so close that Kidder and Albright returned to St. Paul for aid. There they persuaded Norman W. Kittson, a trader of great influence in the Red River Valley, to throw the votes he controlled to the Sioux Falls candidates. With this support the Sioux Falls ticket was naturally successful. On the other hand, D. R. Bailey, after considerable research, could find no evidence that the Missouri settlers had voted; rather, they revealed their displeasure by refusing to vote and by ignoring the legislative proceedings at Sioux Falls altogether. Ibid., pp. 133–47, and Bailey, *History of Minnehaha County*, pp. 19–23.

68. The alleged number of votes for Kidder was 1689; Lounsberry, *History of North Dakota*, p. 222.

scrip" to use on six of the company towns, while five other town-sites had been located and improved. The secretary also voiced some of the company's hopes: he spoke of Sioux Falls as a future railroad terminus as well as the territorial capital. Then he urged the company to expand its activities into the field of navigation, for the Big Sioux was navigable and the Missouri had already been sounded for navigation. "There are more than two thousand miles of navigable waters bordering and within the ceded portion of Dakota, and this Company will have already secured the most desirable centers for trade and commerce and *governmental organization* on all these rivers. The question of adding to our land enterprise a system of navigation, will of necessity force itself upon the new administration of this Company, and its importance is worthy of their consideration." [69] The secretary's report presents some idea of the virtual monopoly control which the Dakota Land Company officials had in mind for Dakota Territory.[70]

The second squatter Assembly met at Sioux Falls on November 4, 1859. Theoretically the councilors and representatives came from six organized counties, which included the settlements at Yankton and Vermillion, but actually most of the legislators were from Sioux Falls.[71] W. W. Brookings, manager of the Western Town Company, became president of the council, and Albright of the Dakota Company became Speaker of the House. The Assembly adopted the Minnesota Territorial Code of Laws for the squatter territory and chose Albright's paper, the *Democrat,* as the official organ of both houses.[72]

The sudden death of Governor Masters on the eve of the election had left the squatter government with no chief executive, but after some bickering the Assembly chose Albright to take his place, and the session proceeded according to plan. The program of the second Assembly was much more bold in its scope. The members

69. "Sioux Falls Settlement," p. 178.
70. Allan Nevins found Missourians following a similar technique in Kansas: "Missourians were well aware that Kansas was deficient in wood and water. By taking possession of the timber claims along the streams, they believed they could dominate the economic and political destinies of the country; for who could farm a Kansas holding without wood for building fences and fuel, and water for stock?" *Ordeal of the Union,* 2, 310.
71. Goodspeed, 6, 217–18.
72. Ibid.

introduced bills for the granting of ferry and railroad charters, for building roads, and for defining county boundaries. They passed laws for establishing supreme and district courts. They memorialized Congress for land offices and for territorial status, and requested their delegates to secure an appropriation of $6,000 from Congress to cover the cost of the squatter government during the year 1859.[73]

While the Assembly was in session only a few weeks, and though it never really carried out any of its acts, the Missouri River settlers became greatly alarmed. In November 1859 the residents of Yankton and Vermillion held a public meeting and passed resolutions stating that they would not support "squatter officers."[74] Ex-Delegate Fuller wrote from Yankton—where the Dakota Company had sent him to spy on the town boom activities of its rivals—that Captain Todd and Mr. Frost were visiting the river settlements to hold meetings and secure petitions which would counteract the Sioux Falls bids for political and economic supremacy.[75]

Any power which the squatter officers may have possessed steadily diminished after the adjournment of the Assembly. The federal government as well as the Missouri settlers "looked with more surprise than compassion on these early political freaks of Dakotians," wrote Moses K. Armstrong, an early settler of Yankton.[76] Delegate Kidder, like his predecessor Fuller, was unable to secure recognition in Washington in 1859-60. The final blow to the Dakota Company's ambitions came with the Republican victory in 1860, for the firm had staked all its hopes on the success of the Democratic party. Galusha Grow, the Republican chairman of the House Committee on Territories, strongly opposed the company and referred to its squatter government experiment as little more than a "vigilance committee."[77]

The Dakota Land Company's efforts today seem a harmless but rather interesting frontier experiment in self-government which

73. Bailey, p. 24.
74. Goodspeed, 6, 218.
75. A. G. Fuller to F. J. De Witt, November 6, 1859, in "Settlement at Sioux Falls," p. 146. De Witt was a member of the Dakota Land Company.
76. Armstrong, *History and Resources of Dakota, Montana, and Idaho* (Yankton, 1866), p. 36.
77. *Congressional Globe*, 36th Cong., 2d sess. (December 12, 1860), p. 80.

failed. Actually it was a business venture whose originators were determined to use the processes of local government as a medium to establish supreme control over the economic and political life of an entire territory. The majority of the directors of the Company—and those of the Western Town Company, too—were either professional politicians or men with legal or journalistic training.[78] They were especially conscious, therefore, of the structure of local government and of the functions which that structure could be made to perform. While they proposed to use democratic processes, their aims were anything but democratic. For this reason the Sioux Falls squatter government throws a revealing sidelight on the nature of extralegal government on the American frontier. Such extralegal governments are generally described as spontaneous but necessary institutions called into being for the protection of the individual and his property. The Dakota Land Company government went two steps further: (1) it used the institution of government to *create* property and wealth—an aspect of frontier government of which Todd and Frost were also conscious—and (2) it saw government as an instrument which could be used not only to *protect* the individual and his property but to *control* them as well. Governor St. Clair had anticipated this very development in 1799 when he wrote that a frontier, if left to govern itself, would create one "democratic in its form and oligarchic in its execution." His prophecy almost came true in Dakota in 1859. As a frank advocate of this broader conception of the business possibilities lying within the realm of frontier government, the Dakota Land Company had great and prophetic significance.[79]

The inhabitants of Pembina, a trading post and customs port in the Red River Valley of the North constituted a third group

78. Governor S. A. Medary of Minnesota, Delegate J. P. Kidder, Editor S. A. Albright, Byron M. Smith, Judge C. E. Flandrau, James M. Allen, and F. J. De Witt, all of the Dakota Company, answer to the above description. Mayor Hetherington, W. W. Brookings, G. P. Waldron, and William Tripp of the Western Town Company were also professional politicians in 1859 or became public office holders a short time thereafter. See Lounsberry, p. 215, and "Sioux Falls Settlement," p. 180. See P. W. Gates, "Frontier Landlords and Pioneer Tenants," *Journal of the Illinois State Historical Society*, 38 (1945), 1, for an account of the speculating politician on the frontier.

79. See below, Chap. 9.

of traders, natives, settlers, and speculators who were interested in securing territorial status for Dakota. Pembina, unlike either Sioux Falls or Yankton, had existed as a settlement from the time of Lord Selkirk's experiment of colonizing the Canadian Plains.[80] Although periodically flooded by the muddy Red River, Pembina had been a fur-trading center since 1819 and by the 1850 census returns claimed to have a population of more than a thousand persons.[81]

The majority of the inhabitants of Pembina were half-breeds of French, Scotch, and Indian descent; and to a much greater degree than those along the Missouri these *Bois Brulé*, and even the full-blooded Indians of the Red River Valley, had taken on a veneer of French customs and habits.[82] "Their dress is singular," wrote a member of Captain Long's expedition in 1823, "but not deficient of beauty; it is a mixture of European and Indian habits," consisting of a blue capote with a hood, a calico or painted muslin shirt, moccasins, and leather leggings.[83] Catholic missionaries had been much more active in this region than along the Missouri, and by 1855 they had established several permanent missions in the Red River area.[84] These factors and the long presence and activity of the Hudson's Bay Company within the Red River Valley combined to make Pembina a different type of settlement from that of Yankton or Sioux Falls. Further, the nearness to the Canadian border and the fact that the Red River was a natural connecting link between the Canadian plains settlements—such

80. H. G. Gunn, "The Selkirk Settlement," *North Dakota Historical Quarterly*, *1* (1926), 46–60. Gunn states that the first bona fide settlement was made at Pembina in 1819. See E. H. Oliver, ed., "The Canadian Northwest, Its Early Development and Legislative Records," *Publications of the Canadian Archives* (Ottawa, 1914), Vols. *1, 2*, for a documentary account of the Selkirk Colony. See also Lounsberry, pp. 40–52.

81. *Census of 1850*, pp. 1006–7; see also Briggs, *Frontiers of the Northwest*, p. 361. It should be noted that census figures on the frontier were usually padded to make the country seem more settled to prospective immigrants and to allow for a larger representation in territorial assemblies.

82. Quaife, *Army Life*, pp. 65–7, 261.

83. William H. Keating, compiler, *Narrative of an Expedition to the Source of St. Peter's River, Lake Winnepeek, Lake of the Woods, etc. . . . . Performed in the year 1823 . . . under the Command of Stephen H. Long* (Philadelphia, 1824), 2, 44.

84. Vernice M. Aldrich, "Father George Antoine Belcourt, Red River Missionary," *North Dakota Historical Quarterly*, 2 (1927), 30–52.

as Winnipeg—resulted in Pembina's being as much a Canadian frontier town as it was an American one.[85]

On the other hand, the Pembina and Red River inhabitants were well acquainted with the mysteries of American frontier politics. When that area had been a part of Minnesota Territory from 1848 to 1858, the Pembina settlers had been active as "Moccasin Democrats" in the Assembly. Powerful and paternalistic leaders like Joseph Rolette, Norman W. Kittson, and later, Charles Cavalier, had so organized the Red River region politically that the inhabitants usually voted as a single bloc in elections.[86]

The residents of Pembina were also familiar with the American custom of townsite booming. As a part of Minnesota Territory the eastern portion of the Red River Valley had been the scene of townsite speculation in the early 1850's, and by 1856 the boom had spread to the west bank of the river.[87] The Panic of 1857 sharply curbed these activities, however, and before its effects had worn off, the exclusion of the west bank of the Red River from the new state of Minnesota further contracted settlement and speculation. But having once tested the sweet fruits of a boom period, the traders and settlers along the west bank were as anxious as the Sioux Falls squatter government for territorial status. This desire was whetted by the knowledge that Governor Stevens' proposed northern rail route to the Pacific crossed the heart of the Valley and would connect all the Red River settlements with St. Paul and Chicago.

Two other factors made territorial status even more desirable: (1) in 1857 the Hudson's Bay Company, deciding to abandon its old trade route to Europe, secured permission to import its supplies through the Great Lakes and across Minnesota to the Red River, and from there by steamboat to Winnipeg.[88] The new route

85. John P. Pritchett, *The Red River Valley, 1811–1849* (New Haven, 1942), pp. 263–71; see esp. p. ix. Pritchett stresses the interrelationship which the Red River has promoted between Canada and the United States, and compares its importance as a connecting link between the two countries to that of the St. Lawrence River and the Richelieu Basin on the east coast and to the Columbia River on the west coast.

86. Forrest, "Mythical Cities of Southwestern Minnesota," p. 246. The influence of fur-trading companies and federal patronage usually caused the votes to go one way.

87. Briggs, p. 362; Daniel S. B. Johnson, "A Red River Townsite Speculation in 1857," *Collections of the Minnesota Historical Society*, 15 (1915), 411–34.

88. Briggs, p. 363.

promised to bring wealth to Pembina and the Red River area in the form of transportation contracts and facilities, and should a railroad connect the Red River with St. Paul and the East, the entire fur trade of the Canadian Northwest would pass through the Valley. (2) The Red River inhabitants held a slim hope that Congress would create two territories out of the unorganized remainder of Minnesota Territory and that St. Joseph's, a small fur-trading post west of Pembina, would be chosen as the capital of the northern territory. In May 1858 some two hundred citizens of Pembina petitioned Congress to this effect.[89]

It is revealing to find that the 1858 petition to Congress was written in French and that the names of its two hundred signers were predominantly French or French-Indian. Depending upon the aid of Minnesota politicians in Congress and upon the political influence of the more important English-speaking traders, the Pembina residents did little other than follow the traditional frontier method of petition, although in 1859, at the request of Norman W. Kittson, they participated in the second Sioux Falls squatter election. But this was the last unusual action which they took in the struggle for territorial status.[90]

Pembina, Yankton, and Sioux Falls were three distinct types of frontier settlement. Pembina represented the long-standing native frontier element of traders and half-breed Indians who, seeing the inevitability of settlement, did not hesitate to adjust to the new situation and ally themselves with the prospective speculator or the future government official. The enterprises of Frost and Todd at Yankton, on the other hand, were typical of those of the merchant-speculator who banded together a small company to exploit the wealth to be had from the settlement of a new community. Finally, the monopolistic activities of the Dakota Land Company at Sioux Falls reflected both the traditional methods of large scale speculators and the tendencies toward corporate business methods and wholesale exploitation of an entire region which the railroad and the post-Civil War business corporation would soon make a familiar part of American life.

While the settlements were different in form and the struggle

89. "Petition from the Citizens of Pembina," May 1858, MS in Papers of the Committee on Territories of the U.S. Senate, National Archives.
90. Albright, pp. 133–47.

for recognition varied in its pattern, the aims of the three Dakota groups were fundamentally the same. Each group hoped to reap rewards not only from settlement but also from the federal government's policy of protection of the frontier by army units, from its provisions for transportation developments in the form of railroad grants, and from patronage through political and administrative offices. And that the federal government should virtually subsidize frontier settlement in these ways the politically conscious citizens of Pembina, Sioux Falls, and Yankton agreed with a singular unanimity.

The first memorials and petitions from Dakota made little impression on a Congress grown weary of all territorial bills since the Kansas-Nebraska controversy. Because of the relationship of the territorial question to the slavery issue, it took three years of agitation in Congress to secure the organization of Dakota and two other western territories, Nevada and Colorado.

The Dakota Land Company made the initial attempt in May 1858, when Alpheus G. Fuller appeared before the House of Representatives with a memorial asking that he be seated as the delegate from the "Territory of Dakota." [91] But after a lengthy discussion Congress decided that the part of Minnesota remaining outside of the new state should continue to be represented by the territorial delegate who was incumbent when the new state was formed. W. W. Kingsbury, the old delegate, was determined not to lose his seat to Fuller, and Congress sustained his view.[92] Those supporting Fuller asserted that the creation of the state of Minnesota ended the legal existence of Minnesota Territory and that a new delegate must be chosen for a new territory.[93]

Even in this first struggle the contending factions in Congress and within the future Territory became apparent. While it was obvious that Fuller had no right to a seat, a vociferous minority

91. *Cong. Globe,* 35th Cong., 1st sess. (May 27, 1858), p. 2428.
92. Ibid., pp. 2660–1, 2677–9.
93. The discussion became further involved when the question arose: could legally organized counties which were now attached neither to a state nor to a territory legally elect a delegate? The House Committee on Elections considered these questions and decided that precedents existed in the cases of Michigan and Wisconsin Territories whereby the delegate could retain his seat after part of the territory had become a state. The House approved the committee's report and allowed Kingsbury to complete his term of office. Ibid.

on the House Elections Committee—James Wilson, Ezra Clark, Jr., and John Gilmer—steadily maintained that he did. All three men were either Free Soilers or members of the "American" party, who felt that the Sioux Falls government was antislavery in sentiment and therefore should be supported.[94] It was true that all of the settlers and officials of the Sioux Falls area were from Minnesota, Iowa, or other nonslave states, while both Todd and Frost were southerners. Yet Galusha Grow, one of the leading advocates of territorial organization without slavery and an ardent foe of all frontier speculators, opposed Fuller. Grow was well aware of the Dakota Land Company's connections with the Democratic party in Minnesota, and one of the more prominent men in the rising Republican party, he could not allow a Democratic machine to be established in Dakota.[95] Moreover, the Democrats themselves disagreed over the recognition of the Sioux Falls government. Captain Todd, a Democrat, declared in a letter to the Committee on Elections that the counties now outside of the state of Minnesota had voted overwhelmingly for Kingsbury in 1857 and that they still considered him as their duly elected delegate. This was Todd's method of defeating the aims of Fuller and the Dakota Land Company and of bettering the chances of his own settlements on the Missouri River.[96]

In December 1858 the Sioux Falls government presented a second memorial for the recognition of Fuller. In support of this memorial Senator Henry Mower Rice of Minnesota introduced a bill in the Senate for the organization of Dakota Territory.[97] Rice had lived on the Minnesota frontier since 1839 and had been a lobbyist in 1849 in Washington, where he had worked for the creation of Minnesota Territory. As a Democrat he was surely in contact with and speaking for the Sioux Falls politicians. As a speculator in railroads and railroad lands in Minnesota he was also interested in pushing any piece of legislation which would make the northern route to the Pacific coast more acceptable.

94. Ibid., p. 2661. A perusal of the brief available biographies of Wilson, Clark, and Gilmer reveals no other motive for their support of the Sioux Falls delegate and government.
95. See Galusha A. Grow in the *DAB*.
96. *Cong. Globe*, 35th Cong., 1st sess., p. 2661.
97. Ibid., 2d sess. (December 20, 1858), p. 138.

For that reason Rice favored the Sioux Falls and Red River settlements over those along the Missouri. Rice had been largely responsible for securing railroad land grants for Minnesota in 1857, and his brother, Edmund, was actively engaged in building Minnesota railroads.[98] Both men were naturally for the creation of a territory west of Minnesota which would most benefit that state and whose lines of communication would lead from St. Paul and not up the Missouri River.

A month later, February 8, 1859, the Chairman of the Senate Territorial Committee, James S. Green of Missouri, reported adversely on the Rice bill and on all the petitions from the Sioux Falls Assembly and the citizens of Pembina.[99] Green was doubtless an acquaintance—if not a friend—of D. M. Frost of St. Louis, Todd's partner in the Frost-Todd Trading Company. Like Green, Frost was a leading Democrat in Missouri state politics throughout the 1850's, and naturally commanded some political influence with the Senator.

In the first session of the Thirty-Sixth Congress, Senator Rice again attempted to secure the passage of a bill to organize a "temporary government" in Dakota, but with no success.[100] Meanwhile an increasing number of petitions were pouring in from the Missouri River settlements, and Frost and Todd were in Washington lobbying for a bill to locate the capital of the territory on the Missouri River.[101]

It was not until May 11, 1860, however, that another bill of organization reached the floors of Congress. On that day Galusha Grow reported three bills for the organization of Nevada, Colorado, and Dakota. The House quickly tabled the first two, but the Dakota bill caused a new eruption of the territorial question. When Eli Thayer, the controversial representative from Worcester, Massachusetts, and the originator of the Kansas Emigrant Aid Society, proposed to table *it*, too, the motion provoked an outburst from Congressman Samuel R. Curtis of Iowa, who made

98. Henry Mower Rice and Edmund Rice in the *DAB*. Edmund believed in running railroads in advance of settlement and by that method to determine the path or line of settlement.

99. *Cong. Globe*, 35th Cong., 2d sess. (February 8, 1859), p. 877.

100. Ibid., 36th Cong., 1st sess. (December 29, 1859), p. 287.

101. Armstrong, *History and Resources of Dakota Territory*, p. 36; and *History of Southeastern Dakota*, p. 18.

a plea for its passage and for the organization of the whole West. It was an area of lawlessness, he said, since Congress refused to let government proceed there. Curtis intimated that Thayer's motion was not prompted by antislavery feeling at all, but by the desire to see the territories remain public domain, which could be disposed of in the form of railroad land grants.[102]

To this attack Thayer replied somewhat obliquely with an exposition of his own solution to the territorial problem. He had urged since the time of the Kansas-Nebraska issue that the West could best be settled by private colonization companies, whose aim would be to make a profit from the business of settlement. In every case, he felt, the northern settlement companies would win out over the southern ones, and thus by allowing for the practice of "popular sovereignty" in these colonized territories their governments would inevitably be nonslave and the whole question of slavery in the territories would be resolved. In questioning the right of congressional control over territories and the right to use army units for protection of the frontier settlers, he asked: "What do they want with our protection? . . . And if they do want it, what protection would they get except a government of broken-down politicians, which the president of the United States would send them?" These politicians "have usually been worse to the people of the Territories than the frogs and lice to the people of Egypt (Laughter)." They go out to the territories to "fill their own pockets with gold of the General Government; to trade with the Indians; to speculate in town lots; and often one of the methods by which they accomplish their ends is by stirring up Indian wars."

> These people of Dakota are as well off to-day as they would be if they had our territorial officials over them.

102. *Cong. Globe,* 36th Cong., 1st sess. (May 11, 1860), p. 2070. Curtis himself may have been an advocate of the Sioux Falls government, since the Western Town Company of Sioux Falls had its headquarters in Dubuque, Iowa. Curtis' suggestion that Thayer was a speculator in railroad lands or was at least pro-railroad in his land policy may have stemmed from the fact that Thayer was on the House Committee on Public Lands. Thayer later became a land agent for a New York railroad company. See Eli Thayer in the *DAB.* J. T. DuBois, in his *Galusha Grow* (New York, 1917), p. 186, says Thayer was in the railroad equipment business in 1859–60. Grow made puns about Thayer's attempt to "locomote" legislation.

They have known no Indian wars. The Yanctons and the
Sioux are all quiet. But organize the Territory, and send
out your executive officials; and then, sir, these speculators
will greatly desire an influx of Government gold. There
is no method so sure and so convenient to produce that
result as to stir up an Indian war. It will be done, sir, to
raise the price of town lots. The Yanctons and the Sioux
will come down on the white settlements and we shall hear
of the terrible inroads of the savages. Then, sir, a heart-
rending appeal for protection. Then, sir, a regiment of
soldiers and a million dollars. Then, sir, damages and pen-
sions and war claims to the end of time. They are better
off to-day than they can be with these Government speculators turned loose upon them.[103]

Thayer's account—of the future inglorious history of Dakota
Territory and of all territories—and the opposition of the southern
Democrats were together enough to kill the chances for the organization of the region in the spring of 1860. A bill introduced
by Grow for the organization of the Red River area as the Territory of Chippewa also failed.[104]

The Dakota question did not reappear in Congress until the
second session in 1860. On December 12 Thayer, as a member of
the House Committee on Public Lands, reported a bill which
would provide for the creation of a Dakota Land District and
for a delegate therefrom as selected by its squatter government.[105]
In the intervening months between the first and second session
of Congress, Thayer had apparently become convinced that the
Sioux Falls government corresponded with his ideas of "company
colonization" and "self-government" within territories, and for
this reason he became one of its vigorous defenders. Thayer explained that his bill would allow (1) for the survey and sale of
the public lands of Dakota and thus give immigrants a chance to
purchase and secure homesteads, and (2) would bypass the ques-

103. *Cong. Globe*, 36th Cong., 1st sess. (May 11, 1860), p. 2074.
104. Ibid., pp. 2079–80, 2081. The "Chippewa bill" was consistently opposed
by John S. Phelps of Missouri, who argued that there were no people in the proposed territory.
105. Ibid., 2d sess. (December 12, 1860), p. 80.

tion of territorial organization by accepting the one which the people of Dakota had created for themselves. He concluded with a request that the Sioux Falls delegate, Jefferson P. Kidder, be given his rightful seat in the House.[106]

Thayer, who was already in trouble with his own party (Republican) for supporting a version of popular sovereignty, did not seem to realize that his bill, should it become law, would reap tremendous advantages not only for the Dakota Land Company but for the Democratic party as well. The acceptance of a "squatter government" which was affiliated with the Democracy of Minnesota would have put a whole territory into the hands of the party that had just suffered national defeat in the November elections and local defeat in Minnesota. The bill was certainly a clever and daring scheme, proposed as a last-ditch fight by the Dakota Land Company against its rivals in Dakota and against Republican encroachment and control of the new territory. It was an attempt to use a form of "popular sovereignty" for private and partisan advantage in an area where no slavery could possibly exist. In four short years the Douglas conception of "popular sovereignty" had become a sophisticated political mechanism which could be the means to almost any end, and in less than seventy-five years the colonial system of the United States had almost succumbed to this absurd fetish for localism in government.

To Galusha Grow fell the task of opposing so unorthodox a bill. Against its first purpose he argued that the bill created a new office where the Surveyor General of Minnesota already had jurisdiction. Against its second aim he replied that the government then organized in Dakota was really nothing more than a "vigilance committee," that the Thayer bill would not legalize it, nor would any court recognize it. Finally, Grow replied to Thayer's argument of May 11 by asserting that Congress must be the "primary law-making power of these Territories." [107]

Grow then explained the plan of the Republican-controlled Committee on Territories to organize all the remaining territory

106. Ibid.
107. 'Ibid., p. 81.

in the West and to end the entire issue at one stroke. He proposed five new territories: (1) the region around Pike's Peak, (2) the region near the Washoe Silver Mines (Nevada), (3) Arizona, (4) Dakota, and (5) the region above Dakota. While upholding Congressional supremacy in territorial affairs, Grow hoped that the organic acts of these new territories would allow legislative enactment of a law over the gubernatorial veto by a majority vote. He also suggested that the acts permit the citizens to elect their own officers when a population of 25,000 should settle in a territory.[108] Lastly, Grow, who had once been the law partner of David Wilmot, indicated that antislavery provisos would be included in the organic acts, but, he added, it might be possible to vote such provisos down.[109] In view of Grow's powerful opposition and his counterproposals, Thayer referred his bill to the Committee of the Whole rather than to Grow's Committee on Territories. But even there the Thayer bill failed, and with it failed the hopes of the Dakota Land Company.[110]

Dakota elicited little discussion in Congress again until February 15, 1861. On that day Senator Green introduced two bills to provide for a temporary government and for the creation of the office of surveyor general in Dakota and Nevada Territories.[111] Although the evidence is indirect, it appears that these bills had the approval of Grow and of the Republican party. Green, though an ardent proslavery Democrat, seems to have decided to work with the opposing party in order to present territorial bills which would be acceptable to both Houses, and in doing so he secured the help of W. H. Seward as well as Grow.[112]

With the cooperation of Republicans and conciliatory Democrats, the slavery issue in territories did not appear in the debates until February 26, 1861. It seemed as if a conspiracy of silence had been imposed on the subject as one of many efforts being made to conciliate the seceding South. On that day, however, when bills for the organization of Colorado, Nevada, and Dakota

108. Ibid., pp. 80–81.
109. Ibid., p. 81.
110. Ibid.
111. Ibid. (February 15, 1861), p. 897.
112. Ibid., p. 923.

came before the Senate, Douglas of Illinois noted that while the bills agreed with noninterference with slavery in the territories, they had no reference to slavery in them. He wondered what the cause was for this omission.[113]

Senator Green objected to Douglas' bringing up this question and explained that the Colorado bill did provide for the slavery question by stating that the "Territorial Legislature shall pass no law abolishing or impairing the rights of private property." To this Douglas replied that the clause simply meant that southern senators would interpret the clause as approving slavery, while the nonslave senators would see it as not dealing with slavery. Thus it would be a question for the courts and could be appealed to the Supreme Court.[114]

At this point Senator Green submitted a House amendment to the Colorado bill allowing writs of error or appeal from the territorial courts in all cases except those dealing with slavery. Douglas' answer to this amendment was that such an arrangement would suit the Republicans, since Lincoln was to appoint the territorial judges, but that by this system the law concerning slavery would change every time the national administration changed. For this reason Douglas objected to the amendment, but the Senate concurred in the House amendment by a vote of 26 to 18.[115] The same day bills for Dakota and Nevada passed with the amendment attached.[116]

Between February 26 and March 1, when the House passed the territorial bills, several conferences took place, the result of which was that Green, Grow, and the leading Republicans agreed to ignore the slavery question entirely and to drop the House amendment to which Douglas had objected. Grow admitted this compromise, and Senator Benjamin Wade in a speech defending the action stated:

113. Ibid. (February 26, 1861), p. 1205.
114. Ibid., p. 1205.
115. Ibid., p. 1206. It is revealing to find the number of Republican Senators voting for such an amendment: Cameron, Chandler, Clark, Collamer, Dixon, Doolittle, Fessenden, Foot, Foster, Grimes, Hale, Harlan, King, Morrill, Sumner, Trumbull, Wade, Wilkinson, and Wilson.
116. Ibid. pp. 1206–8. An attempt by Douglas to submit his own bill for Nevada received a crushing defeat (31 against, 4 for).

The different sides of this chamber could not agree in carrying out the principles that they contend for. The one side intended to make the Territory slave territory; and the other contended that there should be a prohibition of slavery in the territorial bill. Finally we agreed informally . . . we talked the subject over, and both sides feeling the necessity of having a territorial organization there, agreed that there should be nothing said about slavery in the territorial organization, one way or the other, and the bill was framed with that view.[117]

Such a decision, James G. Blaine wrote, amounted to a virtual sanction of "popular sovereignty" by the Republican party.[118] Douglas himself realized this, and as the Dakota and Nevada bills were being considered in the Senate before final passage he remarked how his original position in the Kansas-Nebraska controversy was being adopted by his political opponents.[119]

The final fight to pass the territorial bills occurred in the House of Representatives on March 1, 1861. Amid great confusion, cries of order, motions for adjournment, and motions to hear the Committee from the Peace Conference, Grow succeeded in being recognized by the Speaker. At an almost breathless pace he presented the Nevada bill and mentioned that it had no slavery clause in it. Motions to table or to postpone the bill failing, it passed with a vote of 95 to 52. In the same manner the bill for Dakota passed without debate or even a number vote.[120]

In this hasty fashion, with a minimum of debate and an evasion of the slavery issue, the Territories of Dakota, Nevada, and Colorado came into being. It is an unexplained inconsistency why the Republicans, who owed their political existence to the determined stand they had taken on slavery in the West, should abandon it at the last moment.[121] As David Potter has observed:

117. David N. Potter, *Lincoln and His Party in the Secession Crisis* (New Haven, 1942), p. 278. Wade was speaking specifically here of the Colorado Organic Act.
118. *Twenty Years of Congress* (Norwich, Conn., 1884), *1*, 271.
119. *Cong. Globe*, 36th Cong., 2d sess. (February 26, 1861), p. 1208. See also J. G. Randall, *Lincoln, the Liberal Statesman* (New York, 1947), pp. 19–21.
120. *Cong. Globe*, 36th Cong., 2d sess. (March 1, 1861), pp. 1330–5.
121. Blaine, *Twenty Years of Congress*, *1*, 269–70.

"Radical Republicans and administration Democrats had agitated the territorial question for a decade, and had thus brought the country to the brink of war. By a profound irony, they now at last voted together, a few weeks before the bombardment of Fort Sumter." [122] Blaine called this evasion "one of the singular contradictions in the political history of the country." [123] The commonly accepted explanation by the Republicans in Congress has been that it was part of the conciliation policy which they followed in the final days before the outbreak of the Civil War. Blaine himself accepted this view and added that "the Republicans did it the more readily because they had full faith that slavery never, could secure a foothold in any of the Territories named." [124]

When the first volume of Blaine's *Twenty Years of Congress* appeared in 1884, Grow took issue with Blaine's comments on Republican inconsistency and defended the course the party had taken in 1861. Any bill with an antislavery clause would have been impractical, Grow stated, for there was great need of territorial organization because of the pressure of thousands of immigrants. Moreover, Grow wrote, the great battle between "Freedom and Slavery for supremacy in the Territories had been fought and won in Kansas, and the people had elected a Chief Magistrate on Freedom's side, so that the influences of National Administration would no longer be wielded for the extension of human bondage." [125]

In terms of the immediate North-South crisis of 1861, the creation of new territories without a slavery clause may seem a part of the general Republican conciliation policy. From a broader view of a developing national policy by a Republican administration the Acts take on a new significance. Grow himself stated that

122. *Lincoln and His Party,* p. 278.
123. *Twenty Years of Congress,* 1, 269–70. Blaine attempted to surround the abandonment of the antislavery proviso by the Republicans with great mystery, but he did not state that the motive behind the abandonment was any other than conciliation of the Southern Democrats.
124. Ibid., p. 271; Potter, pp. 277–8. Blaine felt that the Republicans actually owed Webster an apology for all their attacks upon him after his seventh of March speech, for in 1861 they had adopted precisely the same course that Webster advocated.
125. Blaine, 2, 677–8. These pages contain an interesting analysis of Grow's defense by Blaine.

the "pressure of immigrants" forced the territorial question. It was, then, the fulfillment of a campaign promise made to foreign elements in the United States which partly motivated these Acts.[126] Grow had been extremely active in the West in 1859 among the foreign-born German settlers, and especially so in Minnesota, where he had distributed thousands of handbills in German which told of his proposed homestead bill. To make such a bill mean anything, new regions of the West to which the Homestead Act could apply had to be opened; hence his great concern for the organization of Dakota, Nevada, and Colorado and all the remaining territory of the West. The interrelation of the land distribution question and the territorial question is so great—and this is particularly true in Grow's career—there can be no doubt that his activity on behalf of territorial organization coincided with his plans for the Homestead Act of 1862.[127] Grow's lifelong opposition to speculation in public lands by monopolists or railroad groups may serve as a further explanation of the integral connection between the territorial and land questions.[128]

The more general and long-range reasons—such as the nationalist and strategic military ones in the event of a North-South

126. By the adoption of a homestead plank in their 1860 platform and by winning the confidence of the foreign elements in the West, the Republicans were able to secure many more votes in the 1860 election. W. E. Dodd, "The Fight for the Northwest in 1860," *American Historical Review*, 16 (1911), 774–8, has gone so far as to say that "the fate of the Union" was decided "not by native Americans but by voters who knew least of American history and institutions." George M. Stephenson, *Political History of the Public Lands from 1840 to 1862* (Boston, 1917), pp. 222–6, provides a good summary of the methods used by the new Republican party after 1856 to capture the foreign vote of the Midwest.

127. James T. Du Bois, *Galusha A. Grow, Father of the Homestead Law*, New York, 1917; see esp. chap. 11, "Organizing the Farmers' Frontier," which is an account of Grow's effort to push through the territorial bills of 1861; see also Helene Sara Zahler, *Eastern Workingmen and National Land Policy, 1829–1862* (New York, 1941) for references to Grow's fight for a homestead law: pp. 147, 148 n., 160, 161, 167, 173–4, 176, 180. The most complete treatment of the agitation and background for a homestead act is George M. Stephenson, *The Political History of the Public Lands from 1840 to 1862*, Boston, 1917; see esp. pp. 195–9 for an account of Grow's Homestead Bill of 1860. The arguments against the bill by the South were revealing and pointed up the relation of the bill to the organization of new territories. Southern Democrats stated, for example, that the bill provided a bonus to induce men to immigrate to "new territories" and to go there with the condition that aid societies should pay for their expenses to get there. See also Roy M. Robbins, *Our Landed Heritage, the Public Domain, 1776–1936* (Princeton, 1942), pp. 203 ff.

128. Galusha A. Grow, in the *DAB*.

war in 1861—have already been mentioned as factors which moved the Republicans to organize the West in 1861. Grow himself stated that "concentrated settlement . . . was the main desideratum to assure defense, the centers of organized government offering a natural stronghold." [129]

Finally, the pressure of the lobbyists themselves had an appreciable effect on Congress in 1861. The Nevada and Colorado Acts, like the one for Dakota, represented the result of several years of agitation by the mining population in each of those territories. The Congressmen from the western states were almost unanimous in their advocacy of government for the new regions.[130] The refusal to heed such agitation could have resulted in the establishment of "squatter governments" like those of Sioux Falls and the Territory of Jefferson all over the West.

In the case of Dakota, the influence of Frost and Todd on Green and the Missouri congressmen was probably considerable. Todd was in a particularly favorable political position after November 1860 because of his kinship to Mary Todd Lincoln, wife of the incoming president. The Minnesota and Iowa delegations in Congress, also, finally supported the organization of Dakota Territory, even though they could not secure an official recognition of the Sioux Falls government. Jefferson P. Kidder, the squatter delegate from Sioux Falls and a former lieutenant governor of Vermont, did not hesitate to use his influence with the Vermont delegation in Congress. Behind these men stood a horde of small-town politicians from all parts of the United States who were anxious for office in the new territories; and cooperating with them was the usual number of merchants interested in the Indian and army trade, as well as speculators in lands and in railroad lines. These forgotten men, anonymous but powerful, and unceasing in their wants, were often two or three times removed from the high official they hoped to influence; they were not rich enough to bribe or outstanding enough to overwhelm; thus they had to make their mark in American history by unending pressure,

---

129. See above, p. 17. Du Bois, *Grow, Father of the Homestead Law*, p. 185.

130. The vote on various territorial bills in the period 1858–61 reveals a sectional vote, the West voting for most of the organization bills, with the South and East opposed. After 1860 the Republicans of the East joined with the West and with conciliatory Democrats to push through the several territorial acts.

by cajolery, by horse trading. They were the commission men or, better, "phase capitalists," who were shrewd enough to make money on a coming event, bold enough to assume the risk, and mendacious enough to salvage something if their scheme did not pay off. It is no wonder, then, that these bills became law in the midst of the greatest crisis the Union had ever faced, and that Buchanan himself signed them two days before his term ended. On March 2, 1861, the Territory of Dakota became a fact, and with its recognition a new era began in the regions of the Upper Missouri and in the territorial history of the United States.

Chapter 2. The Founding Fathers: 1861–66

> The patronage which the government bestows on new territories is one of the sources of their growth which ought not to be overlooked. Instead of making the territory a dependency and drawing from it a tax, the government pays its political expenses, builds its roads, and gives it a fair start in the world.　　　　*C. C. Andrews, 1856*

WHEN ABRAHAM LINCOLN became President on March 4, 1861, the new Republican administration found itself so overwhelmed by the double tasks of running a government and prosecuting a Civil War that the appointment of territorial officials was made with little consultation or consideration of ability. In a Washington filled with harassed and fearful congressmen, insistent office seekers, and rumors of impending chaos and treachery on every side, an applicant needed only a short note or a verbal endorsement from Seward, Chase, Davis, or some other prominent Republican to secure an office in one of the new territories.[1]

Of the appointed territorial officers, that of the governor was by far the most important. It was his duty to represent the federal government within the territory while at the same time supporting the demands of his adopted constituents and acting as *ex officio* Commissioner of Indian Affairs for the tribes within his territory. And now the threat of Confederate invasion or raids, such as those which Arizona and New Mexico were to experience, gave the governor military duties as well.[2]

Captain J. B. S. Todd was the most obvious candidate for the governorship of Dakota. A resident of the frontier for some twenty years, with a considerable knowledge of the Sioux Indians and a personal stake in the future of the Territory, Todd seemed the

1. So many endorsements, decisions, and appointments were made verbally during the hectic days of the spring of 1861 that little written evidence exists to reveal how many contenders there were for territorial office. Letters concerning territorial appointments are to be found in the U.S. Department of State, Territorial Papers, 1861–73 (TP, Dakota Letterbook) and the U.S. Department of State, Appointments Division, Letters of Application and Recommendation, 1861–77 (TP, Dakota Appointments), National Archives.

2. The role of the governor is discussed in E. S. Pomeroy, *The Territories and the United States, 1860–1890* (Philadelphia, 1947), pp. 16 ff.

ideal man for the position. His efforts in Washington to organize Dakota on his own terms indicated that he had political ability. A slender man of pleasant appearance and somewhat florid style of speech, he had what his contemporaries were apt to describe as a "noble countenance." He was easily at home in all Washington social and political circles. Straight-backed and dignified, with an impressive beard, he combined many of the qualities of a Kentucky gentleman with those of a professional West Pointer.[3] But carrying his silver-headed cane and wearing elegant pale gloves, he hardly seemed the type who would choose to settle the bare Dakotas. And since he was a Democrat, Lincoln could ill afford to appoint him to an office which traditionally went to a political spoilsman. Moreover, he was a cousin of Mrs. Lincoln's, and his appointment might have laid the President open to charges of nepotism at a time when Lincoln's prestige was already peril- ously low. Todd's position was further weakened when his ex- partner, Colonel Frost, made an audacious attempt in the spring of 1861 to seize St. Louis for the Confederacy.[4]

Lincoln chose instead Dr. William Jayne, his neighbor and family physician in Springfield, Illinois. Jayne not only was a trusted friend of the President but had the good fortune to be the brother-in-law of Senator Lyman Trumbull of Illinois as well.[5] A tall, lanky man of thirty-six years, with a hawklike nose and piercing eyes, Jayne possessed a strong temper and so little political subtlety that he was to split rather than unite the infant Republican party of Dakota in its first years. In his fight to seize political control of Dakota, he ran up against Captain Todd, whose more adroit maneuvers finally forced Jayne to return to Spring- field in defeat. In a brief but accurate analysis of Jayne, one of his colleagues described him to Salmon P. Chase as "a neighbor of the Pres't, a clever man, a tolerably shrewd ward politician, but without any appreciation of statesmanship and wholly unable to meet the present crisis." [6]

3. See above, p. 36; also Doane Robinson, *South Dakota* (Chicago, 1930), *1*, 256, for a brief allusion to Todd's activities in Washington in 1861.

4. See above, p. 37. Frost joined the Confederate forces and received a com- mission as a brigadier general.

5. Kingsbury, *Dakota Territory, 1,* 178, 181, 183, 273–4. Goodspeed, *The Province and the States, 6,* 222–3; Robinson, *South Dakota, 1,* 256.

6. Judge Philemon Bliss to Hon. John C. Underwood and Salmon P. Chase, Yankton, D.T., October 26, 1862, Salmon P. Chase Papers, in Library of Congress.

William Jayne: first governor of
Dakota Territory (1861–63),
founder of the
Dakota Republican Party,
and delegate to Congress (1863–64)

Two Founding Fathers of Dakota Territory

Newton Edmunds: second governor of
Dakota Territory (1864–66)
and a leader in political and business
affairs throughout the territorial period

Jayne's qualities have been described in some detail because in addition to his duties as governor, he was the founder and titular leader of the fractious Republican party in Dakota. Further, much of the political history of the western territories centers on the struggles of the governor against the delegate, the Assembly, or, in many cases, both. Jayne's administration unhappily was not an exception to this general situation.

The other federal appointees—the territorial secretary, the three territorial judges, the federal marshal, and the attorney-general—were also of great importance in shaping the nature of Dakota politics. Virtually all of the first appointees were politically ambitious young men with a smattering of legal training. They had received their appointments through some influential member of the Republican party and consequently were not responsible to the territorial citizens, the governor, or a particular department of the federal government. The result was that the early executive and judicial branches of the territorial government were so politically independent of one another that their administration bordered on anarchy.[7] Out of the eight federal officials first sent to Dakota, for example, at least three of them, and perhaps more, took office with the serious expectation of becoming the next governor or territorial delegate.[8]

Not one of these officials saw his appointment in a bureaucratic light or would have considered himself as a trained civil servant or an expert administrator to a colonial region.[9] The position was merely a stepping stone to a more important office or, as was often the case, a base from which a recently defeated politician might operate to recoup his political fortunes.

The first Chief Justice of Dakota, Philemon Bliss, was a repre-

7. The federal government did little to remedy this anarchy. "There was more than lack of administrative impulse, attributable possibly to decentralization and to the press of other affairs; there are evidences of a policy of non-intervention." Pomeroy, *The Territories and the United States*, p. 12.

8. Secretary John Hutchinson, Chief Justice Philemon Bliss, Attorney General William Gleason, and possibly Surveyor General George Hill expected to succeed Jayne. See TP, Dakota Letterbook, 1861–64, and TP, Dakota Appointments, 1861–66.

9. The territories from 1861 to 1890 were important to the federal government for patronage reasons mainly, which explains the lack of a territorial or colonial policy and largely explains the attitude of the appointees. It also reveals one of the basic differences between the British and American colonial system during the 19th century.

sentative of this latter type. A former abolitionist Congressman from Ohio, Bliss owed his judgeship to political friends, among whom were Salmon P. Chase, Benjamin F. Wade, and Frank P. Blair.[10] Bliss had high hopes of replacing Jayne as the territorial governor. He succeeded in forming a strong anti-Jayne faction within the local Republican party, but his enemies held up his obvious machinations to ridicule so many times that his chances for higher office were ruined.[11]

The attorney general, W. F. Gleason of Maryland, also had gubernatorial ambitions. But Gleason, whom Kingsbury has described as a "fastidious gentleman of the Henry Winter Davis school" and who neither smoked nor drank, found frontier politics so unpleasant that after a few months he accepted a consulship at Bordeaux as a position more befitting his tastes.[12]

Perhaps the most likable of the first federal officials were John Hutchinson, the territorial secretary, and George Hill, the surveyor general. Hutchinson, a small, nervous, but quite affable man, was a personal friend of William Seward. It was Seward's influence, he proudly admitted, that had secured him the secretaryship. Hutchinson's appointment file reveals that he would have preferred to become secretary of Washington Territory, and if that was not available to receive a consulship to one of the German states—just so long as it paid $2,000 a year.[13] A Minnesota lawyer by profession, he had acquired his political training as an active abolitionist in Kansas, where he served as speaker of the House of Representatives in the Topeka Assembly.[14] A man of some principle and capability, he also wished to replace Jayne, but he was to follow a frustrating and thankless career as secretary instead. Later he became so disgusted at the undis-

10. Letters endorsing Bliss are to be found in the U.S. Department of Justice, Appointments Division, Appointment Papers, Dakota Territory, 1861–62 (Justice Appointment Papers, Dakota).

11. Kingsbury, Dakota Territory, 1, 376–8.

12. Ibid., 1, 177, 182–3. See also J. B. S. Todd to Lincoln, February 1863, Justice Appointment Papers, Dakota. In a letter showing remarkable candor (W. E. Gleason to Lincoln, May 1863), Gleason asked for a judgeship in Dakota because it paid more. He received the appointment.

13. Kingsbury, Dakota Territory, 1, 181–2. See also Hutchinson letters in TP, Dakota Appointments, 1861–65, esp. J. S. Hutchinson to Seward, March 15, 1865.

14. Cyrus Aldrich, William Windom et al. to Lincoln, March 7, 1861, TP, Dakota Appointments, 1861–65.

ciplined antics of the Dakota politicians that he resigned from office and accepted a consulship in Leghorn, Italy.[15]

George Hill of Michigan was probably a more typical frontier official than any of the preceding men. A large jovial fellow with an overweening affection for alcohol and an unfailing instinct for speculation, Hill saw the office of surveyor general as a means to make a personal fortune in frontier lands. If one may believe Kingsbury, a Dakota journalist and historian who was Hill's contemporary, Hill "sold" every surveying contract to the highest bidder, who usually turned out to be an old friend from Michigan. Hill was, nevertheless, a leader of a faction of politicians within the local Republican party, and as a speculator interested in selling land to immigrants he was largely responsible—through persuasive speeches and pamphlets—for convincing the outside world that Dakota was inhabitable.[16]

Most of the federal officials set out for Dakota with no idea where the new capital was to be, so they made their destination Sioux City, Iowa. There they learned, in May 1861, that Governor Jayne had chosen Yankton, "Captain Todd's town," as the capital. Doane Robinson, one-time state historian of South Dakota, has stated that Jayne's choice was determined by Mrs. Lincoln's personal request that her cousin's settlement be favored.[17]

As Jayne, Hutchinson, Gleason, Bliss, and the other officials either steamed up the Missouri or rode along its banks that spring, they found themselves in a gently rolling, almost flat country of black earth covered with a thick sod of tall plains grasses.[18] In the hollows along the river and creek banks grew ash, cottonwood, and willow trees in great abundance, but the lack of trees

15. Kingsbury, *Dakota Territory*, *1*, 182.
16. Ibid., *1*, 183; U.S. Department of the Interior, Appointments Division, Applications and Papers Pertaining to Surveyors General of Dakota and Florida, 1865, File 3, 1262 (Interior Appointment Papers, Dakota Surveyors General). Hill had the entire Republican party of Michigan behind him when he was appointed. The charges against Hill for malfeasance in office were contained in a letter from J. B. S. Todd to James Harlan, July 23, 1865. Kingsbury and Armstrong indicate that the charges were true. Kingsbury, *Dakota Territory*, *1*, 314; Armstrong, *Early Empire Builders*, pp. 78, 128. See also Briggs, *Frontiers of the Northwest*, p. 370.
17. Robinson, *South Dakota*, *1*, 256–7; he does not cite the source of his information.
18. C. L. White and E. J. Foscue, *Regional Geography of Anglo-America* (New York, 1943), p. 586; S. S. Visher, "The Geography of South Dakota" *Bulletin of the South Dakota Geological and Natural History Survey*, 8 (1918), 1–117.

beyond the banks gave the terrain a barren appearance. This barrenness was perhaps emphasized by the absence of larger game such as the buffalo, for white and Indian hunters had nearly wiped out these animals in this region as early as 1850.[19]

The first settlements had begun to make their mark. At more than one creek or river crossing the travelers discovered a ferry, operated by a pioneer farmer who would take them to the other side for fifty cents.[20] In the river lowlands, or "bottoms" as they were called, Norwegian families from nearby Minnesota or from Wisconsin had already established several small closely knit communities.[21] At Elk Point, a settlement only twenty-five miles northeast of Sioux City, but in Dakota, a small but prosperous group of French-Canadian farmers had settled.[22] Vermillion, the next village along the way, boasted a sawmill operated by Jacob Deuel, a squaw man. Many Norwegians were taking up claims near Vermillion, and James McHenry had opened a general store to serve the town's rapidly increasing population.[23]

At Yankton the officials found a community of less than three hundred souls living in sod huts or rude log cabins. Though town blocks and lots were marked, only the most rudimentary streets existed. Yankton seemed less like a capital city than a mere camp site for trappers who might if they so wished load the major part of the town on their backs and move on to some other locality. On the town's main street, Broadway, stood a few of the cabins and the small law office of Captain Todd. Near the center of the town was the Ash Hotel, where the three most valuable things in Yankton were to be found: beds, whiskey, and food cooked by a white woman, Mrs. Ash, the wife of the proprietor. Even so, these three items were obtained under rather disheartening conditions. Two or three people had to share the beds, the floors were still of packed earth, and the inner walls of a room were usually blankets

19. Garraghan, *Jesuits of the Middle United States*, 2, 451–2. For an excellent account of the decline of the buffalo in the Northwest see Briggs, *Frontier of the Northwest*, pp. 125–80.

20. Ibid., pp. 256–357.

21. G. Bie Ravndal, "The Scandanavian Pioneers of South Dakota," *Collections of the State Historical Society of South Dakota, 12* (1924), 309. Ravndal states that the early Scandanavian settlers were Norwegians from Dane County, Wisconsin; Winneshiek, Iowa; and Goodhue County, Minnesota.

22. Kingsbury, *Dakota Territory, 1*, 152.

23. Ibid., p. 127.

or skins stretched across part of a larger room to make several sleeping compartments.[24] Governor Jayne himself found living quarters so scarce that he had to share his bed with the attorney general for the first six months.[25]

How the officials reacted to the capital city one can easily surmise. Kingsbury believed that they were all disappointed when they "came face to face with Dakota and into real possession of their offices." [26] A first glance at the Yankton citizen must have proven even more disappointing. Almost all of the inhabitants were young men in their twenties or thirties, unmarried, and quite used to frontier hardships. A majority of them sported mustaches or beards, wore a colorful mixture of Indian, pioneer, and American dress, and carried a variety of sidearms, knives, and other instruments of protection. Half-breeds, full-blooded Indians, sojourning fur trappers, squaw men, speculators, Frost-Todd agents and traders, lawyers and surveyors, agents from the nearby Yankton and Brulé Indian reservations, and army couriers passing through town to Fort Randall up the river—these constituted the motley population.

The early citizens seemed to be engaged in almost every occupation but that of farming; indeed, most of them were still quite dubious about the agricultural possibilities of Dakota. They were more interested in the booming of town lots, trading with Indians, or holding some government office or contract. The absence of a strong agricultural group within the early Yankton population which would provide the community with a basic food supply and source of local wealth led many into an excessive interest in speculation—schemes of the wildest sort—and on the social side, they engaged in huge fights and drinking bouts to ward off the boredom and disgust that could so easily overwhelm the spirited inhabitants of an isolated frontier town. Any deviation from the norm was welcomed with almost pathetic eagerness as a source of amusement, excitement, or ridicule.

One of the chief outlets of the pent-up energy of the Yankton and Dakota nonfarming citizens was a great interest in politics,

24. Ibid., p. 194; Armstrong, *Early Empire Builders*, pp. 35–6.
25. Robinson, *South Dakota*, 1, 257.
26. Kingsbury, *Dakota Territory*, 1, 183.

as a calling or avocation. Traditionally political-minded, the American pioneer in Dakota was to make politics—the only organized general sport on the frontier—his main preoccupation throughout the territorial period. So great did this interest become that it led many Dakotans to view all their problems in a political light and to pose their solutions in political terms and action. The fact that they did not categorize economic, social, and political institutions, combined with the mobility and amorphousness of these institutions, partially explains this development and, incidentally—some twenty years later—makes the attempt of the Alliance and the Populists to redress their economic grievances by political action seem much more logical.[27] But there were other important reasons for the Dakotan's obsession with politics, as the activities of the Sioux Falls squatter government have indicated. A study of the early territorial period will bring these to light.

Governor Jayne had been in Yankton only a week, and had not yet made a census of the population so that legal elections could be held, when a self-styled "Union Party Mass Convention" met in Vermillion to choose one A. J. Bell as the Republican candidate for territorial delegate. A few days later a similar meeting occurred in Bon Homme, a settlement thirty miles west of Yankton. There the candidate, C. P. Booge, appeared simply as a nominee of the "Peoples' Party." Captain Todd also entered the delegate race, but he posed as an "independent" rather than as a Democrat and laid heavy stress upon his close relationship to the new President in Washington. He prevented a convention from nominating him, for he felt it would be wiser not to divulge his political strength too openly to the new Republican officials in Dakota.[28]

The importance of the delegate's role in territorial politics is difficult to exaggerate. As the single elected representative in Washington of an entire territory, he was the clearing house for most of the territorial-federal business. Through his office flowed rivers of patronage of every sort, and if it did not flow freely, he

27. See below, Chap. 9.
28. Kingsbury, *Dakota Territory*, 1, 184–6; Armstrong, *Early Empire Builders*, p. 32; Robinson, *South Dakota*, 1, 265–7.

was promptly defeated in the next election. In an excellent study
of territorial administration, Earl S. Pomeroy recently wrote:
"General interest in elections for delegate probably attests to the
influence and importance of the post as well as to the pleasures
of life in Washington. Party battles were as fierce as in the elections for senator and representative; party issues were drawn as
broadly as in the states." [29] Such campaigns naturally laid bare
the form of territorial politics and thus are of particular value in
understanding the politics of Dakota.

The most striking characteristic of the early Dakota delegate
campaigns was the absence of a true party organization behind
any of the candidates; instead, there existed only small local factions who supported a candidate because he had promised them
a specific reward. In many cases the members of a faction had
little relation to membership within a single party, and after an
election such factions would disband or even shift their alliance
if reward did not appear.[30] Only in the last ten years of the
territory's existence were party machines and organizations able
to bring these ever-shifting factions, or "combinations" as the
Dakotans preferred to call them, under control.[31] Political conventions usually consisted of a group of factions that had temporarily agreed on a candidate and wished to present a harmonious
front for a few weeks by adopting the name of a national party
and paying lip service to its platform.

The first Dakota delegate election was even simpler; it was
merely a test of the personal strength and influence of the three
candidates. Only the Bell faction went through the formality
of adopting a platform.[32] Two newspapers were established for
the duration of the campaign to support the candidates and each
was paid out of the candidate's pocket. The *Weekly Dakotan* at
Yankton was the Todd organ, and the Vermillion *Republican*
devoted its energies to Mr. Bell's election. Mr. Booge, it was

29. Pomeroy, *The Territories and the United States,* pp. 82–8.
30. Armstrong, *Early Empire Builders,* pp. 131, 139, describes some of the factions in Dakota.
31. See below, Chaps. 7, 8.
32. Robinson, *South Dakota,* 1, 265–6. The "Union Party" had as one of its platform planks a stern denunciation of monopoly. It was directed not toward big
business, however, but toward Todd's control over the Territory and toward Sioux
Falls ambitions.

commonly reported, "relied upon his fast horses and stump speakers." [33] It was common knowledge that a large majority of the Dakotans were Democrats, so that the decisive vote for Todd, when the election occurred in September, was not surprising.[34] Todd's victory, however, was not a Republican defeat so much as an affirmation of the fact that the settlers wanted the most economically powerful and politically influential man in their midst to represent them in Washington.

Although the election of the members of the first legislative Assembly in September 1861 was a spirited affair in each of the legislative and council districts from Pembina on the Canadian border to Bon Homme, the most southwesterly white settlement in Dakota,[35] the shaping of political factions and even the major reasons for their existence did not become apparent until the Assembly convened in March 1862.

Meanwhile political activity in the Territory became moribund during the winter of 1861–62. The federal officials returned to their eastern homes, the local newspapers ceased publication after elections were over, and a fear of Indian attacks and raids occupied the minds of the settlers and the few immigrants who appeared that winter. For exciting news and political action, the Dakotan would have to await the spring thaw and the convening of the Assembly.

Three weeks before the first Dakota Assembly met in March 1862 an anonymous newsletter appeared in the Sioux City *Register* which told of the happenings in the frontier capital of Yankton. The federal officials had returned; a company of militia had been organized to meet either an Indian or a Confederate attack; and, the correspondent continued, "wire-pulling and pipe-laying has commenced for officering the two Houses. *Politics are discarded.*" [36]

This report was quite accurate, for Governor Jayne and the local

33. Armstrong, *Early Empire Builders*, p. 32.
34. Kingsbury, *Dakota Territory*, 1, 185.
35. See map above, p. 29.
36. Moses K. Armstrong was the correspondent. A pioneer journalist and politician, Armstrong wrote a series of pro-Democratic articles for the Sioux City *Register* which reveal his great keenness of observation. He used the pseudonym "Logroller" but everyone in Dakota knew the author. The quotation is from the Sioux City *Register*, February 19, 1862; italics are mine.

Yankton politicians, a majority of whom were Democrats, were busy striking agreements and "deals" which completely ignored party lines. Their aim was to control the coming session so that they could permanently locate the territorial capital at Yankton, for by the Organic Act the Assembly could, at will, revoke Jayne's choice.[37] The Sioux Falls forces, now led by W. W. Brookings and G. P. Waldron, were still strong despite their recent defeat in Washington, and they had not abandoned the hope that Sioux Falls could be the capital.[38] At the same time the settlements of Vermillion and Bon Homme were large enough now to compete with Yankton for the honor. Moreover, Vermillion had four councilmen in the Assembly while Yankton had only two.[39] Thus Jayne and his colleagues, and Captain Todd and *his* supporters in the Assembly—M. K. Armstrong, D. T. Bramble, John Stanage, and C. F. Picotte—joined forces to obtain an agreement from the various sectional factions to leave the capital where it was.[40] Their method of persuasion was obvious: they distributed the honors of Assembly office to the Bon Homme faction in return for their cooperation. George M. Pinney, a Bon Homme Republican who also had an interest in Vermillion, became the speaker of the House after pledging his word in writing that he would not oppose Yankton. J. H. Shober, a wily and shrewd lawyer who had brought one of the earliest colonies of settlers to Bon Homme, was made president of the Council. In this way the Vermillion forces and Brookings and Waldron, who had been elected to the Assembly by the Sioux Falls district, would be unable to secure a majority vote for removal. To guarantee further Yankton's hold on the capital, Vermillion was to be the site of the territorial university and Bon Homme was to have the territorial penitentiary.[41] When the Assembly convened, the formal

37. See the Organic Act for Dakota, in Kingsbury, *Dakota Territory, 1,* 170–3.

38. Brookings and Waldron were both officials of the Western Town Company, which had located alongside the Dakota Company at Sioux Falls.

39. Robinson, *South Dakota, 1,* 268.

40. C. F. Picotte, a Yankton half-breed educated in St. Louis, was sergeant-at-arms of the Council. He had aided Todd in securing the Indian treaty of cession in 1858 and had received $30,000 for his efforts. As a leader among the local half-breeds and the Yankton Indians, he possessed considerable political influence. Kingsbury, *Dakota Territory, 1,* 250–2.

41. Armstrong, *Early Empire Builders,* pp. 63–4; *House Journal of the Legislative Assembly of the Territory of Dakota, 1862* (Yankton, 1862), pp. 1–10; D. Robinson, *History of South Dakota* (Yankton, 1904), *1,* 192–3.

election of these picked officers was carried out without a hitch, and even the lesser offices such as that of clerk and fireman were farmed out among the Bon Homme and Yankton members with little trouble.[42]

To discern the emerging patterns of frontier politics in Dakota it will be necessary to treat only three aspects of the Assembly proceedings of 1862. First, a brief analysis of the individual make-up of the Assembly itself, an account of its collective attitudes, and its role in territorial politics will be helpful. Second, by discussing the capital location question, one of the abiding and chief political issues during the entire history of the territory will become apparent. Third, a short mention of the more significant legislation passed by the Assembly should throw light on other points of political difference.

In treating the make-up of the Dakota Assembly it is important to remember that its members were very conscious of the fact that they were laying the foundations of representative government in a new area of the Northwest. They likened themselves to the Pilgrims at Plymouth and to the Founding Fathers at Philadelphia. They half believed the glowing predictions of greatness, both for the Territory and for themselves, that Governor Jayne enunciated in his first address before the Assembly.[43] They all shared a belief that they had been particularly chosen to shape the destiny of Dakota.

But in order to establish the political and economic institutions, the first assemblymen felt that they must have the power to do so. Hence they showed an unfailing antipathy to federal control

42. *House Journal* (1862), pp. 1–10.

43. Jayne informed the Assembly that in Dakota "We have combined the pleasant, salubrious climate of Southern Minnesota with the fertility of soil of central Illinois. . . . I venture the prediction, that the wheat granary of this continent will yet be found in the valley of the Red River and Saskatchawan." Dakota would be settled as quickly as Indiana, Illinois, Michigan, Missouri, Wisconsin, and Iowa, he felt, for "shall we not judge the future by the past." Moreover, the Pacific railroad would bring the trade of the Orient through its borders and the Big Sioux could be harnessed to drive all the machinery of the New England mills. Jayne then prophesied that the United States would direct all nations in fifty years, that it would have a "government with a hundred millions of loyal subjects, carrying the beneficent influence of her arts and her civilization upon the wings of her commerce, over every sea and ocean, to every continent and isle, which smiles beneath the genial rays of the sun." *Council Journal of the Legislative Assembly of Dakota,* 1862 (Yankton, 1862), pp. 15–30.

by the governor or by other appointed officials. They voiced the traditional frontier demand for "local" and therefore "truly democratic" self-government. Hidden beneath such phraseology was the ambition to achieve supremacy over territorial executive, legislative, and judicial powers, to ignore completely any concept of checks and balances in government, and to deny any separation between government and private enterprise. To achieve these ends more than to curb tyranny they bombarded Congress with petitions for checking the veto power of the governor, for his popular election, and for a law permitting only territorial residents to be eligible for the office. The Assembly was, indeed, the focal point of every type of faction, political, economic, and otherwise.

So obvious were the various factions and lobbies who tried to influence the Assembly, from both within and without, that Frank M. Ziebach, a pioneer editor of Yankton, organized these groups into a "Third House of the Assembly," which met while the regular Assembly was in session and parodied its actions. Indeed, Ziebach became known as the "Squatter Governor," and every Dakotan knew what it meant to be called a member of the "Third House." [44]

It would be misleading to say that the average assemblyman adhered to these beliefs or patterns of action in any grim and deliberate manner, for he was first of all an opportunist, flexible in his ambitions and shifting in his loyalties. The average legislator was such a young and active man that the sessions often resembled a college fraternity meeting. On various occasions these frontier solons brandished pistols to get recognition from the speaker, or had drinks sent in from a nearby saloon. Of the thirteen members of the House of Representatives only six were over thirty years old and of these six only two were over thirty-five years of age. John L. Tiernon, who replaced Pinney as the first Speaker of the House, was a mere twenty-two, and the oldest of the hired officers was only thirty.[45] The Council presented a similar roster of young legislators, their average age being thirty-two.[46] With an exuberance that demanded informality, and some-

44. Kingsbury, *Dakota Territory*, 1, 210.
45. *House Journal* (1862), pp. 1-7.
46. *Council Journal* (1862), pp. 1-6.

times produced anarchy, these loud and lusty legislators set the wheels of Dakota government in motion.

Eight of the House members claimed to be farmers, but a majority of these were actually land speculators or agents. Two were surveyors, one a lawyer, one a trader, and Waldron of Sioux Falls described himself as only a laborer though he was actually the treasurer of the Western Town Company.[47] In the Council, on the other hand, only one farmer could be found, in the company of five lawyers, two merchants, and one engineer.[48]

The birthplace of the legislators was even more instructive. In the House three of the members were Irish immigrants, two were from Norway, one was from Canada, and the rest came from Missouri, Ohio, Indiana, Pennsylvania, New Hampshire, Vermont, and New York.[49] The Council differed from the House on the question of national origin, however, for every member was a native-born American, with a majority coming from the northeastern states.[50]

The fact that most of the members of the Assembly were born in the United States meant that they possessed an ethnic homogeneity and a familiarity with American political traditions that gave them an advantage over the politically naive Scandanavian and Bohemian settlers who were to make up a large segment of the territorial population. What is more, a majority of these native Americans appear to have had a common Protestant New England background. The result was that the transplanted New Englander, whether he was from Maine or from Indiana, brought with him some of the social and political institutions of his home state and set them up in Dakota. And although these men did not form the greater number of the Dakota population in 1861 or later, they contributed a disproportionate number of local political leaders, who in turn partly fashioned political traditions.[51]

This so-called "American group" also became associated with

47. *House Journal* (1862), pp. 1–2.
48. *Council Journal* (1862), pp. 1–2.
49. *House Journal* (1862), p. 1.
50. *Council Journal* (1862), p. 1.
51. House and Council *Journals* (1862–63); W. H. H. Beadle,"Memoirs of General William Henry Harrison Beadle," *South Dakota Historical Collections, 3* (1906), 99–102; Herbert E. Gaston, *The Non-Partisan League* (New York, 1920), pp. 11–13.

the Republican party and thus were the main recipients of federal patronage throughout the territorial period. A judicious use of this patronage won over most of the Scandanavian and Bohemian village political leaders, who in turn persuaded their constituents to vote in single blocs for the Republican party.[52]

A few members of this first Assembly deserve individual attention. Fortunately for the historian, Moses Kimball Armstrong, an amateur journalist with a keen appreciation of frontier politics, was a member of the Assembly, and he has recorded, in a rough humorous style, biographical sketches of his colleagues and a brief account of the proceedings of that none too august body.[53]

Armstrong himself was a member of the House in 1861 and was the leader of the Todd Democrats. Though only twenty-nine, he had behind him ten years of experience on the frontiers of Iowa, Minnesota, and Dakota. As early as 1855 he had surveyed land in the Red River Valley; before that he had written articles booming infant towns in Minnesota and had used his journalistic abilities in political campaigns, both local and national.[54]

Armstrong remains today one of the most appealing of the colorful figures of which Dakota history is full. His disarming candor was so tinged with humor that few opponents could take offense. Unlike Todd, whom he was to replace as the leader of the Dakota Democracy, Armstrong made his political moves with unabashed openness, using charm and wit where Todd had relied on "influence" or adroit maneuvers.[55]

Quite in contrast to the urbane Armstrong was Speaker of the House George Pinney, a young lawyer of tremendous ambitions

52. Gaston, *Non-Partisan League*, pp. 11–13.

53. These sketches first appeared in the Sioux Falls *Register* under the pseudonym of "Logroller." Armstrong saved clippings of the articles, which he put into a scrapbook now deposited in the Minnesota Historical Society. When he published his *Early Empire Builders of the Great West*, 1901, he included the sketches. His writings today have a special value, for in addition to his descriptive ability and political insight, he was more interested in factual history than in reminiscences or sentimental history. He was one of the founders of the Dakota Historical Association and one-time President of the Minnesota Historical Society. See pp. v–vi in *Early Empire Builders*; also his *History of Southeastern Dakota*.

54. From clippings in Armstrong Scrapbook, MS in possession of the Minnesota Historical Society, St. Paul.

55. In an undated letter Armstrong wrote to an editor, "I came to this territory to make money, and not to fawn or cringe at the feet of the people, for the sake of office or political favors." Armstrong Scrapbook.

and few scruples. The pugnacious and scheming Pinney had been the organizer of the "Union Party" which had backed A. J. Bell for the delegateship in 1861. That failing, he had allied himself to Jayne and the Republican party. But since the Republicans in the first Assembly were not only unorganized but in the minority, Pinney's power there was limited, and he turned his attention to obtaining federal office. He succeeded in 1862 when he became United States Marshal for Dakota.[56]

In the Council the number of able men was greater. Shober, the shrewd lawyer from Bon Homme has been mentioned. The outstanding personality was Enos Stutsman, a very small but fiery member from Yankton who had successfully lived on the frontier for years despite the fact that he was almost a dwarf because of abnormally short legs. Stutsman thrived on large political and speculative schemes in the best western tradition. As he hobbled about Yankton on his canes like a frontier Toulouse-Lautrec, he considered himself an equal to all comers. Armstrong has described how Stutsman, in reply to an insult or a challenge, would spring upon his opponent, knock him to the ground, and there, where they were equals, thrash him.[57]

Politically, Stutsman had been a Democrat and had been associated with Todd in the Yankton Town Company.[58] But when he saw that the federal officials of Dakota might be of more aid to him than local political popularity, he cast his lot with that of Jayne and became for a time the Governor's secretary.[59] Stutsman's eagerness for political power almost places him on a level with Burr or Houston. He envisioned himself as the leader of a northern territory carved out of Dakota and roughly equivalent in size to the present state of North Dakota. He wrangled the job of customs collector at Pembina to further his scheme.[60] Later he dabbled in the Louis Riel Half-Breed Rebellion in the hope

56. Robinson, History of South Dakota, 1, 193–4; Kingsbury, Dakota Territory, 1, 184, 206 ff.

57. Kingsbury, Dakota Territory, 1, 144, 463; Armstrong, in the Bismarck Tribune, December 28, 1887.

58. Armstrong, Early Empire Builders, p. 29.

59. William Jayne to Enos Stutsman, June 30, 1862, "Official Papers of the Governors of Dakota Territory," MS, State Department of History, Bismarck, North Dakota (Governor's File, Bismarck). See also Armstrong, Early Empire Builders, p. 34.

60. Armstrong, Early Empire Builders, p. 53; see also Armstrong in the Bismarck Tribune, December 28, 1887.

that Western Canada would annex itself to the United States and he could be one of the founders of a northwestern empire.[61] Such were the dreams of the short, half-crippled lawyer from Indiana, who always signed his letters, "Your little friend, Stuts."

In the agent of the Western Town Company, W. W. Brookings, the Council had another leader. After graduating from Bowdoin College, Brookings had come west to Dubuque, Iowa, to make his fortune. There he became a stockholder in the company which located at Sioux Falls. With a grim puritanical zeal Brookings had cast his lot with the Sioux Falls Squatter Assembly of 1858 and had served as the president of its council. The defeat of the squatter government only made him the more persistent as a boomer for Sioux Falls. Like Stutsman he was crippled; part of both feet had been amputated, after having been frozen in a blizzard in 1859 while he was racing to the Missouri River to establish a townsite claim for his company.[62]

To Brookings the Assembly of 1862 was merely another instrument to use in booming Sioux Falls and advancing his own fortunes. More than almost any person in Dakota he saw political office as the means of promoting economic ends. He joined the Republican party, since it controlled territorial patronage, and in the first Assembly he was one of the few to vote consistently on a party basis; but later when the party refused to serve his ends, he caused a breach in its ranks which rendered it politically helpless for over four years.[63]

While the remainder of the assemblymen were not outstanding, they were by no means the passive followers of Todd, Jayne, Brookings, or the others. Downer T. Bramble, a shrewd and hardworking Yankton merchant, for example, was an impassioned opponent of Jayne.[64] The two Norwegian members of the House, Burgess and Jacobson, refused to join any faction and voted independently on every issue.[65] Since they did not make policy, they need not be treated at length here.

61. Ruth Ellen Sanborn, "The United States and the British Northwest," *North Dakota Historical Quarterly*, 6 (1931), 36–8. Miss Sanborn refers to Stutsman as the leader of the "American intrigues."
62. Kingsbury, *Dakota Territory*, 1, 99; Robinson, *South Dakota*, 1, 538.
63. See below, Chap. 4.
64. Armstrong, *Early Empire Builders*, pp. 67–8.
65. Ibid., p. 70.

One of the chief causes of political difference in Dakota was the capital location issue. As a local manifestation of political conflict based upon geographic sectionalism, which has been so constant a theme in American history, it was to be expected. From the agreement which located Washington on the Potomac to the sordid fight between opposing land speculation groups over the site of the Nebraska territorial capital, one can trace the story of this issue and see behind it similar motives for political and economic gain.

The situation of a political capital was very important in an area where industry was unheard of, where there was little proof that agriculture could exist successfully, and where no mineral wealth had been found in great quantity in 1861. Rather, trapping, Indian trade, speculation, and political office were the sources of income. These sources were intimately bound up with the federal government, since it possessed direct sovereignty over the territory and controlled its various livelihoods through the Indian Bureau, the Land Office, and the Departments of State, Interior, Justice, and War. Only in this way can the great preoccupation with issues like those of capital or even county seat location for nearly fifty years in Dakota be made intelligible.[66]

When the Dakota legislators considered the bill to make Yankton the permanent capital, Armstrong wrote that "Excitement ran to a high pitch during a few days on the last stages of the bill." "A little blood was shed, much whiskey drank, a few eyes blacked, revolvers drawn, and some running done."[67] At the last minute Speaker Pinney, who held the balance of power, became so enamored of his ability to make any Dakota village the seat of government that he disregarded his agreement with the Todd

66. The capital issue was still being fought in South Dakota as late as 1905. Of similar struggles over capital location Avery Craven writes: "Kansas settlers, like other frontiersmen, usually found their funds exhausted before their new land began to yield a surplus. The control of government and the salaries from public office often measured the difference between failure and holding on. Control of government also gave the power to locate county seats, to determine the location of the territorial capitals, and to influence the lines along which the railroads would run. The Kansas struggle was, to some extent, a conflict between two frontier groups for just such advantages. Slavery differences aggravated but did not produce the interests involved. Disputes over lands contributed even more to the struggle." *The Coming of the Civil War*, p. 362.

67. *House Journal* (1862), pp. 100–13; Armstrong, *Early Empire Builders*, pp. 63–4.

forces to favor Yankton. In a surprise move he united with the Pembina, Sioux Falls, and Vermillion forces to place the capital at Vermillion. Pinney's coup almost succeeded, but after a rapid reorganization of factions, Yankton remained the capital.[68]

The fury of the betrayed Todd men knew no bounds. They moved to unseat Pinney as the speaker, but they could not muster the necessary two-thirds vote. They concocted a plan whereby they would forcibly unseat Pinney, throw him out of the window, and while he was recovering from bodily injury, elect a new speaker. Upon learning of this plan, Pinney requested Jayne to station soldiers from the local militia in the House to aid him in retaining the chair. At the appearance of the soldiers the House adjourned in protest and the Council demanded an explanation from the governor. Jayne, seeing that the Assembly would not be cowed, replied that Pinney had "cowardly and scandalously" misrepresented the facts to him; therefore he ordered the withdrawal of the soldiers.[69]

Pinney then submitted his resignation as speaker and the Todd Democrats elected John L. Tiernon, an army officer from Fort Randall, in his place.[70] The colorful episode did not end there, however, for the sergeant-at-arms of the House, determined to carry out the original plan to unseat Pinney, hurled the exspeaker through a closed window when the two happened to meet in Robeart's Saloon one day. A few days later, Delegate Todd personally attacked Pinney, whereupon the latter voluntarily jumped through another window and "ran as but few lawmakers could run." [71]

The capital issue with all of the rough entertainment which it provided was only one of the sectional problems that plagued the Assembly. The various capital factions had within them factions struggling over the location of county seat towns, territorial institutions, and roads.[72] It is safe to say that all the Assembly members had invested in land in Dakota, or planned to

68. Armstrong, *Early Empire Builders*, p. 66.
69. Ibid., p. 64; Kingsbury, *Dakota Territory*, 1, 206.
70. Armstrong, *Early Empire Builders*, p. 66.
71. Ibid., p. 69; Robinson, *History of South Dakota*, 1, 193.
72. *House Journal* (1862), pp. 100, 103, 105, 118.

live partly by legal transactions involving land. Although this
gave them a common interest, it resulted in as many political
factions as separate settlements, for each had the aim of en-
hancing the value of the land and business of his particular community. Such an approach acted to restrict true party development.

The sectional issue took still another form in the controversy
over the apportionment of seats in the Assembly, the number of
which had been limited by federal law; hence each legislative
district was interested in revising apportionment so as to permit it
to have the largest number of representatives and councilors. Never
was gerrymandering practiced with more avidity. A political deal
could produce a new county or legislative district overnight—
or just as quickly abolish one. The hope of increased representation caused many of the counties to return the most preposterous
census reports when Dakota was organized.[73] An excellent example of the extremes to which the districts went occurred in the
second Assembly. A few days before adjournment, the Assembly
passed a fair apportionment law. The Red River delegation, thinking that no new measures of importance would arise, departed
for home. These men were barely out of the Yankton town limits
when several anti-Todd factions united to pass a new apportionment bill which would have deprived the Red River Valley of
all representation whatsoever! The resulting extra seats were given
to Bon Homme County, now a stronghold of Governor Jayne's.
Fortunately the passage of the bill required a two-thirds vote,
and it failed when the speaker, who was Armstrong, had to cast
the deciding ballot.[74]

In two other pieces of legislation the basis for Dakota political
differences became apparent. One of them concerned a bill to
exclude negroes from the Territory. "No persons of color, bond
or free," the bill read, "shall reside upon the soil of Dakota Territory," and should any attempt to do so, they must leave within
twenty days or be jailed.[75] The bill originated as a result of a

73. William Jayne to Seward, Annual Report (1862), TP, Dakota Letterbook.
74. *House Journal* (1862–63), pp. 192–3; Armstrong, *Early Empire Builders*,
pp. 97–8.
75. Armstrong, *Early Empire Builders*, pp. 69–70; *House Journal* (1862), p.
157.

recommendation in the governor's message urging that slavery be abolished in Dakota by law.[76] The Democratic Assembly instead passed one which made a travesty of Jayne's views by forbidding negroes to reside in Dakota. The bill passed the Council with a five to three vote, the Republicans Betts, Boyle, and Brookings opposing it. In the House it failed when two old-line Democrats joined the Republican members in voting against it.[77]

The vote disclosed a split between the frontier and eastern elements in the Assembly, and therein lay the nearest thing to conflict in principles that could be found in Dakota politics for the next five years. The Dakotans followed the progress of the Civil War with a tremendous interest, and though few if any in the Territory ever openly favored the Confederacy, the Democratic frontier element in Dakota cared little for the principles upon which the abolitionists and the Republicans had taken their stand, or upon which the nation had divided in 1861.[78] They knew that Dakota would never have a negro population; nevertheless, they refused to allow even the "imaginary negro" his right to live in an "impossible place." The federal officials and those recently arrived from the East, whether of Republican or Democratic leanings, felt that they must oppose such an attitude, although it might be only an academic issue in Dakota.[79] Ex-Speaker Pinney dismissed the whole attempt to pass such a law as merely the "legitimate offspring of four gallons of villainous whiskey." [80] Armstrong wrote, however, that because of this law "Party politics have been sprung in a tangible form." [81]

The frontier-eastern cleavage became much clearer in the voting on the General Half-Breed Bill. Realizing that the half-breeds and trappers of mixed blood formed a considerable segment of the population and recognizing them as a possible powerful polit-

76. See Governor Jayne's address in *Council Journal* (1862), pp. 21–2. Jayne concluded his antislavery remarks with the plea, "Let us by a prohibitory enactment express our repugnance to an institution which today convulses the continent; arrays a million of men in arms, suspends business, prostrates trade, and paralyzes all the industrial interests of the country . . . "

77. Armstrong, *Early Empire Builders*, p. 70.

78. Robinson, *History of South Dakota*, 1, 194, cites a case of supposed disloyalty which ended in full acquittal.

79. Bliss, Jayne, and Hutchinson had all been abolitionists.

80. Armstrong Scrapbook; from the Sioux City *Register*, April 22, 1862.

81. Ibid., article dated April 30, 1862.

ical ally, the Todd Democrats attempted to pass a bill which would allow any half-breed who could read, write, or speak the English language to become a citizen of the Territory.[82] The alarm of the federal officials and of the Republicans in the Assembly was great. News of the proposed bill aroused so much interest that parties of men and women journeyed all the way from Sioux City, Iowa, to watch the spirited proceedings of the two Houses. Passage of the bill meant that the "Moccasin Democrats" would rule Dakota, and that factional though it might be, the Democratic party would be unbeatable, since it was estimated that the half-breeds were the largest single ethnic group in the Territory outside of the Indians themselves. The bill passed the lower House by one vote, but in the Council, because of the personal intervention of Jayne, it failed by one vote.[83] In Dakota the East had won its first political battle over the West.

There is a delightfully ironic inconsistency in the positions taken on the negro and the half-breed bills. The Republican officials, while urging freedom and the granting of some rights to the negro slave, stood ready to kill any grant of political rights to the half-breed. On the other hand, the frontier Democrats, by forbidding the negro to live in Dakota, ostensibly for fear he would constitute a racial and political problem, hoped to use a local racial group as a means to achieve political power.

Finally, the economic legislation of the first Assembly illustrated another facet of Dakota politics. Eager to advance the economic development of the Territory while at the same time controlling this development, the legislators passed broad homestead and debt-exemption laws which were calculated to attract the immigrant.[84] The Assembly held up the incorporation of the Missouri and Niobrara Valley Railroad Company, formed by Erastus Corning, Elihu Washburn, Isaac Pendleton, and other eastern promoters, until they had made every member of the Assembly a partner! Then it granted the company an extremely

82. Armstrong, *Early Empire Builders,* pp. 73–4. It is possible that Charles F. Picotte, the half-breed sergeant-at-arms of the Council, was behind this bill.
83. Armstrong reports having seen Jayne in the streets "logrolling" to defeat the bill. *Early Empire Builders,* pp. 73–4.
84. *General Laws of the Territory of Dakota,* 1862 (Yankton, 1862), pp. 299, 410, 480.

liberal charter! [85] The laws for establishing townsite claims were likewise very liberal, since each member stood to benefit by them. Again, in the memorials to Congress the Assembly pleaded as one man for the location of army distributing depots in Dakota, for more military forts, for cavalry, for road grants, and for a treaty with the Brulé Sioux by which the Sioux would cede the Black Hills. They urged that the federal government encourage the Hudson's Bay Company's use of the Red River route to the east coast, and they ended their memorials in this session with a request for new mail routes. [86]

No sooner had the Assembly adjourned and the campaign for the election of the second Assembly and a new delegate begun than news of a general Indian outbreak in Minnesota struck terror into the hearts of the Dakota settlers. [87] Maddened by many years of broken promises, the machinations of crooked agents, and the ever-increasing pressure of white settlement, the Minnesota Sioux resorted to war to redress their wrongs. Within a few days two hundred miles of frontier settlements along the Minnesota River were under attack. [88] Though the neighboring Yanktons remained neutral, the Santees and other Dakota tribes raided farms near Yankton, and the Sioux Falls settlers upon hearing of the massacre at New Ulm, Minnesota, completely abandoned their town, many fleeing into Iowa or the more settled parts of Minnesota. Yankton built a stockade and blockhouse, and every man went armed. Rumors that Confederate agents were behind the Indian attack caused many to see the outbreak as more serious than it really was, but in September 1862 the army found the situation grave enough to create a Department of the Northwest under General John Pope, late commander of the Army of Virginia. [89]

Strangely enough, the Indian menace, immediate as it was, failed to divert attention of those remaining in Dakota from the

85. *Private Laws of the Territory of Dakota*, 1862 (Yankton, 1862), pp. 21–8.
86. See *General Laws of the Territory of Dakota* (1862), pp. 505 ff.
87. For a detailed treatment of the causes of the outbreak see Doane Robinson, "A Comprehensive History of the Dakota or Sioux Indians," *Collections of the State Historical Society of South Dakota*, 2 (1904), 252–68; see also C. E. De Land, "The Sioux Wars," op. cit., *15* (1930), 9–32.
88. Robinson, "History of the Sioux Indians," pp. 275 ff.
89. This belief was unfounded, but many nevertheless believed it to be true; see F. L. Paxson, *The Last American Frontier* (New York, 1924), pp. 227, 243–4.

political campaigns of 1862; indeed such a tremendous interest was manifested that a sufficient explanation is difficult to find.[90]

The two contestants for the delegateship were Todd, who sought reelection, and Governor Jayne, who had come to prefer Washington politics to those of Yankton. Jayne had succeeded in organizing most of the federal officials and the Bon Homme, Sioux Falls, and Vermillion Republicans into a sort of temporary machine which would support him.[91]

Todd had the support of the regular Democrats, such as Armstrong and Shober, of the frontier elements around Fort Randall and further up the Missouri, and of Judge Bliss and Attorney-General Gleason, each of whom harbored a personal animosity toward Jayne. Bliss and Gleason were welcome visitors to the Democratic ranks, since it enabled them to appear as a fusion group under the name of the "Peoples' Union" party and thus escape the anti-union tag which was pinned to the Democratic party throughout the Civil War.[92]

The platform of the Republicans consisted largely of patriotic utterances and a repetition of the national party planks. Todd's, while expressing equally fervent patriotic sentiments, was designed to fit local prejudices. It denounced Jayne and the other officials as nonresidents who spent the major portion of their time and salaries in the East. It asked that the governor's veto be curbed and that Congress provide a timber tract of land along with every homestead. Finally, with a stroke of the western genius for opportunism, the platform requested that soldiers should be allowed to pick their own officers. This plank had some appeal for nearly every male over twenty-one in Dakota, since they had been mobilized into the territorial militia to protect the settlements from Indian raids.[93]

During the campaign the absence of party lines once again was

---

90. "The year of 1862, notwithstanding various other diversions, including the Indian war, was a year of politics in Dakota Territory": Robinson, *South Dakota, 1,* 273. Armstrong reported that while the first Assembly was still in session, "Outside chalking and peg-driving had already commenced on the delegate election this fall. I have heard of a dozen who would consent to serve their constituents in that capacity": *Early Empire Builders,* p. 74.

91. Robinson, *History of South Dakota, 1,* 198.

92. Ibid., p. 198; Kingsbury, *Dakota Territory, 1,* 217.

93. Kingsbury, *Dakota Territory, 1,* 221–30.

apparent. Some of the delegates to the Republican convention which chose Jayne also appeared as delegates to the Democratic one. One of the trustees of the defunct Dakota Land Company, F. J. De Witt, decided to urge Todd's election.[94] The main issue was over which of the candidates had the most influence with President Lincoln, his physician or his wife's cousin.[95]

On election day, September 1, with the Indian crisis at its height and with the settlements resembling armed camps, nearly every citizen in the territory—and many who were not—"voted early, late, often, vociferously and muscularly." [96] When Secretary Hutchinson and Judge Bliss canvassed the votes for delegate, they found so much evidence of fraud, especially ballot box stuffing, on both sides that they were at a loss as to what to do. With all the votes counted as valid, Jayne had won by less than a twenty-five majority. The two canvassers were certain that Jayne had been elected, but some of the Jayne ballots were so obviously fraudulent that they had to be thrown out. The problem became further involved when the Red River Valley returns failed to appear because of the difficulty of a messenger traveling through the hostile Indian country, so that no final decision could be made. On November 16, after the time had passed when the Red River votes could be legally counted, Bliss and Hutchinson declared that Jayne had won by sixteen votes.[97]

A few days later, a messenger bearing the Red River votes arrived in Yankton. He brought news that a major portion of them were for Captain Todd. It was as if no election had taken place.[98] Accusations flew between the candidates; Bliss and Hutchinson were attacked by both sides. Todd announced that he would contest the election and proceeded to take depositions from voters in areas where the voting had been fraudulent. Jayne countered by doing the same. Judges of election were examined and evidence of vote buying, midnight voting, false returns, and willful misleading of the Norwegian settlers about their right to vote all

94. Ibid., pp. 222–3.
95. Robinson, *South Dakota*, 1, 274; and *History of South Dakota*, 1, 197 ff.
96. Robinson, *South Dakota*, 1, 274; Kingsbury, *Dakota Territory*, 1, 230.
97. Kingsbury, *Dakota Territory*, 1, 230; Robinson, *History of South Dakota*, 1, 199.
98. Robinson, 1, 198.

appeared.[99] At Fort Randall the investigators discovered that a company of Iowa soldiers stationed there had been given leave on election day "to go plumming"; instead, they had "gone voting" for Jayne.[100]

So provoked were they by attacks and by new revelations of fraud that Bliss and Hutchinson later decided that Todd was the legally elected delegate, but in urging his recognition to the Congressional Committee on Elections they felt constrained to add that "the effrontery with which the elective franchise has been habitually trifled with in this Territory would surprise your honorable body, only as you refresh your recollection in relation to the Territorial election in Kansas." [101]

The delegate controversy so affected politics that the second Assembly, which met in December 1862, was simply the cockpit in which the fight continued. The Council, with Stutsman as its president, held angry sessions. A complete breakdown of parliamentary procedure and legislative organization occurred in the House. Only eight of its fourteen members had uncontested seats, and of these eight four were Jayne men and four were for Todd; consequently, there was a tie vote on every motion for five days. Under Secretary Hutchinson's guidance as temporary speaker—the situation must have reminded him of his previous experience as speaker of the House in Kansas—the House finally investigated enough contested elections to allow four new members to be seated. But the deadlock continued, for the vote was now a six-to-six tie. Then on December 9 the six Jayne members rose in a body, left the House, and thus destroyed a quorum. Later that day these six and three pro-Jayne contestants organized a separate House of Representatives, which the governor recognized as the official one. It proceeded to hold its sessions in Bramble's store down by the Yankton levee.[102]

The Council now declined to recognize the pro-Jayne House while Jayne refused to acknowledge the Todd House, which continued to meet in the capital building. The Todd House then con-

99. Report No. 27, *House Miscellaneous Documents,* 38th Cong., 1st sess., pp. 1–117.
100. Ibid., pp. 60–3.
101. Ibid., p. 138.
102. Kingsbury, *Dakota Territory, 1,* 258–61.

sulted Attorney General Gleason for a legal opinion on which body was competent to sit. Gleason ruled against his enemy the governor, declaring, "There is not in the whole range of Territorial history such an example of official presumption." [103] Jayne chose to ignore Gleason's opinion.

On the seventeenth day of the session the two factions, under the pressure of Hutchinson and the Council, finally worked out a compromise plan. Armstrong, a Todd Democrat, would replace as Speaker A. J. Harlan, a Todd Republican, and several of the contested seats would be given to the Jayne men.[104] In this way the Assembly was finally organized.

The second Assembly accomplished little in the way of legislation, for bitterness over the delegate contest, apportionment, county seat locations, and contested seats troubled the session until adjournment. The members found some diversion, however, in considering applications for a legislative grant of divorce, which they laughingly referred to the "Committee on Internal Improvements." This type of legislation evoked strong opposition from the more devout Lutheran members, who thought that such flippant proceedings made a mockery of all marriage, but since they were in a minority and the bachelors formed a majority in both Houses, their protests went unheeded.[105]

By far the most instructive law which passed the Assembly limited the working time of women and children in the mechanical and manufacturing trades to ten hours a day. The same limit applied to any labor contract concerning women which did not mention specifically the number of working hours. Manufacturers could be fined for violating the act, and the proceeds were to be used to support schools.[106] Such an act affected a nonexistent group in Dakota in 1863, but sitting in his sod hut or log cabin,

103. *House Journal* (1862–63), p. 53.
104. The lack of party lines was never better illustrated than in the contest for Speaker. The contenders were A. J. Harlan and A. W. Puett, both of whom were radical Republicans. Harlan, however, had supported Todd in the campaign and therefore acted with that group in the House, since Todd wished to use the Assembly to aid him in his contest for the election. Kingsbury, *Dakota Territory, 1*, 258–9.
105. *House Journal* (1862–63), pp. 181, 198; Armstrong, *Early Empire Builders*, pp. 95, 97. A liberal divorce law was enacted in 1862–63, but further attempts to make the marriage bond less binding were vetoed by the governor.
106. *General Laws of the Territory of Dakota* (1863), chap. 49, p. 241.

the assemblyman saw himself as a favored being who could at least extend his sympathy to the poor factory worker in the East. Such an attitude was inconsistent with his approach toward the negro slave and the half-breed, to be sure, and it was partly intended as a lure to attract settlers from the working classes of the Eastern cities, but it also suggested that labor-reform sentiment could reach even into the wilds of Dakota.

The adjournment of the second Assembly marked the end of a brief period of naive optimism that had attracted many an ambitious young man to Dakota. Fear of the Indian caused the immigrant who had hoped to settle there to turn eastward again in 1863. From Yankton that year Armstrong wrote in great alarm that "a crazy panic has fallen upon the Norwegian settlement, and many are loading their teams to leave the territory." [107] He begged that a few soldiers be sent "*immediately* to steady the nerves of the people and prevent an impending stampede." [108] But the few who stayed and farmed saw their crops wither under a scorching drought in the summer of 1863. The newly discovered gold fields of Montana lured more of the population away.[109] Moreover, Iowa colonizing agencies sought to give Dakota a bad name so that immigrants would settle in Iowa. The final blow came when the Army officials in charge of the Indian campaigns urged that settlement be prohibited in Dakota until the Indian problem had been solved.[110]

With no immigrants to buy land or goods and with few fur collections being made, the business of the Territory came to a virtual halt. The federal government remained the one source of revenue and sustenance to see the more hardy and ambitious citizens through this "starving time." The political effects of such a situation can hardly be exaggerated. The federal officials and the delegates came to play an abnormally important role in all ter-

107. Armstrong, *Early Empire Builders*, p. 111.
108. Ibid., p. 111; italics are Armstrong's.
109. Briggs, *Frontiers of the Northwest*, p. 367. Several companies were formed by Yankton groups to exploit the gold fields and the trade it would bring the Missouri, but they never succeeded. See Armstrong, *Early Empire Builders*, pp. 96, 105, 107.
110. Briggs, *Frontiers of the Northwest*, pp. 367–9.

ritorial affairs and by taking full advantage of their favored position to assume almost dictatorial powers. The settler and the
local politicians, realizing their predicament, usually decided that
to vote Republican was the better part of valor, so that in the
Assembly election of 1863 those factions going under the name
of Republican won nearly every seat.[111] Even Yankton County,
Captain Todd's personal preserve, went Republican.[112] This was
to be the case for the next three years. The third Assembly was
largely Republican; and under the controlling hands of Stutsman
in the Council, Puett in the House, and the able new governor,
Newton Edmunds, it catered to Delegate Jayne's wishes.[113] The
slightest deviation—and they were frequent—caused the culprit
to be branded as a "Copperhead." [114] So strong was the official
power that the Republicans succeeded in 1864 in depriving the
Red River Valley of all representation in both the House and the
Council. This was a punishment to that area for voting Democratic in the 1863 election.[115]

Such tactics naturally aroused resistance, but an attempt by
Chief Justice Bliss and Attorney General Gleason to form a fusion
party of War Democrats and anti-Jayne men failed to have much
effect.[116] In a letter to the Sioux City *Register*, Armstrong complained: "The political parties of the territory are in a bewildering
chaos of disorder. No strict party organization has ever been
effected, and hence we find men shifting their political signboards
to suit the gale of every annual election." [117] Each party, he felt,
was "an amalgamation of men of all political proclivities," and
each was molded by patronage instead of principle: "It matters
not into how many little cliques and feuds a party may be divided,
the leader of each squad considers himself the head and front of
the 'Great Union Party' of the territory." The result of such a

111. Armstrong, *Early Empire Builders*, pp. 128–9.
112. "The Republican party brought to bear all their heavy guns upon this, the
capital county, and drove our gallant party into defeat," wrote Armstrong, op. cit.,
p. 129.
113. Edmunds was Jayne's choice for his successor; see William Jayne to Lincoln, September 16, 1863, TP, Dakota Appointments.
114. Armstrong, *Early Empire Builders*, p. 181.
115. Ibid., p. 140.
116. Ibid., p. 138.
117. Ibid., p. 129.

situation was, Armstrong concluded, that "we are consequently supplied with a large ratio of dictators—the political doctrine of each of whom it is treason to disobey." [118]

Not until the spring political conventions of 1864 did the opposing factions seriously attempt to break the power of the "patronage loyalists," as the Jayne group was called.[119] At that time three conventions were held. The first, under the name of the Republican and Union party, nominated as delegate Dr. Walter A. Burleigh, Indian agent for the Yanktons. Burleigh had the support of Jayne and the administration Republicans such as Hill, Stutsman, Brookings, and Edmunds.[120] Next, a fusion party consisting of "non-abusive Republicans" and "War Democrats," to use Armstrong's terms, organized as the Territorial Union party and nominated Judge Bliss as their candidate. Then startling news reached Dakota: the contested election of 1862, which had dragged on in Congress for two years, had suddenly ended when the House Committee on Elections declared Todd to be the rightful delegate.[121]

In his newly advantageous position Todd announced that he would run a third time. In a matter of hours after this information was spread about, the Democratic supporters of Judge Bliss changed their allegiance to Todd. The remainder of the Bliss group then met with the Burleigh party in a territorial mass convention, joined forces to combat Todd, and chose Burleigh as the candidate of both parties.[122] Furious at being passed over in favor of a political parvenu from an Indian reservation and disgusted by the fickleness of his Democratic supporters, Bliss left Dakota, his political hopes dashed. Meanwhile a People's Union convention met at Vermillion under the auspices of Armstrong, Shober, and other faithful Democrats to nominate Todd formally.[123]

Although Jayne had lost power, the administration Republicans in Dakota had used their patronage well. Every newspaper

118. Ibid., pp. 131, 139.
119. Ibid., p. 138.
120. Kingsbury, *Dakota Territory*, 1, 368–79.
121. Armstrong, *Early Empire Builders*, p. 138.
122. Kingsbury, *Dakota Territory*, 1, 368–79.
123. Ibid.

Walter A. Burleigh: doctor, lawyer, Indian agent, and territorial delegate (1865–69)

Two Vigorous Frontier Politicians

Moses K. Armstrong: pioneer surveyor and journalist, leader of the Dakota Democratic party, and territorial delegate (1871–75)

in the Territory was so dependent upon government printing contracts for its existence that no paper dared support Todd. The application of the copperhead stigma to the Democrats had had its effects too. Dr. Burleigh, also, was an able campaigner who spent campaign funds with a princely air and who promised great things for Dakota.[124] He was aided by the shrewd maneuvers of Jayne's chosen successor, Governor Edmunds, who was a pioneer resident of Dakota and understood the interests and needs of his constituents.

Burleigh was elected by a clear majority, and Todd himself agreed not to contest the election when the new delegate promised that he would not use his office to hurt the interests of the Frost-Todd Trading Company.[125]

The fourth Assembly reflected the delegate election in its membership. Once again Stutsman, who also acted as the Governor's private secretary, became president of the Council. Brookings, this time a member of the House, became the speaker. Since both men worked in close harmony with Governor Edmunds, the session of 1864–65 was largely a cut and dried affair. So thorough had Edmund's control become by the fall of 1865 that every candidate, including Armstrong and a dozen other lifelong Democrats, who ran for the fifth Assembly ran on the Republican ticket! The Democrats had assumed, for the time being, the role of a major faction within Republican ranks.

In a summary of Dakota politics from 1861 to 1866, the outstanding characteristic was the lack of a true party organization. Instead, factions formed to gain immediate rewards and—based upon political and economic sectionalism, upon the personality of the factional leader, and upon the gap between those holding to frontier political habits and those attempting to introduce eastern political beliefs—dominated the scene. The delegate elections, the Assembly sessions, and the political activities of the territorial officials pointed up these differences.

Under the tremendous impact of the Indian Wars of 1862–66, however, the power of the Assembly, the single democratically

124. For a brief biographical treatment of Burleigh see below, pp. 109–10.
125. Kingsbury, *Dakota Territory, 1,* 379.

elected branch of the local government, declined precipitately, while that of the federal officials and the delegate did exactly the opposite.

The basic reason for arrested party development in Dakota and for the great imbalance of its governmental branches was probably a unique one in American territorial history. It was simply that Dakota, unlike all previous American territories, had no proven value as an agricultural region, or, as of 1865, no known rich mineral deposits, such as Colorado or Montana possessed, to make settlement worth while.[126] Nor was a transcontinental railroad certain to pass through Dakota. The prevailing attitudes that the soil could support only a small population was strengthened by a lingering belief in the Great American Desert legend and by the fact that during the years 1862–67 the territory suffered from yearly drought. The early settlers did not know that their arrival coincided with the end of a wet-weather cycle; thus they gathered a mistaken impression about the climate of the territory.[127] A severe grasshopper plague in 1864 not only seemed to confirm their worst fears but had a devastating effect on all favorable propaganda hitherto given out about the possibility of settlement in Dakota.[128] Under such conditions the homestead law was of little value.

Washington was in essence subsidizing a government which had few citizens, no income, and a highly questionable future. In such a situation the Territory had to lead a chameleon-like existence, taking its political hue from a Republican Congress. Territorial government came to assume a role of vital economic importance and the field of politics offered the one sure means of livelihood to those who remained in Dakota. Only the fact of complete dependence could explain how the part Indian, part French-Catholic, part frontier-American, nonagricultural group which was the backbone of the Democratic party in Dakota could so suddenly be replaced by a newly arrived, American-Scandinavian, Protestant, pro-agricultural group which constituted the

126. Persistent rumors of gold in the Black Hills were rife in 1865, but no proof existed and the Black Hills were completely inaccessible. Briggs, *Frontiers of the Northwest*, pp. 25-6.

127. Ibid., pp. 366–9.

128. Ibid., pp. 368–9; Kingsbury, *Dakota Territory, 1*, 342–52.

local Republican party there, or that the former group should join the latter so quickly. The normal pattern of political evolution was interrupted in this region which had so recently been part of the Great American Desert.

During the period of dependence the frontier's fine disregard for the division-of-power theory of government resulted, it seems, in a breakdown of the democratic process rather than in a more vigorous practice of it. In any event it was a remarkable example of how mobile, fluid, and absolute the power of politics could be in a frontier community.

The events of 1861–66 also produced a "colonial" or "territorial" attitude in Dakota political circles. Many Dakotans decided to seek political power through appointive office. It became more important to have influence in Washington or with the territorial officials than to be politically popular in Dakota. Later such men grew to rely so heavily upon the nonelective offices of the territorial system that they opposed statehood, since it would destroy the key to their power. They were like colonial officials who were fearful that their colony might become self-governing and thus dispense with their services.

Naturally a local animus against the nonelective official developed in Dakota as it had developed in every preceding territory. More generally this animus became the spearhead for a "home rule" campaign which later took the form of a statehood movement. Since both the territorial Republican and the Democratic parties had a federal administrative faction as well as a home rule faction within their respective ranks, the development of the party system was further impeded. But the struggles of these two groups both inside and outside of the party boundaries helped to produce some of the most colorful episodes in the history of the Northwest, and clearly exposed the nature of frontier politics.

Chapter 3. Divided Republicans: 1866–70

> In the great squabble for office and place, you Slope men need not
> count me in. I have tried office and find it does not pay, and, as a mere
> experiment, I intend to . . . see if I cannot make an honest living!
>
> *Enos Stutsman*

BY THE SPRING OF 1866 it was apparent that in Dakota hard times
could not last forever. The warring tribes of the Missouri Valley
were negotiating for peace.[1] Surveyor General Hill had persuaded
a colony of one hundred New York farmers to move to Dakota.
Although crops were uniformly poor until 1867, other settlers
began to trickle in soon after the Civil War ended, to take advantage of the Homestead Law.[2] Meanwhile the territorial delegate, W. A. Burleigh, joined Hill in writing pamphlets and making
speeches in the East, in which he urged settlers to migrate to
Dakota.[3]

The period of economic stagnation began to end when the
army expeditions under Generals Sully and Sibley created such
a demand for foodstuffs and supplies in the Upper Missouri
Country that nearly every merchant and farmer remaining in
the Territory sought to profit by an army contract.[4] The number
of steamboats engaged in supplying the army forces increased
greatly. Local farmers began to raise more cattle for sale to the
army commissary, and some devoted their entire energies to
ranching.[5] The fortunes of Dakota again looked up when Congress

1. Negotiations with several tribes were completed in the fall of 1865, and many
more accepted treaty obligations in the spring of 1866. Official accounts of the
fighting in Dakota may be seen in *Official Records of the War of the Rebellion*
(Washington, D.C., 1880–1900), 48, Pts. 1, 2. A summary of the peace negotiations may be seen in "Ending the Outbreak," *Collections of the State Historical
Society of South Dakota*, 9 (1918), 409–41. See also Textor, *Relations between the
U.S. and the Sioux Indians*, pp. 104 ff.

2. Briggs, *Frontiers of the Northwest*, pp. 455–8; Kingsbury, *Dakota Territory*,
1, 332–4.

3. Briggs, *Frontiers of the Northwest*, pp. 456–7.

4. Armstrong, *Early Empire Builders*, pp. 146–8.

5. See testimonial letters in *House Journal of the Fifth Session of the Legislative
Assembly of the Territory of Dakota*, 1865–66 (Yankton, 1866), pp. 163 ff.; see also

provided a grant for the construction of three territorial roads, one of which led from Sioux City, Iowa, to Fort Randall via Yankton. So desperate were the Dakotans for aid of any sort that several of the territorial representatives and councilors gladly accepted jobs on the project, and the expenditure of the road grant funds was a major political issue in the Assembly of 1865–66.[6] Pointing out the close connection between politics and army contracts, Armstrong wrote in doggerel:

> No politician yet is dead,
> Nor ever will be, long as *Hay*,
> And Corn, and Cordwood fill the way.[7]

In the political field, too, many changes occurred and new men and new issues appeared. The Army's prosecution of the Indian war had a very important effect on territorial politics; for example it clarified the Dakotan's view of the Indian problem and his plan for its solution. This view was best exemplified in the efforts of Governor Newton Edmunds to bring peace to the Upper Missouri Valley.

Edmunds had come to Dakota from Michigan in 1861 as a clerk in the office of Surveyor General Hill. He had obtained this minor position through his brother, C. E. Edmunds, commissioner of the United States Land Office during the Lincoln administration. By quietly making friends of the Dakota federal officials and by playing upon the local prejudice for a governor who was an actual resident of the Territory—as he himself was—Edmunds became Jayne's successor in March 1863. Jayne himself had written both Senator Trumbull and President Lincoln the most glowing endorsement of Edmunds, and it is probable that Lincoln acted upon Jayne's advice.[8] Edmunds' contemporaries agreed that

---

the very complete report on the stock business in the *House Journal* (1867–68), pp. 318 ff.

6. Ibid. (1865–66), pp. 93–4, 242, 246, 255; *Council Journal* (1865–66), pp. 90, 194–5, 219–21. A furious debate grew out of the suspicion that one of the road superintendents, G. C. Moody, had embezzled part of the federal appropriation.

7. Armstrong, *Early Empire Builders*, p. 147.

8. Edmunds received almost unanimous support for his appointment as governor. The letters in the Appointments Division of the State Department indicate that Dakota Democrats and Republicans endorsed him. Governor Jayne wrote his brother-in-law, Senator Trumbull, January 4, 1863, that Edmunds would be "in-

it was a wise choice. Shrewd and cautious, he appears not to have been particularly ambitious for political office for himself. Rather he used his appointment to aid territorial development, to establish himself in the infant business circles of the Territory, and to intrench himself as a benign and respectable boss of a segment of the local Republican party. From his office in the Yankton bank, which he opened after his term as governor ended, Edmunds exerted considerable control over territorial politics for the next twenty years. Dignified and courteous, and somewhat solemn, he was perhaps a perfect example of a New England squire in western politics.[9]

In his first message to the Assembly of 1864 Edmunds criticized the Army's method of quelling the Indians as being too cumbersome and slow. He recommended instead that a line of military posts be erected across the southeastern part of the Territory to keep the Indians out.[10] A year later he was more vehement in his denunciation of the government's Indian policy. He called the campaigns of Generals Sully and Sibley expensive and useless.[11] In large measure Edmunds was correct, for every campaign had failed to produce clear-cut victories. The armies advanced so slowly that most of the hostile Indians had little trouble in avoiding them.[12]

Edmunds' objections had other grounds than the poor tactics of the Army. The presence of several thousand troops on the march against warring Indians gave Dakota a bad name and impeded settlement. Moreover, the Indian Bureau had either ceased to function or had been subordinated to the Army's will

---

valuable to the Government, the Territory, and the Republican party." Jayne wrote Lincoln, September 16, 1863, that Edmunds would save the Territory from the Copperheads. See TP, Dakota Appointments, Edmunds File, 1863–66.

9. Robinson, *History of South Dakota*, 1, 287.

10. *Governor Edmunds' Annual Message to the Legislative Assembly*, December 1863 (Yankton, 1864), printed pamphlet in the W. R. Coe Collection of Western Americana of the Yale University Library.

11. *House Journal* (1864–65), pp. 29–43.

12. W. S. Waddel, "The Military Relations between the Sioux Indians and the United States Government in Dakota Territory, 1860–91" (Master's thesis, Department of History, University of South Dakota, Vermillion, S.D., 1931), unpublished copy deposited in State Department of History, Pierre, South Dakota. Mr. Waddel found that the governors of Iowa, Minnesota, Dakota, and Nebraska all advocated Edmunds' plan of distributing troops along the frontier in small posts instead of using them in aggressive campaigns. See especially p. 36.

in the Upper Missouri, and the great number who were affiliated with the Indians as traders, agents, and supply men wished for a return of peaceful conditions. Edmunds, who was much more conscious of his powers as *ex officio* Indian commissioner than Jayne had been, agreed with this view.[13] The Army must not exterminate the red man but serve as an instrument to protect the whites by forming a barrier between the Indian territory and the white settlements; reservations and annuities should be provided for the Indians, and efforts should be made to civilize them, although the majority of Dakotans in 1866 seriously doubted that the Sioux could really be civilized. Implicit in Edmunds' conception of the problem was the ever-diminishing power of the red man. Delegate Burleigh agreed with Edmunds when he told the House of Representatives: "The future of that country [Dakota] is already fixed; the fate of the Indian is sealed as effectually and as materially as was that of the Canaanites before the advancing armies of Israel as they moved forward to possess the promised land of their inheritance." [14]

The army barrier then was to be a mobile one, gradually pushing the Indians back, slowly decreasing their number and their area of free action until this process of extended attrition should bring every remaining native under the complete control of the Indian Bureau. Edmunds felt that this could be achieved by making separate treaties with the Missouri tribes and by impressing them with a few immediate gifts and the promise of annuities. He knew that most of the Indians by this time were in a starving condition and would negotiate. He was convinced that the Army's insistence upon treating the warring Indians as sovereign enemies to be defeated in battle and brought to terms was so much nonsense.[15] Regardless of how much it might rankle both the Eastern and Western mind, Edmunds believed that it

13. Edmunds notified the Indian Bureau that Jayne and Hutchinson had virtually ignored the Indian affairs of Dakota and that when he had assumed office, only two of the seven agents under his control were on their posts, and that no one of them possessed a permit of leave. Edmunds to Indian Commissioner W. P. Dole, November 23, 1863, U.S. Office of Indian Affairs, Chronological Files (1863) Dakota, National Archives (OIA, Chron. Files, Dakota).

14. *Cong. Globe,* 39th Cong., 1st sess. (June 8, 1866), p. 3056.

15. "Ending the Outbreak," *Collections of the State Historical Society of South Dakota,* 11 (1918), 409 ff.

was better to bribe a tribe into peace than to have recourse to the more traditionally honorable and more expensive method of war.

With these views in mind, and backed by the governors of Minnesota, Iowa, and Nebraska, Edmunds journeyed to Washington in the early spring of 1865. There Lincoln endorsed his policy; and with the support of Thaddeus Stevens and Delegate Burleigh, Edmunds secured an appropriation of $20,000 and the appointment of an Indian Commission to treat with the Missouri tribes.[16] At that point, however, Edmunds ran into the hostility of the military and to some extent that of the army contractors who were finding a lucrative business in supplying the Indian expeditions. In reply to a letter requesting army cooperation in the peace negotiations, General Pope of the Department of the Northwest wrote that "I have the honor to inform you that there are no Sioux Indians in Dakota Territory with whom it is judicious to make such treaties as you propose." [17] Edmunds reported Pope's reply to Secretary of the Interior Harlan, who in turn consulted with Secretary of War Stanton over the conflict in policy, but no compromise seemed forthcoming. Indeed, that disagreement quickly ballooned into a public debate between War Department and Indian Bureau advocates as to who should control the Indian. A proposal that the Bureau control the "peaceful tribes" and the Army the "warring tribes" proved completely unworkable. In a furiously indignant letter to General U. S. Grant, Pope wrote, "Either the War or Interior Department should have the sole management of Indian affairs. The divided jurisdiction leads to nothing but evil." [18] Delegate Burleigh, a supreme opportunist, saw that the issue was a popular one and joined the Bureau in its attack upon the Army. For a time the debate became the chief article of interest in the Northwestern press, with the Army bearing the brunt of criticism.[19] Dakota Indian agents published out-of-context segments of their correspondence with army officials to show how implacably inimical and uncompromising the mil-

16. "Ending the Outbreak," pp. 409–12.
17. Ibid., p. 416.
18. Ibid., p. 428.
19. Ibid., p. 421.

itary were toward all Indians, both warring and peaceful.[20]

After Lee's surrender to Grant on April 18, 1865, a new factor appeared in the campaign against the Army: the military were accused of fomenting trouble with the Indians in order to keep the large standing army called into being by the Civil War. A large-scale offensive against the Indians, the Dakotans argued, was what the Army wanted as the excuse to retain its size and its great importance in national affairs. When General Pope asked Sully to investigate the sources of such charges, Sully replied that "Burleigh and Company" were behind the whole movement.[21]

Burleigh's and Edmunds' reasons were not hard to find. Both men had become convinced that Dakota could be settled; thus they opposed the Army policy of "no settlement" until the Indian was under complete control, for that might take several years. The local politician also saw the Army as an independent government agency which could not be brought under territorial control the way the Indian Bureau could.

While the debate over the Indian peace question raged, General Sully made a fifth expedition into the heart of the Sioux Country, but once again no clear-cut battle or victory resulted. With this failure the Army was forced to compromise and allow Edmunds to begin talks with the Missouri tribes in October 1865.[22] During the fall and winter of 1865–66 Edmunds and the Indian Commission, with the ubiquitous Armstrong as its secretary and a Chicago *Tribune* reporter in attendance, brought 16,020 Indians of the Yanktonnais, Brulés, Two Kettles, Minneconjous, Sans Arcs, Ogallalas and Blackfoot tribes under treaty obligations. The Indians agreed to cease hostilities, to withdraw from overland routes, and to locate permanently on reservations.[23] For this accomplishment the entire Territory looked to Edmunds as a personal savior.

Indian hostilities did not end until 1867 in parts of Dakota,

20. Ibid., pp. 421, 424 ff.
21. Ibid., p. 422; see also *Official Records of the War of the Rebellion, 48,* Pt. 2, p. 766.
22. "Ending the Outbreak," p. 441; Goodspeed, *The Province and the States,* 6, 247. Textor, *Official Relations between the U.S. and the Sioux,* pp. 104–8, gives the substance of most of the treaties and makes some valuable comments.
23. Goodspeed, 6, 246; see also texts of treaties in *The Statutes at Large of the United States, 14,* 695 ff., 723–49.

but the 1865–66 negotiations left the Dakotan with a clear idea
of how to approach the Indian question. By using the presence
of the Army—located in permanent forts—as a continual threat
to the Indians, he could, with the aid of the Indian Bureau, gradually contain the Indians by the processes of settlement, economic
attrition through annuities, and perhaps by civilizing. On the
whole this policy was more anti-Indian than it seemed, for it
was based upon the premise that a good Indian was not necessarily a dead one but a weak live one who could be exploited.[24]

The desire to exploit the red man in this way was one of great
antiquity, of course, but in Dakota it was of decided import because the possibilities of eking out a livelihood in agricultural
pursuits alone was still highly dubious. Indeed, the whole Army-
Indian Bureau debate eventually centered on the question: could
all of Dakota be settled? Once again the white man's lingering
belief in the Great American Desert legend benefited the Indians,
for the Dakotan feared that extermination of the Indians might
remove a valuable source of federal income to the local settler.
Thus for the first time in the history of the American western
movement, the Indian's continued presence was desirable. The
age-old American aversion to a living Indian was never stronger
than in 1866–67, and the conviction was still strong that he would
eventually die off, but the unprecedented problem of inhabiting
a semi-arid region was a significant factor in shaping the so-called
"peace-policy" and in the western acceptance of it.

The Dakotan's advocacy of a peaceful policy toward the Sioux
was perhaps an early major and often overlooked factor in the
national movement for a new Indian policy after the Civil War.
The "peace policy" of the Grant and later administrations was
certainly motivated in part by western dissatisfaction with Army
methods in Dakota and elsewhere from 1862 to 1867. But there
was one very basic difference. The strong eastern demand for a
peace policy which was being expressed at this time was based

24. Even the idea of placing the Indian on a reservation was qualified by the
Dakotan. When Congress made the Black Hills area a permanent reservation for
the Indians of the Northwest, the Dakotans protested bitterly. No good land must
be given the Indians, but the useless parcels on the west bank of the Missouri
should be given them instead. See "Memorial to Congress," in *General Laws and
Private Laws for Dakota Territory* (1867–68), pp. 275 ff.

on humanitarian and reformist grounds. The western—or at least Dakotan—impetus came from a desire to exploit as well as the desire to try new techniques of control. In the campaign for a peace policy the efforts of these two dissimilar groups coincided, but once the demands became official policy based upon the eastern philanthropic premises, only conflict could result.

As the Dakotans and leaders from other territories intrigued to change national Indian policy, an important change on the local scene also occurred. By taking the side of the Indian Bureau and its local agents, that faction of the Republican party led by Edmunds and Burleigh built up an alliance with the local Indian officials and traders which lasted for many years. Such an alliance —tenuous though it often was—explained in large part why the traditionally Democratic frontier vote of the traders and trappers so suddenly turned to favor Republican candidates as early as 1863.[25] The combined forces of the Indian and territorial officials naturally increased their influence in Washington, where one group could count upon the other to support its requests for funds or other aid. By the end of Edmunds' first term, in fact, rumors and secret charges were reaching Washington that the governor had formed an efficient ring of agents who had to correlate their activities with Edmunds' political and personal wishes in order to keep their positions.[26]

The local alliance eventually became so powerful that Carl Schurz endeavored to clean up some of the corrupt Indian rings in Dakota when he was appointed Secretary of the Interior in 1877. But he ran into a thousand protests. The entire officialdom of the Territory turned upon him in wrath; the territorial newspapers, with one exception, spoke as a single voice in opposing the well-meaning secretary. Calumny after calumny was heaped upon the head of the unfortunate Indian inspector who dared to

25. The extremely close relationship between the territorial politician and the Indian agent in Dakota is revealed in the diary of Henry F. Livingston, agent to the Crow Creek Reservation (near Fort Randall, Dakota) from 1867 to 1878, MS in the W. R. Coe Collection of Western Americana in the Yale University Library.

26. Edmunds' reports to the Indian Bureau in the years 1864-66 indicate that he took great interest in his duties as Indian commissioner for Dakota; before he left office he had hired a clerk, George H. Heartt, to handle Indian business. See Edmunds to Dale, January 1864; January 30, 1865; May 15, 1866. See, too, Edmunds to Commissioner D. N. Cooley, January 1, 1866, OIA, Chron. Files (1864-66), Dakota.

report any irregularity in the distribution of supplies or annu-ities.[27] Needless to say, Schurz' efforts failed. He was attempting to dislodge not only one of the keystones in the arch of power that the Republican party had erected in Dakota, but one of the main supports to the Territory's still shaky economy.

The power of the Dakota factions calling themselves Repub-licans or "National Unionists" was never more complete than in the spring of 1866. To the superficial glance only one party existed and Governor Edmunds and Delegate Burleigh were its leaders. The new territorial secretary Solomon L. Spink, Judges Ara Bart-lett and Jefferson P. Kidder, and the new United States attorney George H. Hand entertained no ideas of insurgency such as Bliss and Gleason had. The affable Hand was so cooperative, in fact, that he became Edmunds' private secretary.[28]

But the Civil War had ended; new settlers were coming in, bringing with them their own political inclinations; the stigma of "Copperhead" could no longer be used against the Democrats, and the "starving time" was over. Yet the real excuse for ending the enforced coalition in which Democrats acted as a wing of the Republican party arose out of the postwar political situation in Washington, where President Johnson found himself at odds with the Radical Republicans over the reconstruction of the South. While Reconstruction, like the Civil War itself, was of little im-mediate concern to Dakotans, the Territory was so dependent upon both the president and Congress at this time that it was inevitable a federal crisis should vitally affect territorial politics.

27. See below, Chap. 6.
28. Solomon L. Spink, appointed Secretary of Dakota in 1865, served until 1869, when he became the delegate to Congress. See Robinson, *Encyclopedia of South Dakota*, p. 678. Ara Bartlett replaced Philemon Bliss as chief justice of Dakota in 1865. He served until 1869. See ibid., p. 61. Jefferson P. Kidder had been one of the original members of the Dakota Land Company, and had served as delegate to Congress under the squatter government at Sioux Falls. After the failure of the Dakota Company, Kidder had entered Minnesota politics and served a term in the Minnesota Legislature (1861–64). Backed by his home state, Ver-mont, and by Minnesota Republicans, Kidder received the Dakota judicial appoint-ment in 1865, which he held until 1875. See ibid., p. 392. George H. Hand, one-time clerk of the Wisconsin Senate, had applied for the position of United States attorney in 1861, but had joined the Union army as a volunteer instead. In 1866, as a good Republican and a veteran, and with the aid of Francis P. Blair, Jr., he secured the appointment. See Justice Appointment Papers (1866), Dakota, Hand File.

Briefly, the dispute focused on the question: should Dakota take the side of Johnson, who alone could appoint territorial officials, or Congress, which alone could appropriate funds?

The whole issue came into the open when the Republican delegate, Dr. Burleigh, decided to campaign for reelection in 1866 on a pro-Johnson platform. The personality of this remarkable man deserves some explanation, for it was because of him that Dakota was so deeply influenced by reconstruction politics. Burleigh was a tall Dakota version of Stephen A. Douglas of Illinois. He slammed, slashed, cajoled, bought, and argued his way through Dakota politics in a manner that his contemporaries would never forget. So vigorous was he that men when walking with him had to run to keep pace with his giant strides. With the possible exception of General Todd and Alexander McKenzie, Burleigh was the most controversial and colorful politician to be found in the entire territorial period. The personification of the ambitious, amoral, rugged individualist seeking a fortune on the frontier, Burleigh saw in politics one of the keys to power and financial success. With an energy approaching fanatic zeal he had assailed doubts about the unfavorable soil and climate of Dakota; with cunning and vigor he had forced the Army to give in on its Indian policy. Yet most of this had been done to enhance his own financial and political career. An investigator sent to observe Burleigh's conduct while the latter was an agent to the Yankton Indians at Greenwood Reservation was so impressed with the payroll padding, graft, and nepotism practiced by this able, jovial doctor who was also a lawyer that his report was written in a tone that sounded less like condemnation than respectful awe. Indeed, the investigator noted, it took a superior imagination to be able to perpetrate so many frauds at one time.[29]

The frontier voter easily overlooked Burleigh's past record and

29. Burleigh appeared in Dakota in 1861 as Indian agent to the Greenwood Reservation on the Missouri River. There he outdid the average agent in fleecing the Indian Bureau and the Indians for all they were worth. His daughter was listed on the payroll as a teacher to Indian children although no school existed on the reservation. His thirteen-year-old son drew eighty dollars a month as a clerk. His father-in-law appeared in the records as a worker. Alexander Johnston, the special agent who reported on Burleigh's actions, wrote with such an appreciation of Burleigh's character that it borders on the witty and amusing. See Johnston's "Report on Indian Affairs in Dakota Territory," Washington, July 16, 1866, OIA, Chron. Files (1866), Dakota.

never questioned his political ability, but even the most hardened constituent found it difficult to condone the genial doctor's campaign methods. Acutely distrustful of his own popularity or of the efficiency of the local Republican party, Burleigh felt that he personally must buy each election, and he spent funds lavishly to bring in the votes. As Kingsbury has aptly noted, he was his own political machine.[30] Such a procedure had a bad effect on any party discipline which might have existed in 1866, and the addition of the reconstruction question was fatal.

Burleigh's decision to support President Johnson was motivated by several circumstances. He had become a personal friend of the president and had used this friendship to control almost all territorial appointments. In a letter to the Attorney General of the United States in 1866, Burleigh wrote: "The President has always given me to understand that as the friend and supporter of his Administration—I should control the Federal appointments in my own District—and I feel confident that he still concedes this to me." [31] The result was that Burleigh appointed more officials than any preceding delegate.

Burleigh had also found that Edmunds' "peace policy," which he had recommended so strongly, had profited him little either politically or otherwise, while Edmunds was now the most popular figure in Dakota. This should explain why Burleigh, without warning, arose in the House of Representatives on June 8, 1866, and denounced the Indian peace policy with great harshness. In referring to the treaties recently negotiated by Edmunds and the commission, he declared: "The consummate stupidity which planned those negotiations is only surpassed by the reprehensible meanness in which their details have been carried out, and the total lack of practical results which have followed." [32] The treaties, Burleigh asserted, would only line the pockets of the "favored gentlemen who are selected to disburse the munificent appropriations of a too confiding Congress." [33] Since Burleigh had recom-

30. Kingsbury, *Dakota Territory*, 1, 542–3.
31. W. A. Burleigh to Attorney General Henry Stanley, August 6, 1866, Justice Appointment Papers (1866), Dakota, John W. Boyle File.
32. Burleigh to the House of Representatives, *Cong. Globe*, 39th Cong., 1st sess. (June 8, 1866), p. 3056.
33. Ibid.

mended these very men, he was attacking his own appointees! [34] Regardless of inconsistencies in his new stand, and questionable statistics—Burleigh argued that only 297 out of a claimed 18,480 Indians had agreed to the treaties—the vigorous Dakotan continued the attack. Eventually it did appear that some irregularities had occurred in the treaty-making and that pockets had been lined, but Burleigh's accusations sprang partly from his anger at the Indian Bureau, which had charges pending against him for his extraordinary conduct while an Indian agent, and partly from his inability to share the spoils of the peace negotiations over which Edmunds as chairman of the Peace Commission and *ex officio* superintendent of Indian affairs had full control. But there was a still further reason for this about-face: Burleigh had received a letter from Enos Stutsman containing the gravest charges against Edmunds in his administration of Indian affairs.[35] These bases for Burleigh's dissatisfaction have been generally overlooked by Dakota historians, who could never explain why Burleigh persuaded President Johnson to replace Edmunds as governor in the summer of 1866.[36] It soon became evident, however, that Burleigh was not so interested in reform as in control, for whom should President Johnson appoint as the new governor

34. Various western Congressmen, like Hubbard and Wilson of Iowa, were quick to note Burleigh's change of views and in reply suggested that his own reasons for denouncing the treaties were venal. Wilson, in fact, read aloud some eloquent testimonial letters from Yankton Indians who had been defrauded by Burleigh when he had been their agent. Despite these counter charges Burleigh continued to insist that the treaties had been falsely represented. He hinted, too, that the United States Indian commissioner and the Secretary of the Interior had been knowing and willing parties to these false negotiations.

35. The charges against Edmunds were made by Charles E. Hedges, a licensed Indian trader who seemed to be chafing under Edmunds' jurisdiction, and from Enos Stutsman, one-time secretary to Edmunds. Stutsman accused Edmunds of fleecing "both Agent and Indians with perfect impunity." He also gave the details of a scheme which Edmunds had proposed to him whereby they could deprive the Indian Bureau of between eighty and one hundred thousand dollars. See C. E. Hedges to W. A. Burleigh, February 2, 1866; E. Stutsman to Burleigh, Yankton, April 18, 1866; and C. E. Hedges to Burleigh, Yankton, May 1, 1866. TP, Dakota Appointments (1866), Edmunds File.

36. In February 1865 Delegate Burleigh had urged Lincoln to reappoint Edmunds as governor, which the President promptly did. See J. R. Hanson and W. A. Burleigh to Lincoln, February 6, 1865; TP, Dakota Appointments (1865), Edmunds File. Lincoln's death relieved Burleigh of his obligations to support Edmunds, and in April he promptly forwarded charges to President Johnson. See W. A. Burleigh to Johnson, April 16, 1866, TP, Dakota Appointments (1866), Edmunds File.

but Burleigh's own father-in-law, Andrew J. Faulk, the editor of a small newspaper in Kittanning, Pennsylvania! [37]

Faulk's appointment and others like it so alienated the Edmunds faction that it, and others, gradually came to oppose Burleigh's stranglehold on territorial patronage by endorsing the Congressional reconstruction policy. Now there were two distinct and antagonistic Republican groups. Thus the Democrats of Dakota suddenly found themselves emerging from the role of a subordinate faction to that of a major one holding the balance of power in what was virtually a three-party system.[38]

The new alignments were evident in the delegate and legislative election of the fall of 1866. W. W. Brookings, leading the Edmunds Republicans, ran on a Congressional reconstruction ticket, while Burleigh ran for reelection on a pro-Johnson platform. The Democrats declined to nominate a candidate of their own and instead declared for Burleigh. Their vote easily swung the election to Burleigh, while in the Assembly election the Democrats gained control of both Houses. General Todd (a short participation in the Civil War had merited him a generalcy) himself won a seat in the House, and Moses K. Armstrong, next to Todd the leader of the Democrats, became the Council president.[39]

The legislative session of 1866–67 was noticeably unexceptional, a characteristic due to the total domination of Burleigh and Governor Faulk over the legislature and to the fact that the Assembly had come to play a very small role in local politics during the starving time.[40]

37. The contrast between the endorsements for Faulk and all other gubernatorial appointees for Dakota is astonishing. Not a single letter appeared from a well-known Washington official or from a nationally known senator or congressman; nor were any of the endorsements other than lukewarm. Despite this fact he received the appointment. See letters recommending Faulk in TP, Dakota Appointments (1866), Andrew J. Faulk File.

38. Kingsbury, *Dakota Territory*, 1, 451.

39. Goodspeed, 6, 592; Kingsbury, *Dakota Territory*, 1, 450–8.

40. Both Governor Faulk and the Assembly were preoccupied with the granting of railroad charters to companies planning to build into the Territory, with petitions to Congress to open the Black Hills to settlers, and a sincere concern for the establishment of public education in the Territory. Perhaps the fairest piece of legislation passed during the sixth Assembly was the organization of Pembina County in the Red River Valley. Thus after three years this region was again allowed to participate in territorial political affairs. For an account of the 1866–67 proceedings see the House and Council *Journals of the Sixth Session of the Legislative Assembly*

Andrew Jackson Faulk: third governor of Dakota Territory (1866–69)

Two Dakota Administrators Involved in Party Struggles over Issues of Reconstruction and Railroad Bonds

John A. Burbank: fourth governor of Dakota Territory (1869–73)

In the election of a completely new Assembly in the fall of 1867, however, the Democrats and the Burleigh Republicans split. The Republicans, with a weather eye on the Radical Congress, which had by now reduced President Johnson's powers drastically, declared themselves in favor of Congressional reconstruction.[41] Anti-Burleigh Republicans gained control of the Assembly, with W. W. Brookings and the much respected Enos Stutsman guiding the Council and House respectively.[42] The Assembly revealed its anti-Johnson bias by passing a joint resolution condemning Edwin M. Stanton's removal as Secretary of War.[43]

The endorsement of Radical reconstruction by the Dakota Assembly when the Dakota delegate was a Johnsonian Republican, coupled with the simultaneous efforts of the local Democrats to achieve recognition as an independent party, foretold a violent political campaign in 1868. The scene was further complicated by the fact that territorial immigration had doubled in 1867, and the new residents were still an unknown political quantity. Good crops in 1868 also allowed the farmer-voter to be more independent in his choice.[44] Finally, the unexpected participation of Laramie and Carter Counties, Wyoming, in the election made accurate speculation impossible. Although an Organic Act for Wyoming had been passed in 1867, the region was still legally a part of Dakota in 1868, since President Johnson had refused to appoint the Congressional selections for federal officers in the new Territory. Thus the turbulent population which had gathered in Laramie to construct the Union Pacific railroad and to seek gold had the right to vote in the Dakota elections, since Laramie

of the Territory of Dakota, 1866–67, Yankton, 1867. The governor's annual message is to be found in the Council Journal (1866–67), pp. 23 ff. The charters of the railroad companies may be found in the General and Private Laws for Dakota Territory (1866–67), chaps. 4, 5, pp. 88 ff., 97 ff. For the condition of public education in Dakota see the Council Journal (1866–67), pp. 76 ff.

41. Kingsbury, Dakota Territory, 1, 488–90.

42. Horace Austin was president of the Council, but Brookings was the real leader. Stutsman became speaker of the house. See House and Council Journals of the Seventh Session of the Legislative Assembly of the Territory of Dakota, 1867–68 (Yankton, 1868).

43. Council Journal (1867–68), pp. 202–3.

44. See the governor's annual message for 1867 in the House Journal (1867–68), pp. 23–39. See also letters on future agricultural prospects in ibid., pp. 304–26; Briggs, Frontiers of the Northwest, pp. 487–8.

was still legally in Dakota Territory. Thousands of voters, then some 800 miles from the tiny capital at Yankton, actually controlled the election, for neither territorial Republicans nor Democrats had any contact with or appeal to these voters.

No less than five candidates appeared for the delegateship in 1868. The Edmunds-Brookings faction, aided considerably by its alliance with a triumphant Congress, met as the Republican party of Dakota and chose S. L. Spink, the territorial secretary, as its candidate. The Spink faction, which already included some of the more wealthy and conservative leaders of the Territory, was joined by several able newcomers: Attorney General Hand, Colonel G. C. Moody, and George Bachelder.[45]

A "Peoples' convention," largely engineered by Burleigh, chose the portly and dignified Jefferson P. Kidder, a member of the territorial supreme court, as its candidate. The appearance of Moses K. Armstrong on the same ticket as a candidate for the office of territorial auditor indicated that the Peoples' convention represented the remains of the Democratic-Republican coalition which had elected Burleigh in 1866. Adopting a platform calculated to appeal to every possible voter, the Peoples' party asked for federal aid to develop railroads, for more cessions of Indian lands, for a revision of the homestead law so that veterans could acquire full title after one year's occupation, and finally, for the reservation of unsettled land for homesteaders instead of being placed on the open market as a large number of the Spink party desired. On the question of reconstruction, however, the Peoples' party remained diplomatically silent.[46]

Still another faction, calling itself the Democratic party for the first time in the Territory's history, convened in September 1868 to nominate Todd for delegate. Yet some of the same delegates appearing now as Democrats had met at Vermillion only two weeks before to choose Kidder. A careful study of the delegates reveals once again that the Democrats were still composed of the native frontier elements, a sprinkling of Irish settlers, and a few merchants who had brought their democratic affiliations with them to Dakota. Aside from an endorsement of President

45. Kingsbury, *Dakota Territory*, 1, 494–5.
46. Ibid., p. 495.

Johnson's reconstruction policy and a denunciation of Congress' usurpation of the executive power, the Democrats wrote a platform very similar to that of the Peoples' party.

On September 23 Delegate Burleigh, chafing under a party pledge to support Kidder and fearful of losing his powerful control in territorial politics, announced that he would run for re-election as an independent candidate. Burleigh had taken the precaution to be in Laramie, Wyoming, when he made this statement, so that he could not be reached by indignant members of the Peoples' party. It was obvious that he hoped to carry the two counties of Laramie and Carter and win the election in a surprise *coup*. Burleigh's defection greatly increased the bitterness of an already violent campaign. Kingsbury wrote that "Public meetings at every hamlet and town were of daily and nightly occurrence." [47] W. H. H. Beadle, the surveyor general, wrote Secretary of the Interior J. D. Cox that during the campaign individuals had been promised specific territorial and federal offices, that the expected patronage had already been parceled out, and that even the "anticipated profits of special contracts under the Surveyor General were agreed upon or expected." [48] The Yankton *Dakotaian*, an ardent advocate of Spink, gladly lent its presses to the Todd forces in the hope that the vote would be more evenly divided between Todd and Kidder and thus ensure the election of Spink.[49] The final pitch of excitement came, however, when General Dennis Toohey of Wyoming, a Democrat, entered the lists only a week before election time.[50]

The vituperative language used by the candidates on the hustings had aroused nearly every voter in Dakota. It was not surprising, then, that they cast some 4597 votes in the 1868 election in stark contrast to the 846 votes returned in 1866. Spink, the choice of the regular Republicans, won with 1400 votes, but General Toohey and Burleigh ran next with a combined vote of over 1700. Their last-minute decision to enter the race had certainly thrown the election into the hands of the Congressional

47. Ibid., p. 499.
48. William H. H. Beadle to Secretary of the Interior James D. Cox, August 3, 1869, Interior Appointment Papers, Dakota Surveyors General, File 3.
49. Ibid.
50. Kingsbury, *Dakota Territory, 1,* 498.

Republicans. Yet even had Burleigh and his followers voted for Kidder, the returns indicate that Spink would have won. But how, after the break-up of the coalition and the split within the party, did the regular Republicans carry the Territory? The answer again lies partly in the situation to be found in Washington in 1868 and again illustrates the powerful political control the national government actually possessed over this frontier region. The voters of Dakota appear to have followed closely the ebbing of Johnson's prestige and the rise to power of the Radical Republicans. What is more, the Territory experienced a Grant boom, although its citizens could not cast a presidential vote. Any group supporting both Congress and Grant naturally was popular. The new immigrants to Dakota were, moreover, homesteaders or veterans who were inclined to vote Republican or for any endorser of Grant. Burleigh's break with Kidder not only divided the opposition vote—it cast doubt on Kidder's integrity. And finally, the unexpected entrance of General Toohey was but the ultimate guarantee that the orthodox Republicans would win.

The triumph of Spink and the regular Republicans is significant in another way, for despite the often factional and amorphous condition of any political organization in the Territory, this particular group was well on the way toward becoming a distinct and professional body. They were, more than ever, a self-conscious group whose livelihood lay in public office and the control of territorial affairs. The majority of the members of the Dakota Bar Association organized in 1866, the relatively well-to-do creditors in Dakota, the Republican-appointed incumbents in office—these made up the faction. With their shrewd appeal to immigrants as being the local branch of the party which provided free land, with their use of the Scandinavian and German bloc vote, with their continuous and professional—rather than seasonal and amateur—approach to politics, and with the tremendous boon of patronage power to fall back on, the administrative Republicans could hardly fail to force the frontier politician of the Todd or Burleigh type to give way. The 1868 delegate election was, then, a second major triumph over the indigenous western politicians, despite a split in the Republican ranks. The experience in office and the consolidation of power through wise use of the patronage during the starving time had paid off again.

The new Assembly was also manipulated by the regular Republicans. Gideon C. Moody, later to be a major figure in Dakota politics, was elected speaker of the House, and W. W. Brookings, a true party wheelhorse, became president of the Council. The impact of the recent immigration was reflected in the House, however, for nineteen out of the twenty-four members were newcomers.[51] While it is doubtful that the regular Republicans could have controlled the House by majority vote alone, the Council, dominated by such old hands as Brookings and Stutsman and having the cooperation of Delegate Spink, was able not only to hold the lower House in line but to block every move made by Governor Faulk and to push through a petition asking for his removal and the appointment of Brookings in his place.

The Assembly of 1868–69 was the last annual session of the Dakota Legislature to be held, Congress having passed a law in 1868 providing for biennial sessions only. As the Assembly adjourned in January 1869, the political prospects for the orthodox Republicans seemed bright. With a new administration in Washington soon to take over, a safely Republican delegate untainted with Johnsonism, an Assembly under party control, and a swelling immigration into the Territory, the Republicans had great cause to be optimistic. It remained only for Grant to remove the amiable but unpopular Governor Faulk from office and to replace him with a leading Republican resident of the Territory.

The territorial policy of the Grant administration—if it had one —proved a bitter disappointment to the Dakotans. This was especially the case after a campaign in which the most extravagant of promises had been made and the most minute parcel of anticipated patronage had been divided. The first blow came when President Grant, upon the suggestion of Senator O. P. Morton of Indiana, appointed Morton's brother-in-law, John A. Burbank, as the new governor.[52] This was the fourth governor which Dakota

51. See the House and Council *Journals of the Eighth Session of the Legislative Assembly of the Territory of Dakota,* 1868–69 (Yankton, 1869).
52. William T. Jackson, "Dakota Politics during the Burbank Administration—

had had in eight years, three of whom were in-laws of prominent politicians in Washington. Edmunds, the only exception, had received his appointment through his own brother, C. E. Edmunds, United States Land Commissioner. Not only was Burbank a true spoils appointee but he assumed the office with the express intentions of making a fortune in Dakota railroad speculation and patronage.[53] With his excellent connections in Washington, he virtually took charge of the patronage of the entire Territory. Delegate Spink, who had expected to control the lion's share of these funds, just as Burleigh had done, suddenly found himself deprived of that very function for which he had been elected. During his two years in office he succeeded in appointing only a few residents to office, and most of these were to very minor positions. Burbank and the Grant administration filled the others with spoilsmen from all states to whom they were politically beholden. Territorial protests, petitions, and memorials from both Spink and outraged Dakotans were of no avail, and Washington's suggestion that by appointing nonresidents they were peopling the Territory with desirable and needed settlers caused only indignation. To add insult to injury, two leaders of the Peoples' Union party, Judge Kidder and U. S. Marshal L. H. Litchfield, both with strong out-of-territory political connections, were reappointed. The new chief justice, George W. French, had been a county clerk in Maine with no experience either as a lawyer or as a judge, but having been a personal friend of Senator Hannibal Hamlin, he secured the appointment. The new territorial secretary, Turney M. Wilkins of Iowa, was a protégé of Grant's friend, General Belknap, and despite his total incompetence and the continual protests of nearly every politician in Dakota, Wilkins remained in office for two years. When he was replaced, it was by none other than Senator Hamlin's own son-in-law, George A. Bachelder. Only Brookings of the regular Republicans received an important post as a reward when, in 1869, he was appointed to the territorial supreme court.[54]

Considering the large number of political hacks whom Grant

1869–1873," *North Dakota Historical Quarterly*, 12 (1947), 111; see also TP, Dakota (1866), John A. Burbank File; Interior Appointment Papers, Dakota (1873–78), File 135, John A. Burbank.

53. Jackson, "Dakota Politics during the Burbank Administration," pp. 111–35.
54. Kingsbury, *Dakota Territory*, 1, 522–3.

and the Radical Republicans had pawned off on the Dakotans, it seemed strange that Grant should choose William Henry Harrison Beadle of Wisconsin as the new Surveyor General of Dakota to replace the convivial Hill. Although Beadle received the post only because an incumbent Wisconsin congressman saw him as a possibly successful opponent in the next Republican primary —for Beadle could boast of a brilliant war record—the choice was a wise one. Beadle accepted this political strategy in good spirit and moved to Dakota determined to make it his home and equally determined to be an honest officeholder. He was pompous, verbose, and inclined to take a self-righteous stand upon all public issues, but Beadle's ability was so great that he came to be a major beneficent and reforming influence in the Republican party of territorial Dakota. On some issues he assumed the stature of a statesman and he was perhaps as responsible as any single man in the Territory for identifying Republicanism with repectability. In gratitude for his successful fight to save the public school lands from both squatter settlement and sale to speculators, the State of South Dakota later was to place his statue in the Hall of Fame in Washington. His was the only appointment, however, for which the Dakotans could thank the Grant administration.[55]

The shortsighted appointments made during the first two years of Grant's term in office were too much for the Republicans in Dakota. Political expediency was thrown to the winds. Burbank and Wilkins saw their jobs more as mere sinecures than did perhaps any appointees in the history of the Territory. Throughout their incumbency they made little or no attempt to be popular with the Dakotans. In May 1870 the Attorney General of Dakota, George Hand, complained to Secretary of State Hamilton Fish that there had been no executive in the territory for six months and that public business was piling up.[56] The State Department's clerk, in checking to see if the complaint was true, found that Burbank had taken grants of leave totaling six months in less than two years' time, and that Wilkins, after having been secre-

55. See Beadle recommendations in Interior Appointment Papers, Dakota Surveyors General (1864–71), File 1262, W. H. H. Beadle. Among the recommendations were letters from the University of Wisconsin, where he had attended college, Andrew D. White, General Lew Wallace, and the Wisconsin delegation in Congress.
56. George H. Hand to Secretary of State Hamilton Fish, May 26, 1870; TP, Dakota Letterbook, 1870.

tary for only a little over a year, had been absent from the Territory four months and nineteen days.[57]

The indifference of Burbank—and of Washington—to local party requests, the memory of five candidates for delegate, and the breakdown of the Republican ranks into Spink, Kidder, and Burleigh factions left the Dakota Republicans chastened even though they had won a nominal victory in 1868. They were determined, therefore, to present a harmonious front in 1870. But two factions continued to disturb the ranks, for Burleigh had returned to the party fold after his defeat as an independent. His impressive record as a political maverick made little difference to a large number of the party who were willing to condone almost anything the jovial and expansive doctor did. But the majority of the leading "administrative" or "regular" Republicans felt that this uncontrollable man was too irresponsible to be trusted again with the party's fate and agreed that Spink must be renominated even though his record was singularly unspectacular. Here again the leader with the personal following, a leader to whom a party was a name only, was to clash with an organized political machine in which a certain amount of continuous rudimentary teamwork was considered to be more important than individual popularity.

The Democrats, seeing the impending battle between the Spink and Burleigh Republicans, encouraged each group not to compromise. By convention time in August 1870 the entire population of Dakota, whether Democrat or Republican, had taken sides in this intraparty fight. The result was to be expected: two sets of delegates—most of them chosen in a highly questionable manner —appeared at the county and territorial conventions. No compromise proposal succeeded, so that Burleigh's supporters nominated him as the Republican candidate for delegate and the Spink Republicans placed the incumbent up for reelection. And since the various appointive federal officers had never troubled to develop either an administrative or a party *esprit de corps*, each picked his own candidate.[58]

57. Ibid.
58. Kingsbury, *Dakota Territory*, 1, 542–51. For an account of the political conventions, see the Yankton *Press* for August 31, September 7 and 14, 1870.

Here was a situation about which the Democrats had dreamed. Wisely they picked Moses K. Armstrong, the pioneer journalist-politician, as their candidate for delegate. Armstrong was so popular and respected that he had the trust and confidence of many of the leading Republicans as well as the Democrats in the Territory. Although it hardly seemed possible, the ensuing campaign was as bitter as that of 1868. Each of the seven Republican newspapers became violently partisan, the *Union and Dakotaian* leading the Burleigh forces while the Yankton *Press* supported Spink.[59] The *Press* paraded Burleigh's past record in each weekly edition. His irregularities while an Indian agent were exposed. He was accused of having introduced Texas cattle into Dakota and thus ruining the local ranchers who could not afford to sell their beef at the low prices which the Texas longhorns brought.[60] Burleigh had fleeced the Territory of $200,000 during his nine years sojourn there, the *Press* asserted on one occasion, and as the result of this embezzlement he was so wealthy that he was like Prince Esterhazy of Hungary, "who cannot count his cattle and can do little more than count his herdsmen." [61] Erratic speeches made by Burleigh while he was in Congress were reprinted from the *Congressional Globe* to show that he was disgracefully drunk when he had delivered them.[62] In one issue the *Press* jubilantly published a letter from a constituent who referred to Burleigh as a "political prostitute." [63]

The *Dakotaian* was scarcely less violent in its denunciations of Spink, who was condemned for his ineptness and his failure to secure a railroad grant for the Territory. Spink lacked the lurid past of Burleigh, however, so that Judge Brookings and others of the Spink faction were attacked in print nearly as frequently as Spink himself.[64] Both papers naturally attacked Armstrong as the Democratic opponent, but most of the fire was exchanged between the two Republican factions.

59. Yankton *Press*, August 10, 1870.
60. Ibid., September 7 and 14, 1870.
61. Ibid., August 17, 1870.
62. Ibid.
63. Ibid., August 24, 1870.
64. Ibid., August 10, 1870. In this issue the *Press* refers to the *Dakotaian* attack; see also the *Press*, August 31, 1870, for further comments upon the *Dakotaian's* attack upon Hand, Kingsbury, Stone, Hanson, Moody, and Brookings as Spink men.

In an extremely close election Armstrong won over Burleigh by only ninety-six votes and over Spink by less than two hundred. Burleigh, as was to be expected, contested the election and the issue was not settled until February 1872, when the House of Representatives recognized Armstrong as the legally elected delegate from Dakota. The first biennial Assembly, meeting in 1870, indicated that the breach in the ranks had not ended, for a Burleigh and a Spink faction appeared there alongside the Democratic faction. The Spink forces, preferring that Armstrong should oust Burleigh in the contested election, joined forces with the Democrats to make it a pro-Armstrong Assembly.[65] With Governor Burbank dispensing the major portion of the patronage as he pleased, neither Republican faction was strong enough, without this weapon, to force the allegiance of the other branch. Until one section of the party could again control a lion's share of the federal patronage distributed through a popularly elected delegate—and therefore someone directly accountable to them—there would be no single Republican party. Again, during the biennial election of 1872, the two factions refused to join. The two groups were so distinct by that time, in fact, and so bitter, that they went by the local names of the "Capital Street Gang" and the "Broadway Gang." Under such circumstances the Democrats were able to repeat their performance of 1870 and return Armstrong a second time as a minority victor in a three-man contest.[66]

In a summary of the period 1866–70 in Dakota politics several important new developments emerge. The Dakotans in these four years evolved their own local Indian policy, which after some struggle they forced the federal government to adopt. This policy was based upon seemingly paradoxical premises: (a) that Dakota could be settled successfully by whites, but (b) that at the same time the continued presence of government-supported Indians was a necessary prerequisite to make settlement possible. Even after ten years a lingering belief in the legend of the Great American Desert was still alive.

It is not surprising in view of this attitude to find that Indian

65. Kingsbury, *Dakota Territory*, 1, 559.
66. Ibid., pp. 661–70.

affairs were considered an intimate and vital part of the political and economic life of the Territory. The Republican alliance with the local Indian agents and with other frontier groups who in some way or another could be influenced by government patronage marked a significant advance in the fortunes of the party. Yet this very alliance was a basic source of trouble, for the agent, the rancher, the trapper, the woodhawker, and the squaw man were inclined to follow personal leaders like Todd, Burleigh, and Armstrong. They were little moved by an abstract appeal to support the party candidate, whoever he might be. Thus while Spink could count upon the Republicans in the towns and the more settled farming areas for support, Burleigh could depend upon the personal loyalty of a segment of the frontier elements. The tradition of personal leadership in frontier politics which made each county politician think and assert that he was, as Armstrong put it, "the head and front of the Great Union Party of Dakota" was only aggravated and made more permanent by the issue of radical reconstruction and the indifference of federal appointees like Burbank or Wilkins toward the goal of a well-organized party. After ten years' time the word "faction" was still a more accurate description of the political groups in the Territory than the word "party." The political unanimity achieved under the Republicans during the starving time had been of the most transitory nature. The prosperity of the late 1860's resulted in a quick return of the undisciplined factions. Surveyor General Beadle admirably summed up the first decade of Dakota politics in a letter to the Secretary of the Interior in 1869:

> Dakota has had a small population. The settlements had been rather compact in a few counties in the South Eastern part. But a few hundred votes have generally been polled. Any well informed citizen in public life could know personally nearly all the supporters or opponents of any particular candidate. In such cases there is apt to be, and here there was much personal feeling generated. The different contests had been largely personal or based upon special territorial interests. Party lines were not drawn and men were not judged by the same rules as in densely populated states during regular political campaigns. The questions

were also largely affected by the enjoyment or hope for a share of the patronage of the General Government. *Where the population is small, business light, and wealth not present this is a large and even controlling item of political and private interest. This has been particularly the case in Dakota where all the leading politicians have been in a large measure connected with the General Government and its patronage.*[67]

The politics of this latest period again demonstrated how extremely uneven and mobile the powers of office could be. During the years 1866–68 the importance of the Assembly had declined while the offices of governor and delegate increased enormously in power. With the election of Burleigh and the appointment of his father-in-law as governor, this latter office became a mere rubber stamp to approve the acts of the delegate. The appointment of Burbank and Wilkins marked still another shift. Now the territorial executive exercised the greatest control over the federal patronage, while the delegate lost tremendous prestige. The Assembly regained some of its powers during these latter two years, but it continued to be overshadowed both by the executive branch and by the delegate. It should be made clear that these shifts in power were due not so much to the differing personalities and abilities of the various officials as to the degree of influence which each had in Washington. The local newspapers never failed to remind their readers that Senators Morton and Hamlin and General Belknap were the true sources of political power in Dakota. As Beadle implied to Secretary Cox, the federal government, whether it realized it or not, continued to be the basic determining factor in the political fortunes of the Territory.

Despite the continuing importance of federal patronage, the new immigration—the population was 14,000 by 1870—the good crop years from 1868–70, and the appearance of Eastern capital in the Territory for the first time resulted in important changes within the parties or factions, in the type of voters, and in the political ideas of the settlers. Leaders of the regular Republican

67. W. H. H. Beadle to Secretary of the Interior James D. Cox, August 3, 1869, Interior Appointment Papers, Dakota Surveyors General (1869), File 3; italics mine.

faction, such as Spink, Hand, Brookings, and Beadle, had attempted to follow the national party line and to maintain a continuous party organization in the belief that this was the surest way to success. Aided by the newly arrived settlers from the East, they laid the foundations for a party which still controls South Dakota today. The Democratic party likewise changed its nature, as a merchant and farm group gradually supplemented or replaced the frontier elements who had elected Todd.

The Assembly, which continued to be made up of only the most able and successful of the settlers, made a convenient mirror to reflect the changing attitudes within Dakota.[68] In 1867 it attempted to repeal the Territory's liberal exemption law of 1862 and to pass a law more attractive to creditors. Since the Assembly at this time was filled with the very men who most nearly approached a creditor status in Dakota, they stood to benefit personally by the repeal. The same attempt had been made by a lawyers' bloc and a "resolute outside interest" while the fifth Assembly (1865) was in session, but without success.[69] This combination had also urged the fifth Assembly to request Congress to throw open certain lands, usually reserved for homesteaders, for sale upon the public market. This resolution had failed to pass by only one vote.[70] In the seventh session a similar group, led by Brookings and Stutsman, again tried to repeal or amend the exemption law of 1862, and a bill considerably restricting exemption passed the Assembly, but Governor Faulk's veto prevented its becoming law.[71] Brookings was unable to override the veto, but he did persuade the Assembly to adopt a law which provided that exemption laws should apply only to permanent territorial residents.[72]

Another division of interests along economic lines appeared in 1867, when the Assembly considered the passage of a herd law

68. Some of the newer members, like the old, had had previous political experience. George A. Hand, a member of the House in 1870, had been senate clerk to the Wisconsin upper house in 1860 and had served as attorney general for Dakota from 1866 to 1869. Another member of the House in 1870, John Hancock, had recently been a member of the Pennsylvania Legislature. For biographical sketches of the members of the 1870 Assembly see the Yankton Press, December 21, 1870.

69. Kingsbury, Dakota Territory, 1, 425–6.

70. Ibid., pp. 427–8; Council Journal (1865–66), pp. 87–8.

71. Council Journal (1867–68), pp. 184–6.

72. Ibid., p. 191.

designed to protect the farmers against the cattle rancher.[73] The
united action of the ranchers prevented this bill from becoming
law, but by 1870 the problem of protecting crops had become
so pressing and the number of nonranching farmers had so increased that the Yankton *Press* demanded that the Assembly take
action.[74] Fencing in a prairie country was more expensive than
the initial cost of the land itself, the *Press* noted; therefore a
herd law restricting the movement of cattle and allowing a farmer
to collect damages caused by unherded cattle was the only fea-
sible solution.[75] After a spirited fight the Assembly passed a law
giving the farmer full protection.[76] The law was, in a sense, an
indication that farming was increasingly successful in the Territory and that the distinctly frontier phase of cattle ranching was
drawing to a close.

Finally, there were signs that the new members of the Assembly during this four-year period had brought with them some
Eastern notions. A prohibition bill passed the Council in 1868,
only to be defeated by the House.[77] Again, in the 1870 House a
bill to permit woman suffrage was introduced, but this time it
received a fifteen-to-seven defeat.[78] It is quite probable that these
bills were considered with tongue in cheek, but their very consideration revealed that these ideas were penetrating the con-
sciousness of Western lawmakers and that it was the post-Civil
War settler recently arrived from more eastern parts who was
responsible for their consideration.

The issues of herd laws, prohibition, and woman suffrage failed
to develop much interest after 1869, however, for the entire Territory became absorbed in what was thought to be the solution
for all of Dakota's problems and the touchstone to wealth and
prosperity for everyone. That touchstone was a railroad which
would connect the Territory with the East.

73. Bill in *Council Journal* (1867–68), pp. 182–83, and *House Journal* (1867–
68), pp. 183–4.
74. Yankton *Press*, November 23, 1870.
75. Ibid., December 14, 1870.
76. Ibid., January 18, 1871. By 1870 grain was being shipped from Dakota
farms down the Missouri by steamboat. The greater part of the agricultural products
were consumed by the inhabitants themselves or sold to contractors supplying Indian reservations and Army posts.
77. *Council Journal* (1868–69), p. 154.
78. Yankton *Press*, December 28, 1870.

Chapter 4. Railroads, Prosperity, and

Corruption: 1869-74

Money Loaned for Eastern Capitalists
Taxes Paid for Nonresidents
Investments Carefully Made for Eastern Capitalists
General Law, Land and Collection Business Transacted
Buy and Sell Real Estate
U.S. Land Business Promptly Attended to
Contests a Specialty

Letterhead of E. P. Caldwell,
Attorney, Huron, D.T.

Westward the course of empire takes its way;
    The four first Acts already past,
A fifth shall close the Drama with the day;
    Time's noblest offspring is the last.

George Berkeley, 1726

ON MANY A PUBLIC OCCASION the Dakota politician treated his constituents to a glowing speech which contained or ended with Bishop Berkeley's verses on America. Although the good Bishop was usually misquoted—the first line of the above stanza receiving an especial maltreatment—neither speaker nor hearer, caught in the throes of frontier eloquence, doubted that "time's noblest offspring" was Dakota itself. The Dakotan thought that only one thing was lacking in 1870 to close the drama and that was a territorial railroad.

It would be difficult to exaggerate the vital role the railroad played in shaping the Territory's political and economic history. The struggle to secure a railroad is, in fact, a key and binding factor which gives meaning to Dakota politics for the years 1869–74. Since the builders of the first line were also the leading political figures in Dakota, regardless of party or position, the railroad issue was often the most important political issue. This was, to be sure, exactly the period when the railroad everywhere became a basically important factor in state and national politics —a time when whole legislatures could be bribed or at least

127

"influenced" to do the railroad's bidding. In Dakota, however, it was as much a case of the Legislature buying the railroad as the other way around. With a completely inadequate supply of lumber and fuel and with no goods to exchange for these necessities except bulky agricultural products which could be marketed profitably only if cheap transportation were available, it was no wonder that the railroad proved a subject of primary political as well as economic importance.[1]

One of the first lures to settlement had been the rumor that the much-discussed transcontinental railroad would pass through Dakota. Governor Stevens' railroad explorations along the forty-ninth parallel were followed by a townsite boom in the Red River Valley.[2] By 1857 the railroad boom in Minnesota caused many a speculator to look westward to Dakota as the possible site for still another boom. The Dakota Land Company of Saint Paul carefully established its holdings in an east-west direction through southwestern Minnesota and southeastern Dakota in the expectation that an important rail line would connect them.[3] General Todd and the first Yanktonians had high hopes, after General Harney's exploration along the forty-third parallel, that the projected Union Pacific would run along the north banks of the Missouri through Yankton, then cross the Missouri and continue westward along the north bank of the Niobrara River, which was until 1868 the southern border of Dakota Territory.[4]

The lack of adequate water transportation made the necessity of a railroad to all plains regions obvious, and Dakota was no exception. Although the treacherous, winding Missouri offered Dakotans an outlet which other western territories did not have, it alone could not suffice, for the seasonal vagaries of the Big Muddy made every voyage up or down its channel hazardous, expensive, and extremely slow.

The first Dakota Assembly granted a charter to the Missouri and Niobrara Valley Railroad Company. The road was to be a

1. The settlers alternated between the plans to tap lumber resources by establishing rail connections between the Missouri Valley and Minnesota, or to open the Black Hills, which could supply a plentiful amount of timber.

2. See above, p. 35.

3. Above, p. 42.

4. See the law for the incorporation of the Missouri and Niobrara Valley Railroad in *Private Laws of Dakota Territory* (1862), p. 21.

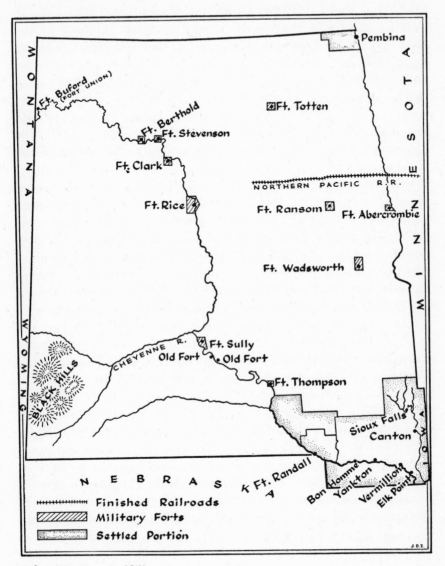

Dakota Territory in 1872.

link in the Union Pacific, connecting Dubuque, Iowa, with Yankton and extending into the Niobrara Valley. Well-known railroad men, such as Erastus Corning, Richard M. Rice, W. B. Ogden, and Elihu Washburn, as well as every member of the 1862 Assembly, appeared on the list of incorporators.[5] The assemblymen had not hesitated to use their office to get in on the ground floor of what they considered a very good business deal. In the subsequent session the Assembly granted more charters and urged Congress to allow the Union Pacific to pass through Dakota.[6] And in each case where a charter was granted, the names of all the assemblymen corresponded to the names of the incorporators.[7]

When news was received that a railroad line was being constructed to Sioux City, Iowa, in 1866, Governor Faulk prophesied a new era for Dakota. The sixth Assembly appointed a joint committee "to devise some means of advancing our railroad and wagon interests" and granted two new charters at this session.[8] The first allowed the Minnesota and Missouri Railroad Company to build between Sioux Falls and Yankton; the second permitted the Dakota and Northwestern Company to connect Sioux City to Yankton by rail, and to continue the line westward from Yankton to Fort Thompson on the Missouri.[9] Again the incorporators were the assemblymen themselves, but in the case of the Dakota and Northwestern, Delegate Burleigh, Secretary Spink, Judge Bartlett, Moses K. Armstrong, and every official and man of means in the Territory were also included.[10] The Assembly enlisted outside talent for the board of directors, however: John I. Blair, builder of the Union Pacific spur to Sioux City, was made president of the Dakota and Northwestern, while his chief engineer, William Walker, was made vice-president. The Board also included the names of A. W. Hubbard, Alexander Ramsay, D. S. Norton, and Ignatius Donnelly. Since all these men were promi-

5. Ibid., pp. 21–7. Jayne in his gubernatorial address in 1862 predicted that the Pacific railroad would bring all the trade of the Far East through its borders. *Council Journal* (1862), p. 18.

6. See the memorial to Congress in *General Laws of Dakota Territory* (1862–63), p. 273; also *General and Private Laws of Dakota Territory* (1864), pp. 149–55.

7. Ibid.

8. *Council Journal* (1866–67), pp. 23, 37.

9. *Private Laws of Dakota Territory* (1866–67), pp. 68 ff., 97 ff.

10. Ibid.

nent Minnesota politicians, the indication was that the railroad schemes were attracting considerable outside interest.[11]

After 1867, when a five-year period of drought ended, the *Journals* of the House and Council were filled with references to railroads. Reports on the progress of the Union Pacific across the country, and upon the extension of the Chicago and Northwestern to Sioux City, created excitement in Yankton similar to that seen during elections.[12] The scope of railroad plans grew swiftly; a House committee reported in January 1868 that some five companies had proposed lines in the Territory, four of which were to run through Yankton.[13] It is probable that the various promoters hoped to repeat the fabulous success story of St. Paul, which had become a city overnight after R. M. Rice had made it the center of a railroad system which fanned out from the capital like the spokes of a wheel.[14]

An unprecedented year of prosperity in Yankton in 1869 and the twin arrivals of settlers and Eastern capital convinced the political leaders that the time was ripe for the actual construction of a territorial line which would connect Yankton to Sioux City. Such a line, in order to be practical, would run through the heart of the settled portion of Dakota. Each platform of the parties demanded a road, and public meetings to discuss the subject were the order of the day.

One of the major difficulties to be overcome lay in the hostility of Sioux City, Iowa, which as a rail terminus, depot, and supply center for merchants engaged in filling army and Indian contracts throughout the Missouri Valley plateau did not wish to lose this business to Yankton as the new terminus. But when W. W. Brookings persuaded the McGregor and Western Railroad to propose a line which would run from LeMars, Iowa, to Yankton by a route north of Sioux City, the merchants of Sioux City became so alarmed that they agreed to cooperate in extending a line to Yankton.[15] By January 1871 the Yankton *Press* was able to report that two companies had organized and had sold a majority

11. Ibid., pp. 88 ff., 97 ff.
12. *House Journal* (1867–68), pp. 2, 97, 110–11, 284 ff.
13. Ibid.
14. See W. W. Folwell, *History of Minnesota* (St. Paul, 1921–30), *1*, 327–50; *2*, 37–58; *3*, 32–57.
15. Kingsbury, *Dakota Territory, 1*, 537.

of their stock. Still the companies were so amorphous that their names, plans, and routes changed several times within a year, but the incorporators, regardless of the railroad, continued to be the chief political figures of the Territory.[16] The Dakota and Northwestern, for example, chose Judge Jefferson P. Kidder as its president and General Todd as its secretary. The Dakota Central, organized in 1868, had many outside investors, but its president was D. T. Bramble, the foremost Yankton merchant and one of the leading members of the territorial Council. Delegate Armstrong was its secretary and engineer.[17]

Constant public meetings to discuss railroads kept the Territory in a state of agitation all spring and summer.[18] Delegate Armstrong asked Congress for a land grant for the road; Governor Burbank journeyed to Washington to push this request.[19] When their efforts proved futile, the Dakotans took matters into their own hands. A committee of Yankton citizens, led by ex-Governor Edmunds, ex-Secretary Spink, Councilman Brookings, and others petitioned the new territorial secretary, George Batchelder, who was acting governor in Burbank's absence, to convene the Assembly in a special session so that it could give Yankton County legal authority to issue county bonds to the proposed railroad, which the railroad in turn could sell in the East for cash. Batchelder complied by issuing a call for the Legislature the same day he received the petition.[20] Five of Yankton's most prominent lawyers drafted the railroad bill, and a week later the special session convened.[21]

At this point a series of incidents occurred to indicate how well planned the strategy of the railroad promoters had been and how identical it was with that of the political leaders of the Territory. The question naturally arose whether an acting governor had power to call a special session—a matter further complicated by the fact that Congress had limited the number of territorial assemblies by law. Burbank, who returned within a day

16. Yankton *Press*, January 25, 1871.
17. Ibid., January 25, 1871.
18. Ibid., February 1, April 12, May 10, June 14, August 2, 1871.
19. Ibid., March 29, 1871.
20. Yankton *Press*, April 5, 1871; see also Batchelder's proclamation in TP, Dakota Letterbook, March 30, 1871.
21. Yankton *Press*, April 12, 19, 1871.

of Batchelder's proclamation, wrote Attorney General A. T. Ackerman for legal advice, but the letter conveniently did not reach Ackerman until the Assembly was already in convention.[22] Ackerman, acting through the State Department, which controlled territorial affairs, wired Burbank that the special session was unauthorized. The version of the telegram which reached Yankton stated that the session *had* been authorized. The Assembly then proceeded with almost prescient haste to pass the cut-and-dried legislation on the day the authorization was received, and before the day was over Burbank had signed the act. The next morning as the Assembly was preparing to adjourn, the corrected version of Ackerman's opinion arrived, but by then the damage had been done. An investigation revealed that somewhere between Omaha and Missouri Valley Junction, Western Union had lost the vital prefix *un,* but beyond that no information was forth coming. Congress further complicated the legal aspects of the whole affair by denying the right of the special session to convene but at the same time approving the bond-issue law which this illegal assembly had passed.[23]

Out of the plethora of paper railroads which the Dakota Assembly had chartered over a ten-year period, the Dakota Southern, organized in the spring of 1871 and supported by the bonds provided by Yankton County, brought the first railroad into Yankton in February 1873. Its directors were, as in the previous companies, a sprinkling of the necessary eastern investors and a number of local public officials, including W. A. Burleigh, W. W. Brookings, J. M. Stone, ex-Governor Edmunds, Delegate Armstrong, and J. R. Hanson.[24]

From its inception the railroad project was a public issue and problem: its promoters were foremost territorial officers and its funds came from citizens acting in a public rather than a private capacity. There was nothing unique about any of these actions, for throughout the country the railroad had always been a topic of public discussion and interest; Congress had treated the Union Pacific as a problem of such magnitude that private individuals

22. J. A. Burbank to Attorney General A. T. Ackerman, April 3, 1871, TP, Dakota Letterbook, 1871.
23. Kingsbury, *Dakota Territory,* 1, 623.
24. Ibid., pp. 625–9.

could not finance the undertaking. Furthermore, it was the custom rather than the exception for counties, especially in the midwest, to subscribe bonds for railroad construction. The difference between the public side of these projects and that in Dakota was one partly of degree, partly of attitude. No one seems to have considered seriously a road which would not have been under political auspices and which would not have had either federal aid in the form of a land grant or local aid through county bonds. The conditions under which the Territory had grown up—that is, the recognition that government itself provided the largest source of income in Dakota and was in a sense its "leading industry" employing the Territory's most able men—inevitably gave the railroad an important political aspect. Finally the prospect of limited returns for a long time was not attractive to the Eastern investor, so that some other means had to be devised to supply the necessary funds.

The need for a railroad had been so great that party or factional lines had been largely ignored. To have opposed any line connecting Dakota with the East would have been an invitation to commit political suicide. Armstrong, Brookings, Todd, Burbank, Burleigh, Spink, and Kidder, all political opponents, were a harmonious and loving brotherhood when the magic word was mentioned. Construction at the Sioux City end was no sooner started, however, than Delegate Armstrong pushed a charter through Congress for a "Grand Trunk" which would absorb every proposed territorial railroad east of the Missouri into one large company. The size and import of the scheme became apparent when it was learned that the incorporators were Governor A. J. Smith, then president of the Northern Pacific, Thomas A. Scott, one of the builders of the Pennsylvania system, Governor Burbank, the new territorial secretary General E. S. McCook, Judge Brookings of the territorial supreme court, Delegate Armstrong, and other officers of the Territory.[25]

The small companies bitterly opposed this monopoly, describing it as a "Great Octopus" rather than a Grand Trunk. General

25. The Grand Trunk Company was organized in 1872. Governor Burbank was president, Delegate Armstrong was vice-president, Secretary McCook was secretary, and Joseph R. Hanson, was treasurer. Kingsbury, *Dakota Territory*, 1, 613.

Beadle, whose own company stood to lose if the plan went through, fought the Grand Trunk at every point. The chief architect of the Grand Trunk appears to have been Governor Burbank. Backed by Eastern investors and his brother-in-law, Senator Morton, Burbank intended to make money by combining railroad building and townsite booming. As his instrument of coercion he used his patronage powers to create a clique of federal appointees who would further his aims.[26] At no time does he appear to have desired popular political control of the Territory or to have been interested in pleasing the rank of his own party in Dakota.

His first move was to persuade the government to locate a land office at Springfield, Dakota, a town which he practically owned. He hardly enhanced his popularity by this act, for most of the businessmen of the Territory had invested in the town of Bon Homme, thinking that it and not Springfield had the best chance of becoming the site of the new land office.[27] Again, in locating the terminal point of the Dakota Southern, Burbank persuaded Congress to place it at his town, Springfield, rather than at Yankton, in the hope that it would replace the latter town as the supply base for the entire Upper Missouri Valley.[28] Of course Burbank was acting in the best Dakota political tradition, but the local citizens did not care to be beaten at their own game. The Dakota Land Company, over a decade before, had in mind a railroad-townsite monopoly similar to that of the Burbank-Grand Trunk incorporators.

The delegate and assembly election of 1872 came in the midst of the growing resentment against Burbank, against the other Grant-appointed officials, and against their railroad speculations. One faction, the so-called "Organization" or "regular Republicans," led by Judge Brookings, stood by the governor, nonetheless, in the hope that by patronage control they might carry the elections. This group received powerful support when Burleigh joined its ranks. The Organization Republicans, also known as the "Capital Street Gang," were opposed by an equally deter-

26. Jackson, "Dakota Politics during the Burbank Administration," pp. 111–35.
27. Ibid., p. 118.
28. Ibid., p. 119; Kingsbury, *Dakota Territory, 1*, 635.

mined group of Republicans, the "Broadway Gang," whose leader was Colonel Gideon C. Moody, an able but fierce and temperamental politician. Moody claimed that his faction represented the true Republican rank and file.

Popular dissatisfaction with the disbursement of the Yankton County railroad bonds which the voters had so willingly turned over to the Dakota Southern loomed as an election dispute in 1872, for it looked as if the railroad directors had used the bonds in some shady dealings. Brookings took the side of the railroad, while Moody became the advocate of the citizens opposing further issuance of bonds to the company. Since other counties were to decide at the polls whether to follow the lead of Yankton County and supply additional bonds, the division on the question was general throughout the Territory. An eleventh hour attempt to achieve party union failed when every county but one presented two contesting delegations at the territorial Republican convention, held at Windsor's Drug Store in Canton. The Brookings men, thinking that they had won control of the convention by fair parliamentary procedure, suddenly found the Moody delegates marching off to a local schoolhouse to hold a rump meeting.[29]

Although Delegate Armstrong had been a Grand Trunk incorporator, he had never been identified as a Burbank man; hence his popularity was greater than ever when he was nominated for reelection by the Democrats. What is more, sober Republicans, disgusted with Burbank and the Brookings-Moody spats, banded together in a local Liberal Republican movement to support Armstrong. They held their own convention at Bon Homme at the same time the Democrats were meeting, and Armstrong was informed of his joint nomination by a delegation of two Liberal Republicans and two Democrats.[30] Just as pro-Grant sentiment had defeated Burleigh in 1868, an anti-Grant feeling, brought about by four years of inept and corrupt territorial officials whom Grant had foisted upon Dakota, reelected Armstrong in 1872. The vote of no confidence in the national administration was seconded by the fact that Moody, though de-

29. Robinson, *South Dakota, 1,* 297–8.
30. *Dakota Herald,* July 23, 1872.

feated by Armstrong, had polled many more votes than Brookings, the Organization Republican.[31]

The campaign itself was as bitter and dirty as any Dakotan had ever seen. Moody, who had once been accused of embezzling funds to pay for a large sheep ranch, was driven from the platform on more than one occasion by a loudly bleating chorus of Brookings men.[32] Beadle, a Moody supporter, toured the Territory denouncing Brookings' railroad schemes.[33] At Sioux Falls, a Brookings stronghold, Moody was not allowed to use the town hall, and he was forced to speak in an abandoned barracks on the edge of town.[34] Each candidate had his own newspaper, and the governor's paper, the Springfield *Times*—a publication pithily described by the Democratic *Dakota Herald* as that "up country smut machine"—entered the lists for Brookings.

The factions eagerly solicited the foreign vote as one method of winning the 1872 election. Rumor after rumor reached the newspapers that this or that Bohemian or Scandinavian leader had been bought.[35] The *Herald*, an Armstrong organ, gleefully reported that the Springfield *Times* had referred to the honest German settlers as the "red-mouthed Dutch," thereby implying that Burbank and Brookings were anti-German. Later, in an editorial attack on Surveyor General Beadle, a Moody supporter whom the *Herald* maintained had assigned surveying contracts in return for bloc foreign votes, it was asserted: "We even now hear it bruited about the streets of this city [Yankton] that Mr. John Langness secured a contract for surveying six townships on the Sioux upon condition that the gross receipts of three of them should be given into the hands of Ole Sampson to control the Scandinavian vote of the Territory for Col. Moody." [36]

The *Dakotaian*, a Moody organ, editorialized that Brookings and the Capital Street Gang were "snakes" who had used money and whiskey to buy votes as well as threats to scare the inde-

31. Ibid., October 15, 1872; see also Robinson, *South Dakota, 1,* 298.
32. Clipping of article on the 1872 campaign written for the Sioux Falls *Forum* (1902?), deposited in the State Department of History, Pierre, South Dakota; see also the *Dakota Herald*, October 8, 1872.
33. *Dakota Herald*, September 3, 1872.
34. Sioux Falls *Forum* (1902?).
35. *Dakota Herald*, September 17, 1872.
36. Ibid., September 24, 1872.

pendent Scandinavians into line. The Yankton *Press,* in terms of equal opprobrium, replied that Moody himself was a "demagogue and a trickster." [37]

The acrimonious feelings engendered by the campaign continued long after the election itself, for Moody contested Armstrong's seat and a large number of seats in the Assembly were hotly contested. The Assembly, representing the three parties, none of whom had a clear majority, was naturally turbulent and accomplished little of a constructive nature. Here the governor and his colleague, Brookings, were able to divide and conquer several factions with promises of patronage. The *Dakota Herald* rightly described it as a "ring legislature" interested only in railroads.[38] Burbank's own efforts resulted in his being made a director of the Dakota Southern.[39] Beadle later complained to Attorney General Williams in Washington that Burbank and the judiciary had also made common cause during the session, "to secure appearance of popular support by all the inducement of promised patronage, favor and prejudice. By signing petitions of certain members for local appointments, and by numerous lobby schemes and influences . . . as well as from those friendly to otherwise . . . they have obtained a deceptive showing." [40] The people stood opposed to both judges and governor, Beadle further asserted, and he urged that they not be reappointed in March.[41]

Two months later Moody entered his own grievance to Williams about the sad state of the territorial judiciary: "You pledged us that we should have *good men* and good lawyers sent to us as judges and we get to constitute our Supreme Court an ass, a knave, and a drunkard." [42] How could they keep a Republican party going in the Territory, Moody asked, if such persons were to be continually fastened upon them? [43] This protest the *Dakota*

37. Ibid., September 17, 1872. The *Dakotaian* and the *Press* were quoted by the *Herald.*

38. *Dakota Herald,* December 17, 24, 1872; January 7, 14, 1873.

39. Kingsbury, *Dakota Territory, 1,* 635.

40. W. H. H. Beadle to Attorney General G. H. Williams, January 11, 1873; Justice, Marshals' Accounts, Dakota, 1873.

41. Ibid.

42. G. C. Moody to Attorney General Williams, March 15, 1873; Justice, Marshals' Accounts, Dakota, 1873.

43. Ibid.

Herald echoed in its statement that "the courts of the Territory are recognized as the most inferior in the entire Northwest." [44] Apparently the wails of discontent had some effect, for in April 1873 Brookings and French—the knave and the ass in Moody's parlance—were removed from the court.[45]

The wave of discontent with governor, legislature, and judiciary washed next over the territorial secretary, General Edwin Stanton McCook. The new secretary had probably been appointed at the request of Governor Burbank, for he was the latter's unquestioning henchman. Before he had been in Dakota a year, the *Herald* summed him up as an "ignorant, vainglorious, drunken lout, who is an eyesore to our people and a depression upon the good morals of this community." [46]

Despite the bipartisan nature of these outbursts, Grant reappointed Burbank in the spring of 1873 and refused to remove McCook. An indignation meeting of Yankton citizens sent the following candid resolution to Washington in reply to such disheartening news: "That the people of Dakota have no use for John A. Burbank as Governor of this Territory, and it is an extravagant and useless waste of money to retain him in that position and pay him the salary provided by law, the Territory being much more likely to prosper without an executive head than with such a one." [47]

While Burbank men like Secretary McCook testified that these unfavorable resolutions were merely the fulminations of a few "Democrats, Liberal Republicans, disappointed politicians and indebted gamblers," the Burbank file in Washington rapidly filled with such remonstrances and only the personal intervention of Senator Morton seems to have kept Burbank in office.[48]

Burbank's reappointment went far to sustain the political excitement and unrest which was now reaching into its second year.

44. *Dakota Herald*, January 21, 1873.
45. Kingsbury, *Dakota Territory*, 1, 634; *Dakota Herald*, April 1, 1873.
46. *Dakota Herald*, March 25, 1873.
47. Resolution in Interior Appointment Papers, Dakota (1873), File 135, J. A. Burbank; see also Jackson, "Dakota Politics during the Burbank Administration," p. 121.
48. O. P. Morton to President Grant, December 7, 1873; W. H. H. Beadle to Secretary of State Hamilton Fish, January 11, 1873; Interior Appointment Papers, Dakota (1873), File 135, J. A. Burbank.

The speculative instincts, stimulated by the wave of prosperity which Eastern capital and a large immigration had brought, only increased the bitterness among the factions as the political and economic stakes grew larger and larger. Then the railroad issue, which had become quiescent when Congress refused to grant land for the Grand Trunk Line, came into the open in a new form. In June 1873 the Yankton County Commissioners, acting as holders of the county's stock in the Dakota Southern, secured a temporary injunction from the Second District Court forbidding the directors of the railroad from selling $1,200,000 worth of first and second mortgage bonds unless the company should give the county some security to protect its particular investment against this watering. The commissioners correctly maintained that Congress had approved the bond issue only on the condition that the county be given $200,000 worth of voting stock. It was in their capacity as stockholders that the commissioners had secured the injunction.[49]

Governor Burbank, one of the directors who had approved the plan to water the stock, was furious at this interference, and he threatened to remove Judge A. H. Barnes, who had granted the injunction, to another judicial district. Since Barnes had replaced Brookings on the supreme court, he had always been in the governor's disfavor. Barnes, nonetheless, knowing that his decision was both correct and proper, refused to be intimidated or silenced. As soon as he could, he reported the incident to Washington, and the new controversy began.[50]

Although Washington forbade Burbank to remove Barnes from the Second Judicial District, the interest in the case led to the discovery not only that the directors had intended to sell watered stock but that the only hard cash which had ever been paid into the Dakota Southern had been from Yankton County and the

49. *Dakota Herald,* August 26, 1873; see also the summary of the Yankton County–Dakota Southern imbroglio in a letter of Attorney General G. H. Williams to Secretary of the Interior C. Delano, November 13, 1873; Interior Appointment Papers, Dakota (1873), File 135, J. A. Burbank.

50. *Dakota Herald,* August 26, 1873. The stock of the Dakota Southern was subscribed to as follows: out of a total of $1,500,000 in capital stock, Wicker, Meckling, and Company had subscribed to $750,000 worth; Burbank, Stone, and Brookings had subscribed $300,000; Yankton County had subscribed to and had paid for $200,000 in stock, while the town of Elk Point had subscribed to and paid $15,000 in stock.

town of Elk Point in the form of bonds. No director had ever paid for his stock, and yet three of these directors, Burbank, Stone, and Brookings, had more voting power than Yankton County. The episode, though much less complicated, was somewhat similar to the *Credit Mobilier* affair which had been exposed in Washington only six months before. Yankton County, like the United States government, had been the chief source of funds for a railroad.[51]

The problem grew in complexity when Brookings, Burleigh, and the Capital Street Gang joined the Governor in the fight against the injunction. Moody, now supported by Spink and the leading Democratic newspaper, declared in favor of the "people" of Yankton County. So much tension and personal feuding developed, however, that the faction leaders themselves began to fear that the Territory's public squabbles would frighten Eastern investors.

To end the dispute a public meeting was called in Yankton for the night of September 11, 1873. Men and women packed the hall that evening to hear the discussion. P. P. Wintermute, a local banker, threw down the first gauntlet when he moved a vote of no confidence in the Dakota Southern. Then a completely unexpected series of incidents followed that ended in tragedy. After Wintermute had made his motion, he left the hall for a drink in the saloon of the St. Charles Hotel, which was close by. There he ran into the territorial secretary, E. S. McCook, one of the chief defenders of the Burbank and railroad faction. The two became involved in a violent argument when McCook crossly refused Wintermute the loan of a dime. Wintermute, claiming that he had been insulted, challenged McCook, who was a huge man of great physical strength. The angry secretary took the diminutive banker—Wintermute weighed only 135 pounds—threw him against a glass mirror, which was completely shattered, and then rubbed the banker's face in the contents of a barroom spittoon. While the struggling Wintermute screamed out threats to kill McCook, the latter calmly left the saloon to wash his hands.

Meanwhile the tempers at the railroad meeting were also run-

51. *Dakota Herald,* August 26, 1873. See also Williams to Delano, November 13, 1873.

ning high. Burleigh, Brookings, Moody, and Spink were engaged
in such spirited exchanges that the chair maintained order with
the greatest difficulty. At this point Wintermute appeared on the
scene, face bleeding, gun in hand, hunting for Secretary McCook,
and before anyone could ascertain what had happened, McCook
walked through the doorway of the hall. Wintermute spotted him
and shot him four times. A panic engulfed the crowded room.
McCook lunged across the room and despite the fact that he was
severely wounded threw Wintermute to the floor, kicked out a
window and tried to pitch Wintermute out of it. Only by great
restraint did several members of the meeting force the bleeding
McCook to remain still while Dr. Burleigh attended his wounds.
But the furious secretary refused to stay still; cursing and swear-
ing, he continued to get up and walk about the room as the blood
poured from his chest. Even the powerful Dr. Burleigh could
not stop this outraged man, and the loss of so much blood from
all this physical action caused McCook's death the next day.[52]

Now the railroad directors and the Brookings group had a
martyr. They trumpeted demands for vengeance from one end
of the Territory to the other. Burbank persuaded the Department
of the Interior to name McCook's father-in-law, Oscar Whitney,
as the new territorial secretary. Whitney had been a clerk in
the late secretary's office at the time of the shooting. This appointment did not help matters, for Whitney devoted his entire time
and energy toward convicting Wintermute. In one instance he
openly interfered with the judicial process when the presiding
judge refused to pass the death sentence. Thus there were trials
and retrials for some three years until Wintermute, by that time
a broken and ruined man, was finally acquitted.[53]

McCook's death was nonetheless a turning point in the political
controversy. The railroad case arising out of the temporary in-

52: The least confused account of the McCook shooting is that of the *Dakota
Herald*, September 16, 1873. Robinson, *South Dakota*, 1, 300, provides details not
mentioned by Kingsbury, *Dakota Territory*, 1, 636. The official account reported
to Washington may be found in letters of Governor John L. Pennington to Secretary of the Interior C. Delano, 1873–75, U.S. Department of the Interior, Patents
and Miscellaneous Division, Territorial Papers, 1873–89, File 200, National Archives (Interior Miscellaneous, Dakota). See, too, Judge A. H. Barnes to Delano,
December 2, 1873, Interior Appointment Papers, Dakota, 1873.

53. Kingsbury, *Dakota Territory*, 1, 718–43, traces the trial in great detail.

junction was settled out of court in the fall of 1873, and the two wings of the Republican party decided to gather in one fold after six years of schism. The political tension further declined when Burbank handed in his resignation in December 1873. The Governor left office an extremely unpopular man, but he could take comfort in certain compensations, for his townsite, his newspaper, and his railroad speculations all had been very profitable.[54]

That the railroad promoters and builders were synonymous with the political leaders and territorial officials in Dakota was obvious throughout the tangled history of the building of the Dakota Southern. This fact implied that the Dakota Land Company's old thesis—that the way to economic success was through political control—was still being followed. It meant, too, that even in the boom period when capital could be had from private as well as public sources, the dissociation of government and business did not occur. With men like Burbank and Brookings holding the reins of power, the association became even more intimate. The reasons for this close relationship have been given in previous chapters, but there were new ramifications and developments in the relationship during the railroad controversy. The territorial government, for example, became an even more integral part of Dakota's economic life. Armstrong took note of this in a public letter to the *Dakota Herald* in 1872:

> The Western Territories are prone to think that they are not liberally treated by the eastern States in Congress. But we in Dakota forget that the people of these same eastern States are usually taxed to pay sixty thousand dollars to sustain our courts in the Territory, $70,000 to survey our lands, $20,000 to run our Legislature, $15,000 to pay our federal officers, many thousand dollars to supply us with mail, several thousand dollars for rent of public buildings, besides stationing troops upon our frontier to protect our settlements, and feeding and clothing 30,000 Indians to keep the peace in our Territory.[55]

54. Jackson, "Dakota Politics during the Burbank Administration," pp. 131–2.
55. *Dakota Herald*, June 4, 1872.

With perhaps as much as a million dollars or more a year being spent in or on the Territory, in which less than 14,000 white persons lived, it was no wonder that government continued to be of great economic importance.[56]

Grant's election in 1869 superimposed upon this existing frontier pattern of government a set of officials possessing the exploitative and speculative attitudes for which Grant's administration and the post-Civil War East became notorious. The territorial citizens rightly called these officials "carpetbaggers," since they viewed the spoils of Dakota in much the same way the carpetbaggers had viewed the South between 1865 and 1876.[57] There was, however —despite the indignant howl put up by the Dakotans—a remarkable affinity between the Grant politician's plan of exploiting government and the Dakotan's. Both were speculative in nature; both ignored the strict boundaries of the law and any limitations upon the power of any office; both reflected a close alliance between government and business.

The similarity between the national and local patterns of political behavior may be even more clearly seen in the struggle between Moody and Brookings, which was actually a conflict between two extremely homogeneous groups. Lord Bryce had said that after the Civil War there was little difference between the two major political parties, that where principle was concerned, both were nearly bankrupt.[58] This parallelism would also suggest that the political characteristics exhibited in Washington during these years reflected a low level of political morality throughout the nation and including the territories.[59] The peculiarly flexible and amorphous territorial system was, in fact, a perfect matrix for corrupt politics, and Burbank's administration was a concrete example of how successful it might be.

The railroad controversy illuminated still another facet of Dakota politics: the continuing existence of two general economic

56. Part of these costs were due to deliberate padding, which in the case of the territorial courts had been developed into a fine art.

57. Pomeroy, "Carpetbaggers in the Territories, 1861–1890," *The Historian*, 2 (Winter, 1939), 53–64.

58. James, Lord Bryce, *The American Commonwealth* (New York, 1927), 2, 21–3.

59. The *Dakota Herald* commented often on the inferior officers in all territories. See February 27, 1872; September 27, 1872; January 28, 1873.

and social groups in the territorial population. In the first days of settlement of eastern settlers the foreign immigrant and the federal officials had combined to oppose a more indigenous western group represented by the rancher, the trapper, the squaw man, and the like. By 1870 this division had become less meaningful, since the frontier fringe was now hopelessly outnumbered by the compact and more populous farming settlements east of Yankton. But now the eastern group itself was split into two factions; and here another kind of differentiation was evolving. It will be remembered that the railroad promoters stated that their lines would allow the farmer to ship his goods to market. Yet the rural voter in Yankton and other counties heartily opposed the railroad bond issue.[60] In view of future economic benefits which the railroad could bring them, the farmers were doubtless being unwise, but they had good reasons for voting as they did. The railroad men and the public officials lived in the towns; they were a non-agricultural group; they were businessmen; and while not possessing the distinctive characteristics of a class, they were a homogeneous combination with a status clearly different from that of the homesteader, the Scandinavian or German immigrant, or even the more successful small farmer or rancher. They were the men who had been able to pay cash for the bloc vote of the foreign settlements, who had Indian and army contracts, who went East once a year or who at least sent their families there for a visit fairly often. They were, in short, a small-town lawyer, merchant, public-official oligarchy, and they ran the Territory.

The leveling features of frontier life prevented many true differences from arising between these two groups, and the chances to join the ruling junta were so numerous that no one with ability was hindered; nonetheless the rural segment felt there was a difference. Consequently they voted against the railroad bonds and chose Armstrong over Moody and Brookings and made up the backbone of the Liberal Republican movement.[61] The Assembly provided the only common ground on which the two ele-

60. Kingsbury, *Dakota Territory, 1,* 625.
61. The makeup of the Liberal Republican party was similar to that of the Johnsonian Republicans of 1866. See Kingsbury, *Dakota Territory, 1,* 666–9.

ments could meet, with the result that the sessions were inevitably turbulent. Even so, the rural element, like the indigenous frontier element, was no match for the professional politician's superior knowledge and ability. Thus the assembly—the one democratically elected organ of local government—remained weak in power and could be bought or sold or organized into "rings" or put at the beck and call of a patronage-dispensing governor. The existence of the two groups further explains why the delegate, the only major official popularly elected by the Territory, often won simply because he was amenable to both. A man appealing to one group—as Todd did to the frontier element after 1864 and as Spink did to the oligarchy in 1870—could not win; Armstrong was twice elected because he was trusted by one group and personally popular with the other. Under such conditions true party development continued to be limited, for internal cliques could split the oligarchy without causing it to lose power anywhere except in the elective offices.

While the railroad issues had clarified the nature of the new groups, that very action left the air filled with portents. The Scandinavians and the Germans were becoming less tractable: the Republicans had to give their leaders more and more minor offices in order to keep them within the fold. A perusal of the *Journals* of the House and the Council indicates that an increasing number of Scandinavians and Germans held positions as clerks, firemen, or sergeants-at-arms, or else were being elected to the Assembly itself. The same thing occurred in the case of the elective offices of territorial auditor, treasurer, superintendent of public instruction, and commissioner of immigration.[62]

The Grange movement swept the settled portion of Dakota in 1872, and a newspaper devoted to Granger happenings began publication at Elk Point.[63] Although it was a nonpolitical movement in Dakota, and the territorial officials gave it their blessing, the farmer got from it his first sense of group organization, a phenomenon which was not to occur again till the late 1880's.

62. See for examples the Brookings ticket for 1872, which included Ole Thoresen for auditor, and Ole Botolfson for treasurer, while the Moody ticket proposed O. B. Iverson as commissioner of Immigration. *Dakota Herald*, May 28, 1872.

63. Ibid., July 15, 1872; Robinson, *South Dakota*, 1, 300.

In the meantime the Territory experienced two earth-shaking changes: the frontier jumped from the Missouri to the Black Hills in one year, and a railroad caused the advance of the frontier of the north, westward from the Red River Valley to Bismarck on the Missouri. These new settlements so affected the political geography of Dakota that it even produced a school of political theorists.

Chapter 5. The Political Frontier Moves Westward;

Settlement of the Black Hills: 1874–80

> As you know, there is a good deal of buncombe in all this talk about
> a new country, but I have not heard or read anything over-exaggerated
> about the Black Hills Country. Seeing is believing, and I have seen one
> of the most favored regions that God ever made.
>
> George S. Pelton, 1880 [1]

> The Wild West made its last glorious stand in the Black Hills min-
> ing camps. Deadwood was the riproaring center of frontier lawlessness.
> There the faro games were wilder, the hurdy-gurdy dance halls noisier,
> the street brawls more common, than in any other western town.
>
> R. A. Billington [2]

DESPITE ITS IMPERIAL SIZE and the boasting of its politicians
Dakota had a population in 1870 of less than 15,000.[3] A half-dozen
small western states had attracted five times this population in less
than five years. As the Dakota Southern Railroad crept up the
north bank of the Missouri to Yankton, many settlers declared
that a new era had begun, but there were still many who argued
that Dakota would always be a grazing country, unfit for intensive
farming or a large population. Yet ten years later the Territory
had a population of 135,000 and was knocking at the doors of the
Union for admission as two states. The sudden change had been
brought about by gold, railroads, and the technique of bonanza
farming.

The lure of gold had drawn men to America from the time of
Columbus' discovery of the new world. The firstcomers to Jamestown in the 17th century hunted for gold before they resigned
themselves to an agricultural existence; gold seekers had driven
the Cherokees out of their homes in the Georgia and Tennessee

---

1. Arthur J. Larsen, ed., "A Journey to the Black Hills in 1880," *North Dakota
Historical Quarterly*, 7 (1932), 49.
2. R. A. Billington, *Westward Expansion* (New York, 1949), p. 632.
3. Frank H. Hagerty, *The Territory of Dakota, an Official Statistical, Historical
and Political Abstract* (Aberdeen, S.D., 1889), p. 54.

hills in the 1820's, and the whole world had thrilled to the news that gold had been discovered in California in 1848. Later, discoveries in Colorado, Nevada, Montana, and Idaho had precipitated the most rapid migration and settlement of a new frontier in the history of the United States. Two years after the first prospector appeared in California, the West Coast was a part of the Union. A similar dramatic discovery of gold in the Black Hills of Dakota in 1874 publicized the Territory's charms to the prospector, the settler, and the immigrant and began a ten-year boom period in this backwash of the prairie frontier.

Tree-covered and mountainous, the Black Hills lie some four hundred miles west of Yankton. After the glaring gray wastes of the Badlands, the Hills looked black to the eyes of the pioneer, hence their name. From time to time trappers, explorers, and individual prospectors had invaded them, but none had ever fully penetrated the region. Considered by the Indians as sacred ground, the Hills had become the subject of countless legends and rumors, each of which contained the assertion that gold worth millions lay hidden there. The discovery of gold in the other mountainous regions of the West persuaded men that the Hills must also be a source of the valuable metal. By 1870 the Eastern press had also begun to feed upon the legends and rumors, although the settlers of eastern Dakota were almost as much attracted by the timber reserves of the Hills as they were by the rumors of gold.[4]

A month before Dakota became a territory a group in Yankton formed the Black Hills Exploring and Mining Association, but they never got beyond the organization stage. In the winter of 1866–67, however, when the Assembly was in session and a large number of speculators and men of property were in Yankton, Byron M. Smith revived the company and enlisted a hundred men to explore the Hills. General William T. Sherman, commander of the Division of the Mississippi, expressly forbade the expedition, since the Hills were Indian Territory. Other attempts were also stopped by the Army, and in 1868 the Hills became a "permanent" Indian reservation, much to the disgust of every

4. Briggs, *Frontiers of the Northwest,* pp. 25–41; Kingsbury, *Dakota Territory,* 1, 861 ff.

Dakotan. But the stories of gold continued to circulate. "The Black Hills gold fever and agitation had reached nearly every part of the United States by 1872, and it was apparent that sentiment was growing throughout the country favoring the cession of that region from the Indians. From all appearances, the time was near when the proclamations of civil and military authorities would be disregarded." [5]

The government decided to bring this agitation to an end by sending General George Custer—with 1200 troops and a number of scientists—to the Hills during the summer of 1874 to explore and report on the mineral wealth of the area. When Custer dramatically announced on August 22 that gold did exist in paying quantities in the Hills, the entire West went wild. Charles Collins, an Irish Fenian who ran a newspaper in Sioux City, Iowa, journeyed to Chicago where he enrolled—according to his own count—11,000 volunteers to settle the Hills. Collins hoped that the Hills would be settled by Irishmen who would become wealthy enough to hire a private army to free Ireland from the British. While Collins pursued his fantastic plan, migrants with no thought in mind but gold set out for the Hills. Overnight, Yankton and Sioux City became chief outfitting centers for prospectors who were willing to make the dangerous trip through the Badlands and hostile Indian country. Both towns provided free shelter for all transients passing through on the way to the fields. Other gold seekers converged on the Hills via the Bismarck route or by way of Sidney, Nebraska, on the Union Pacific line. Many prospectors came in from the West through Cheyenne, Wyoming. This latter route was especially popular with the miners migrating from the worked-out gold fields of California, Nevada, Colorado, and Wyoming.[6]

The Army's task of keeping miners and settlers out of the Hills was hopeless from the beginning, and when an attempt to negotiate a treaty of sale with the Indians failed in the summer of 1875, the government ended its policy of opposition. By December 1875 some 15,000 people had entered the Hills, more

5. Briggs, pp. 28–30.
6. Ibid., pp. 36–7.

settlers than had migrated to eastern Dakota during the first ten years of its existence as a Territory.[7]

The Hills invasion naturally provoked the fierce Sioux and Cheyenne tribes living in the region to go to war. Between 1875 and 1878 raiding bands of Indians harassed the miners constantly. In the spring of 1876 several Sioux tribes under the leadership of the wily Sitting Bull and the master strategist Crazy Horse refused to return from their northern hunting grounds to their reservations. The population of Montana, as well as that of the Black Hills, so feared these roaming tribes whose lands they had so callously usurped that the Army ordered a three-pronged expedition into the field to bring the Indians back. One of these units, moving westward from Fort Abraham Lincoln on the Missouri, split its forces after making contact with the Indians in the Little Big Horn country. The Indians suddenly attacked the troops under General Custer's command on June 25, 1876. When the now famous battle of the Little Big Horn was over, Custer and over two hundred men had lost their lives. Sitting Bull slipped across the border into Canada, and although most of the Indians eventually returned to the reservations, the Indians were not fully under control until the Battle of Wounded Knee in 1890. The gold rush had undone the work of the peace policy advocates, and the whole Indian problem had to be faced anew.

The fabulous history of the Black Hills gold rush, of the rise of Deadwood and Custer City, of the lawlessness which existed there, of the Indian war which it caused, and of such characters as Jack McCall, Bill Hickok, Poker Alice Tubbs, and Calamity Jane has been immortalized by scores of serious and sensationalist writers and by the motion pictures. The inherently dramatic qualities of a gold rush—the colorful and violent society which it creates out of a miscellaneous population thrown together along some creek bed in a wilderness still inhabited by hostile Indians —is so fascinating that it has become a sizable and important chapter in American history, tradition, and folklore.

The glorification of this most violent of American frontiers has not ended with the mere telling and retelling of the legends and

7. Ibid., p. 35.

the facts. The miners' frontier contributed a pattern of political organization which, it has been claimed, was the basis of government in a large part of the West. H. H. Bancroft, in his *Popular Tribunals,* points out that men in all western mining camps were in a "state of nature" toward one another before the regularly constituted instruments of civil government could reach them. Faced with the problem of law and order, the miner, good Anglo-Saxon that he was, created his own government. Bancroft wrote: "He punished crimes committed against himself if he was able; if not he left them unpunished. But soon came that loyalty which springs from social compact, a compact which delegates certain rights of the individual to society on condition that society will protect him in other rights, the conscience as well as the person gradually becoming bound by it." [8]

Thus the miner struck his first social compact in the form of a camp district, in which the resident miners established rules governing the size of claims, set up a court of arbitration for settling disputes, and created the offices of claims recorder, judge, mayor, and sheriff. Bancroft seems to have believed that the miner reenacted in modern times—and in extremely rapid fashion —the whole story of the origin and evolution of human government. There under the sunny California skies Bancroft saw the German *folkmoot* in action; he witnessed the rebirth of the democratic principle that government must exist only by consent of the citizen. In his preface to *Popular Tribunals* he observed: "During my researches in Pacific States history, and particularly while tracing the developments of Anglo-American communities on the western side of the United States, I fancied I saw unfolding into healthier proportions, under the influence of a purer atmosphere, that sometime dissolute principle of political ethics, the right of the governed at all times to instant and arbitrary control of the government." [9]

In this light two mining-town institutions, the mining-camp association concerned with property rights and the vigilance com-

8. H. H. Bancroft, *Popular Tribunals,* The History of the Pacific States, 31 (San Francisco, 1887), *1,* 42.
9. Ibid., p. vii.

mittee concerned with criminal justice, take on tremendous historical significance. There would seem here to be proof not only that the social contract theory of government is valid in more than a hypothetical sense, but that primitive government had been a democratic process. Bancroft's view is a pre-Turnerian expression of the belief that American democracy was partly a frontier product.[10] Yet Bancroft lays great stress on the fact that the racial origins of the miners had much to do with their gift for self-government. The miner's political genius lay partly in the fact that he was Anglo-Saxon and therefore had a heritage of freedom as well as a love of law and order. It was both by blood impulse and rational thinking that the miner had established government over himself: "Here was a people who might give Solon or Justinian a lesson in the method of executing justice. Some one has said that their practical cast of intellect made the Romans the great law-givers of all ages. With equal propriety we might observe that the California miners by their cast of circumstances, have shown to the world more than by any other people who ever lived how civilized man may live without law at all." [11]

The golden age of the state of nature, followed by the impulsive and rational agreements to a compact, abruptly ended when a special brand of villains—some of them Bancroft describes as "low politicians from the eastern states"—invaded the mining camps and towns and, ironically enough, were elected to public office through the machinery of state or territorial government.[12] He comments upon the results in terms of disgust. "Here was the scum of diverse foreign societies uniting amidst the ebullitions of our new society as naturally as impure particles unite upon the surface of boiling liquid." [13]

Under these men crime flourished, courts were corrupted, and honest people were forced to invoke another principle implied by the social compact: the right of revolution, which in the western camps took the form of vigilance organizations similar to

10. *Popular Tribunals* was first published in 1887.
11. Ibid., p. 143.
12. Ibid., p. 79.
13. Ibid.

the San Francisco Committee of 1855 and the Montana vigilantes of a later time.[14] In discussing this subject, Bancroft is careful to distinguish between the principle of mobocracy and that of vigilance. "Vigilance is the guardian of the government, rather than a government within a government," he wrote. Unlike the mob, the vigilance committee had the feeling that "the eyes of their maker and of all mankind" were upon them.[15] And by exercising the principle of vigilance, Bancroft was certain that the miners had added much that was new and good to the democratic process in America.[16]

Bancroft was not alone in his views. Another California scholar and author, Charles Howard Shinn, graduate of Johns Hopkins and contributor to that University's series of publications on history and political science, had anticipated Bancroft's interpretations. Three years before the first volume of *Popular Tribunals* appeared, Shinn published an article entitled "Land Laws of Mining Districts" in the Johns Hopkins series "Institutions and Economics," edited by Herbert B. Adams.[17] Shinn proposed to show that the land laws of the western mining districts were "a curious chapter in the record of social experiments made by men of our Germanic race." He maintained that by studying Germanic land laws and their modification in Anglo-Saxon England, one could understand the local law of the California mining district.[18] Indeed, Shinn's historical imagination took on an extraordinary perspective when concerned with mining law and the American genius for creating governmental institutions. At one point he could see the ancient English common lands system being revised.[19] From another angle he found that applicable Spanish institutions surviving in California had been adopted by the wise miners, and from still another side he could see in the annual meeting of the claim owners of a district the reflection of the town government of 17th-century New England.[20] Yet Shinn,

14. Ibid., pp. 41 ff.
15. Ibid., pp. 11–12; see also p. 20.
16. Ibid., p. 6.
17. Charles H. Shinn, "Land Laws of Mining Districts," *Johns Hopkins Studies,* 12 (1884), 1–67.
18. Ibid., pp. 6–7.
19. Ibid., pp. 8–9.
20. Ibid., pp. 20–6.

like Bancroft, was convinced that the American miner had contributed much that was new and wise to local government in the West.[21]

> The Camp, the Mining District, the Commonwealth of freemen settled for a time in the close companionship under the lofty snow peaks, breaking each other's bread and sharing each other's blankets—*this* must be accepted as a patent factor in all the beginnings of social order, over an extent of territory five times the size of France. The roots of its growth lie deep-tangled in the soil of *Lex Saxonum*, and capitularies of Karl the Great; they spring more nearly from New England town-meetings and parish meetings of the south and settlers associations of the west, but unlike the latter their influence has outlasted the conditions that gave them birth.[22]

Shinn was to soar to even higher levels of fancy:

> As a chapter in political science the place of the full story of these districts will be recognized when the right men, trained in schools of comparative institutional history, come to the writing of the growth and development of communities west of the Mississippi. The student of sociology will say as he investigates the organization of these early camps: "Here are glimpses of Jean Jacques Rousseau, and the 'Social Contract' theory; here is a harmless and altogether new form of socialism here; here, for a brief space, all the world was 'lawless' according to strict legal interpretations, but wonderfully blessed with the essence and spirit of true 'self-government.' " [23]

In quite different terms but borrowing from both Bancroft's and Shinn's accounts of the evolution of local government in California, the brilliant young Josiah Royce published in 1887 his own version of the struggle to establish an orderly society in California. Royce, seeking the truth, could find it neither in the

21. Ibid., pp. 6–7.
22. Ibid., p. 50.
23. Ibid., p. 53.

old settlers' stories that only chaos existed in the early days nor
in Shinn's picture of a golden age.[24] Nor could Royce attribute
mining camp government and local self-government to the
"marvelous political talent of our race and nation" alone. It
took "voluntary and loyal devotion to society" and, as he expressed it, "the courage, the moral elasticity, the teachableness
of the people." [25] Royce believed that the miner's return to the
so-called state of nature was based not upon necessity but upon
the desire of a man for a few weeks to escape his obligations to
society—an obligation Royce felt to be the greatest a man can
have. In a highly effective way he traced the return of these
escapists to the fold of society.

Despite Royce's specific criticism of Shinn's account of early
mining camp society, he himself used the Shinn and Bancroft
"social-compact-in-evolution" concept. To him the miner's pan
was the symbol of man operating as a separate independent unit
in a state of nature. Then the mining cradle came into use, re-
quiring several men to operate it. Here was a great advance over
the pan, Royce thought, for the cradle meant "that men now had
voluntarily and in an organized way" agreed to work together.[26]
Eventually all mining camps, having passed through several
stages of evolution in both economic and political ways, reached
the point where each citizen became the whole citizen again.
Mob or vigilance law was replaced by state laws: local mining
rules were reluctantly abandoned and those of the state and
federal governments substituted.[27]

The record of the miner's genius for creating his own institutions does not end with scholars, nonetheless. Bayard Taylor,
journalist for the New York *Tribune*, reported in 1849, "Nothing
in California seemed more miraculous to men than this spontaneous evolution of social order from the worst elements of
anarchy. It was a lesson worth even more than the gold." [28]

24. Josiah Royce, *California, from the Conquest in 1864 to the Second Vigilance
Committee in San Francisco, a Study of American Character* (New York, 1948),
p. 215 (Royce, *California*).
    25. Ibid., p. 217.
    26. Ibid., p. 227.
    27. Ibid., p. 249.
    28. Ibid., p. 241.

Shinn was able to find expressions of similar views from court cases, politicians, and scholars.[29]

Two aspects of these accounts should be considered before testing their applicability to the mining society of the Black Hills. First, it should be realized that all these writers were affected by the late 19th-century preoccupation with institutional history. Both Shinn and Royce were associated with Johns Hopkins, the university which fostered studies of institutional history and in particular stressed the germ theory analogy of institutional origins.

At the same time these men were insisting that the true origin of American democratic institutions lay deep in the European past; they were advancing the idea that American democratic institutions, especially those arising in the West, nevertheless had a new, unique, and more democratic quality about them, which could not be explained by heritage alone. It was upon this theme that Frederick Jackson Turner was to speak so brilliantly in 1893. These men, Royce, Bancroft, and Shinn, had, in a way, prepared the ground for Turner, and their writings were to swell the volume of historical material supporting Turner.

Still another factor should be mentioned: in 1948 and 1949 both Royce's *California* and Shinn's book *Mining Camps, a Study in American Frontier Government* were republished to celebrate the California state centenary.[30] The reissue of these books makes it imperative that their contributions and conclusions about the nature of government and politics be tested on a newer mining region, such as the Black Hills, for the authors were convinced that their accounts would explain the evolution of western government in the whole West. Shinn wrote: "Over the western third of the United States, institutional life traces its beginnings to the mining-camp: that is the original contribution of the American pioneer to the art of self-government." [31]

It was true that the mining camp was a basic unit of early self-government in a new mineral region, for as W. J. Trimble has

29. Shinn, "Land Laws of Mining Districts," p. 2.
30. R. G. Cleland, Oscar Lewis and J. H. Jackson are editing the centennial series. See the introduction to Royce, *California,* and to Shinn, *Mining Camps, a Study in American Frontier Government,* New York, 1948.
31. Shinn, ed. 1885, p. 4.

pointed out, territorial government not only was slow in reaching the camps but often never provided a system strong enough to preserve order.[32] The early organizations were usually effected by a mass assembly of the miners in a camp district. They elected necessary officers, such as a judge, a secretary, a claims register or recorder, and sometimes a marshal, a mayor, and a board of aldermen. Generally they also adopted a code governing everything from the size of claims and water rights to naming the streets of the camp and surveying the town lots.[33] The miners themselves often acted as an extralegal court which sat in judgment over claim contests or in criminal cases. At a later stage, if law and order had not been preserved by these earlier methods or if the legal government was corrupt or impotent, a vigilance committee, acting in secret, often took over the task of ending lawlessness.[34] These, in brief, were the extralegal institutions and processes that provoked so much admiration from Shinn, Bancroft, and others. Since the Black Hills experienced in some measure all of these processes of evolution, it is necessary to ascertain what influence upon Dakota politics and institutions they had, if any.

European and American mining law, previous to the California gold rush, was not democratic in tone. Valuable minerals were not public domain as land might be, and even when mines were worked privately, European governments had traditionally claimed a share of the production. The federal government had attempted to follow this precedent when it passed laws dealing with the Missouri and Iowa lead mines. Thus when the western miners wrote codes which assumed that mineral rights were public domain, and set up a crude if theoretically fair law of distribution, they were contributing something new to mining jurisprudence. The codes did contain a belief in abstract justice and equality; they were idealistic; and somehow they had the force of both natural and common law. By this interpretation,

32. W. J. Trimble, "The Mining Advance into the Inland Empire," *Bulletin of the University of Wisconsin*, 3 (1914), 227 ff.

33. Briggs, *Frontiers of the Northwest*, pp. 36–7.

34. See Thomas J. Dimsdale, *The Vigilantes of Montana or, Popular Justice in the Rocky Mountains*, Virginia City, Montana, 1882; Briggs, *Frontiers of the Northwest*, pp. 119–20; Bancroft, *Popular Tribunals*.

government to the miner was primarily a judicial organ administering economic and criminal justice as set down by an absolute code, written or unwritten.[35] The term law meant a pure, disinterested power, an interpreter, an organ not functioning until, like an oracle, it was called upon to do so. A claim would be violated; the miners would hear the case, render justice, and then disband. The police powers of this code operated in much the same way, and since wealth through gold was the aim of every person, government then supposedly had little economic attraction; it had no executive; and in its early stages its officials received no pay.[36]

Contrast this conception of governmental functions with that of southeastern Dakota, where government was not a code of laws or a Jeffersonian institution divested as much as possible of an economic nature, but a vital, welcome part of the economy. Provided with an abundant source of economic security of which every man could partake, the Black Hills settlers and the miners of the entire West, it would appear, had returned to the distrust of government and a renewal of pride in self-sufficiency which the Yankton oligarchy had never endorsed. The conflict between two such supposedly incompatible views of government—both of which were frontier creations—presaged the most violent repercussions in territorial politics and promised to highlight issues of the most basic sort; thus political activity in the Black Hills has a special significance.

The first local government in the Black Hills was organized in May 1875 as the Cheyenne Mining District. After adopting a code of mining laws and providing for the establishment of a town, the miners split over the question of a town name. A large faction of southerners insisted on "Stonewall," while a northern group felt strongly about the name "Custer City." After a close, hard fight the Custer City protagonists won.[37] The following

35. For examples of California mining codes see Shinn, "Land Laws of Mining Districts," pp. 55–7. For a Black Hills code see Laws of Lost Mining District, Deadwood Gulch (printed in Deadwood, D.T., December 2, 1875) in the W. R. Coe Collection of Western Americana.

36. For an example of a miners' government in action see Paxson, "The Territory of Jefferson."

37. Briggs, Frontiers of the Northwest, pp. 36–7.

spring a more thorough organization was accomplished when the miners in mass meeting elected Tom Hooper "Supreme Judge" and E. P. Keiffer "Justice of the Peace." One Dr. Bemis was made mayor, and a twelve-member city council was chosen.[38] In November of the same year the miners held a new election and elected an entirely new set of officers. Meanwhile Deadwood had initiated a "provisional government" along the same lines, and to curb the numerous outbreaks of lawlessness in the city the miners created a peoples' court which was to be presided over by "Judge" W. Y. Kuykendall, a veteran of the Wyoming gold fields. Kuykendall was presiding when the peoples' court tried Jack McCall for the shooting of Wild Bill Hickok.[39]

In any candid assessment of these activities and those occurring in other camps in the Black Hills, several factors should be noted. First, a goodly number of the gold seekers in the Hills were veterans of other mining camps; in fact some had even been in the 1849 rush to California. Of these men it must be said that they had acquired a distinct understanding of the nature of society in a mining region and were well versed in organizing a provisional government and adopting a code of mining law. The Black Hills miners were much more sophisticated about the process of political evolution in a camp than any other group in the West. They already knew that the appearance of any corporate group, such as the quartz miners usually were, or the arrival of non-mining settlers, traders, lawyers, and saloon keepers, meant that their system was immediately rendered inadequate and obsolete and would be replaced by a more general form of local government. Thus every miner was aware that his political creation was of the most temporary and expedient sort. The code might stand six months, or at the longest a year.

This indigenous western population was greatly supplemented by a large number of easterners who had recently arrived from the states where a regularly constituted government was the accepted order. Each of these eastern newcomers brought with him a set of notions or ideas about government and politics

38. Jesse Brown and A. M. Willard, *The Black Hills Trails* (Rapid City, S.D., 1924), p. 341.
39. Ibid., pp. 407–8.

which he reluctantly adapted to fit his new environment. In view of these two factors, how seriously did the miner take the business of an "atomistic society" shaping itself anew? The comments of a Black Hills miner, Harry Williams of Deadwood, are particularly revealing on this subject: "We have no municipal government at all. Every man thinks he is mayor of the town. Every once in a while the boys call a mass meeting, draw up resolutions, etc., and decide to incorporate the town and have a board of aldermen; but at the end of the week nobody knows what has become of the resolutions or the aldermen. We start a new city government every two weeks and bust one every week—if there is any." [40]

Williams threw further light on the attitude toward local government by adding that when a man needs gun wadding he "goes and pays four bits for a paper. Whenever they start a new city government they print a lot of ordinances; then there's a grand rush for the paper." [41]

If these comments, made in the spring of 1877, reflected the attitude of some of the miners, there was evidence that the politically conscious settlers were already after larger stakes. Dr. Carl W. Meyer, a pioneer physician to the Hills, was elected by the miners of Deadwood along with General A. R. Z. Dawson as "delegates" to the territorial Assembly in the fall of 1876. Meyer, a southerner and a leader of the Democrats in the Hills, and Dawson, a Republican, were to secure county organization for the mining districts and prevent the "greedy capitalists" from securing legislation in Yankton which would establish a monopoly over the water rights in the Hills. At the same time, as early as December 1876 Meyer and others were agitating for a movement to create a separate territory out of the Hills and make Deadwood its capital. One of the threats which Meyer used in Yankton to force the governor and the Assembly to grant them county governments was that the miners would create their own territory and call it "Eldorado" unless their wishes were met. [42]

40. Interview with Williams printed in the St. Joseph *Herald* and quoted in the *Dakota Herald*, May 12, 1877.
41. Ibid.
42. The phrase "greedy capitalists" is from a speech by Meyer quoted in the *Dakota Herald*, January 20, 1877. For the threat to create a separate territory see ibid., and the *Yankton Daily Press and Dakotaian* for 1877: April 28, May 3 and 29, October 18, and November 5.

The problem of establishing government in the Hills fell upon Burbank's successor, Governor John L. Pennington, a portly North Carolina newspaper man who had joined the Republican party at the end of the Civil War. After having pursued a somewhat devious political career in the reconstruction of Alabama, he now turned to the more promising field of territorial patronage. Through his friend, Senator Spencer of Alabama, who was also a carpetbagger, he had been appointed to the governorship of Dakota in 1874.

When the Hills settlers began to demand county government, Pennington found himself beseiged by applicants for office. Delegate Dawson wrote in February 1877 urging the governor to make Solomon Star and George Burke commissioners for Lawrence County, which had been organized around the Deadwood settlement. "Mr. Star is from Montana and has been an auditor of that Territory for a number of years, also private Secretary for the Governor, and is a thorough Republican, a merchant and a miner and one of the most competent men for the position in the Territory. Mr. Burke of Crook City is Editor of the Republican paper published in that place and a competent—reliable man well fitted for the position." [43]

Dawson also suggested men for the offices of commissioner of deeds, judge of probate, sheriff, and district attorney. Thomas H. Carr of Gayville claimed that he had been popularly elected recorder of deeds by the miners of the Whitewood District in December 1876 and wished to continue in that office. He enclosed a copy of the "Laws of the Whitewood Quartz Mining District" for Pennington's approval.[44] Other applicants, both from the Hills and from the eastern portion of Dakota, sent in petitions and requests for public office. A. W. Adams of Deadwood informed Pennington in February 1877 that the Deadwood Republicans had held a secret caucus the night before and had endorsed certain men for county commissioner whom Adams felt it his duty to report were not representative of the Republicans.[45] A few days later a petition from the citizens of Custer City arrived, in

43. A. R. Z. Dawson to John H. Pennington, February 17, 1877; Governor's File, Bismarck.

44. Thomas H. Carr to Pennington, February 12, 1877; ibid.

45. A. W. Adams to Pennington, February 21, 1877; ibid.

which they asked that the firstcomers be made officers. Then they presented the governor with their own list. Iowa politicians and Montana men were soon writing to recommend persons suitable for public office in the Hills.[46]

When Governor Pennington, whom the Assembly had empowered to appoint commissioners for the Black Hills counties, chose Yankton men for the job, the uproar from the miners was terrific, and a great animus against the "Yankton ring" developed. Pennington himself was accused—with some justification—of appointing commissioners who were actually in league with him to traffic in the sale of townsites, county seats, and offices. Some of the Hills settlers in humorous protest posted bills in the various camps which read: "NOTICE, County Seats Located, Removed and For Sale. Apply to Black Hills County Commissioners." [47] Stories were circulated and given general credence about the efforts of Pennington and his Yankton cohorts to locate a county seat and land office at Sheridan City, a town largely owned by himself.[48] The *Dakota Herald* printed the rumor that the office of register of deeds in Lawrence County was such a lucrative one that Pennington was thinking of resigning the governorship and taking it instead.[49]

The various men who themselves wanted the office of commissioner avidly spread such allegations about the Hills. A large number of the Hills miners were Democrats by party affiliation and resented Pennington's Republican appointees. They demanded that the commissioners resign as soon as they had provided the rudiments of a county government, and allow a general election. The commissioners insisted that their appointments were to last until 1878, but Judge Granville G. Bennett, brother-in-law to General Dawson, leader of the Hills Republicans, declared that an immediate election was in order and that Pennington's commissioners must resign.[50]

The election, held in the fall of 1877, furnished a revealing

46. Custer City Petition to Pennington, February 24, 1877, Delegation of Iowa Citizens to Pennington, February, 1877; Governor's File, Bismarck.
47. Brown and Willard, *The Black Hills Trails*, p. 353; see also the *Dakota Herald*, June 9, 1877.
48. *Dakota Herald*, February 24, March 24, June 2, August 4, September 5, 1877.
49. Quoted from the *Press and Dakotaian* by the *Herald*, February 24, 1877.
50. Brown and Willard, *The Black Hills Trails*, p. 362.

insight into frontier politics. Fortunately, a young reporter, L. F. Whitbeck, who was the Hills correspondent for the Sidney, Nebraska, *Telegraph*, covered and analyzed the election.[51] In one of his articles he wrote: "'Politics in the Hills?' Lord bless you, yes. Strange as it may appear, this country which only eight months ago, was held and largely occupied by Reds is now the scene of a hot campaign, waged upon the one side by straight out-and-out democrats, and upon the other by an amalgamated array of all sorts under the title of 'People's Party.' " [52]

Dr. Meyer, Whitbeck reported, was the leader of the Democratic party, while Seth Bullock headed the People's party. The Republicans used the name "People's," Whitbeck explained, because it had a larger drawing power than "Republican," which suffered from its association with the "Yankton ring." Each party held a convention and chose candidates for office, the most important of which were those of sheriff and register of deeds. John Manning, proprietor of the Senate Saloon in Deadwood, was the Democratic choice for sheriff, while Seth Bullock, the incumbent sheriff by a previous extralegal election, was the "People's" choice. The Yankton faction which made up a part of the People's party "got left" in the nominations, Whitbeck reported. The local papers quickly took sides, the Deadwood *Times* declaring for the People's party while the *Herald* spoke for the Democrats, or "Muldoons" as the *Times* editor called them.[53]

The excitement caused by the campaign contrasts strongly with those taking place at miners' mass meetings. "Politics being all the rage I have had little opportunity to glean very much other matter of news," Whitbeck stated during the campaign. Later he wrote: "For real genuine fun of the Donnybrook fair order (whenever you see a head hit it) commend your friends to the Black Hills during the prevalence of a political campaign. One has just closed, and greater excitement never raged, even in national politics when the welfare of the entire country was at stake." [54]

---

51. Sidney was the outfitting center for those Hills immigrants coming over the Union Pacific Railroad and for that reason the *Telegraph* kept a reporter in the Hills to cover the latest events and to note the new mining discoveries.
52. Whitbeck's articles are quoted in Brown and Willard, pp. 361 ff.
53. Brown and Willard, pp. 362–5.
54. Ibid., pp. 363–4.

Whitbeck found that issues were nonexistent and personality counted for all. "Talk about mud throwing, why putridity would smell sweet compared with the rakings from the various editorial sanctums." [55] The candidates also resorted to the familiar tactic of ballot-box stuffing. Seth Bullock, whom Theodore Roosevelt once described as "my ideal typical American," arranged for a large number of soldiers from nearby Fort Meade in Sturgis to dress in civilian clothes and act as "repeaters" at the polls in Sturgis.[56] The Manning supporters got wind of the scheme, outbid Bullock for the military vote, and the town of Sturgis went solidly for the Democrats and Manning on election day. Beaten at his own game, Bullock refused to surrender his office to Manning, and for a time Lawrence County had two sheriffs. After the heat of the campaign had worn off, however, Bullock admitted his defeat and Manning became the only legally constituted peace officer.[57]

Meanwhile, a serious movement to organize the Hills as a new territory was proceeding apace. In April 1877 a convention met at Deadwood to discuss the matter, and at a subsequent meeting a month later Dr. Meyer and one Captain Walker were appointed "Delegates to Congress" to present their plans to the federal government. The convention then decided to call the new creation the Territory of Lincoln, and they marked out its probable boundaries before adjourning. In the fall of 1877 a correspondent of the *Dakota Herald* reported that the "people of the Hills are determined upon a territorial organization, and to that end are making strenuous exertions." [58]

In Washington the "separatists"—as the new territory men were called—gained the support of Senator George Spencer of Alabama, Representative William Piper of California, and Senator Alvin Saunders of Nebraska. Lobbyists for the Union Pacific also backed the movement, but no bill ever passed either house and the movement, which continued for many years, finally died of inanition.[59]

55. Ibid., p. 364.
56. Ibid., pp. 364–5; Estelline Bennett, *Old Deadwood Days* (New York, 1928), p. 54.
57. Brown and Willard, p. 365.
58. *Dakota Herald*, October 6, 1877.
59. Kingsbury, *Dakota Territory, 1*, 975.

From this brief account of the first governmental organization on a local level, the first legal election, and the separation movement in the Black Hills, several conditions stand out. First, it would appear that the miners and settlers were vastly more sophisticated, insofar as a knowledge of territorial government was concerned, and vastly more interested in politics and political office, than has previously been assumed. Second, there is evidence that as many of them as could tried to get in on the ground floor of the political system, although gold itself continued to be the main attraction. The excitement over the county elections in 1877 suggests not only that politics were a serious part of a miner's life but that party affiliations were fairly strong, and political leaders who possessed professional experience were there to assume and guide the infant parties. The pattern which the election followed—that is, its emphasis on personality, the great interest in the election, and the attempts to win by fraud—was remarkably similar to that engaged in by the early citizens of Yankton and Sioux Falls. The relative importance of the various offices was different and the direct economic motive for holding office was not nearly so prominent in the Hills as it had been in southeastern Dakota—but the degree of interest in holding office was the same.

Still another conclusion which might be made is that the professional politician, from both the East and the West, came to the mining camp along with the miner himself, the hurdy-gurdy dancer, the saloon keeper, and the lawyer. The politician possessed a knowledge of the peculiar political beliefs of the miners and an understanding of western territorial government. He was, in short, one of the most important and distinct figures in a mining camp, yet one grossly neglected by the political and social historian unless he happened to be a famous hanging judge or the like. From a historical point of view, of all the trans-Mississippi frontier types he most deserves to be studied.

The first sheriff of Deadwood, Seth Bullock, was a good representative of this group. Born in Canada in 1847, Bullock migrated to the gold fields of Montana at the age of twenty. He settled in Helena, where he engaged in mining, ran a hardware store, and was elected to the Montana Territorial Assembly. Later he rode as a vigilante in Montana. In 1876 he joined the rush to the Hills, where he became a public figure almost immediately. A tall, lean man, "with drooping mustache, keen gray eyes, a whimsical humor, a soft voice that spoke English like the educated gentleman he was," Bullock was very popular with the Deadwood citizens, who perennially elected him sheriff. Since he was responsible for weeding out the rough elements in Lawrence County, he became an important force in the Black Hills and in territorial politics.[60]

When Bullock was in Helena, Solomon Star was his partner in the hardware business and like Bullock was active politically. Star was secretary to the governor of Montana while at the same time serving as territorial auditor. When he arrived in the Hills, he sought appointment as a county commissioner, and although he failed to receive this appointment, he succeeded in becoming the clerk of the court in Lawrence County and was elected mayor of Deadwood many times.[61]

Dr. Meyer, General A. R. Z. Dawson, Judge Kuykendall, and others like them had followed similar careers. To this list of experienced politicians could be added the names of those coming from more eastern communities. Major Joseph R. Hanson, Indian agent, a director of the Dakota Southern Railroad, one-time member of the Assembly, and the owner of mines in Colorado appeared as a county officer as soon as the Hills organized.[62] General W. H. H. Beadle was in the Hills as early as 1876, where he secured a county office in an extralegal election.[63] W. A. Burleigh, the ubiquitous, affable, and inexhaustible ex-Indian agent, exdelegate, and ex-railroad speculator resigned the presidency of the territorial Council in the middle of its 1877 session to go to the Hills to speculate.[64] By the spring of 1877 the territorial secretary, George Hand, had joined the other Yanktonians in

60. Estelline Bennett, *Old Deadwood Days*, p. 54. See also Robinson, *Encyclopedia of South Dakota*, pp. 101–2. O. W. Coursey in his *Beautiful Black Hills* (Mitchell, S.D., 1925) treats aspects of Bullock's career.

61. Robinson, *Encyclopedia of South Dakota*, p. 708; cf. p. 229.

62. Ibid., p. 340; Kingsbury, *Dakota Territory, 1*, 977.

63. Barrett Lowe, "The Public Activities of General William Henry Harrison Beadle, 1863–1889" (Master's thesis, Department of History, University of South Dakota, Vermillion, S.D., 1938), p. 34. Unpublished copy deposited in the State Department of History, Pierre, South Dakota.

64. *Dakota Herald*, February 24, 1877.

the Hills, and soon thereafter Senator Spencer of Alabama, doubtless apprised of the promising aspect of the Hills by his friend
Governor Pennington, appeared in Deadwood to engage in mining
and townsite speculation and promote the new territory scheme.[65]
Judge Dighton Corson, a pioneer jurist in Milwaukee and later
a judge in Nevada, arrived in the Hills in 1877 to further a legal
and political career.[66]

The classical illustration of a political man attracted by the
new gold fields was James Clagett, "the silver-tongued orator of
Montana." Born in Maryland, Clagett had migrated with his
parents to Iowa in 1850. There he studied law and was admitted
to the bar in 1858. In 1861, he moved to Carson City, Nevada,
not far from the famous Comstock Lode, and in 1862 he was
elected a member of the territorial House of Representatives.
Upon Nevada's admittance to the Union in 1864 Clagett secured
a seat in the new state's House of Representatives. The news that
gold had been discovered in Montana in 1867 drew him to that
territory, where he succeeded in being elected territorial delegate
to Congress. But when he failed to be returned to that office in
1873, Clagett moved to Denver, Colorado. Since the political
prospects did not seem promising in Denver, he was one of the
first lawyers to hang up his shingle in Deadwood when the rush
to the Hills began.[67]

Although Clagett was not successful in Dakota politics, he
thrived on the intrigues and law suits brought by the large mining
companies against one another until 1882, when he moved to
Butte, Montana, to engage in the mining business. But this, too,
failed to produce large returns, and he migrated next to Idaho.
There, with his past political experience, he was made president
of the state constitutional convention in 1889. He tried to capitalize upon this service by running for the United States Senate
in 1891 and again in 1895, but he was defeated both times. Giving
up Idaho politics as a hopeless job, he moved to Spokane,
Washington, where he died in 1901.

Clagett's life story is not that of a particularly successful figure,

65. Ibid.
66. Robinson, *Encyclopedia of South Dakota*, pp. 136–7.
67. James Clagett in *Biographical Directory of the American Congress* (Washington, 1950); see also the *Dakota Herald,* June 2 and November 10, 1877.

but it is representative of many public figures all over the West. Having lived in five territories, he was an excellent example of the mobility which was a primary feature of political life in the West. His career suggests that a large segment of the so-called indigenous Western population had a very accurate knowledge of the politics of the American territorial system and the benefits to be had by becoming a part of it. It was the Clagetts, the Bullocks, the Stars, and the Spencers who called the turns in the political developments in the camps, who wrote the codes, and who were elected to such offices as register of deeds, county commissioner, or territorial delegate. They were the men who organized political parties in the wild lawless towns situated in some narrow gulch where a shallow creek ran, with a fortune hidden in its wet sands.

The problem of law and order in the mining camps was a grave and a unique one for the West and for the American frontiersman. Many new methods of establishing order had to be tried, but the pattern of politics surrounding such law-making remained similar to that on the agricultural plains of eastern Dakota. In view of this similarity, the general idealized picture of miners writing codes and forming 19th-century equivalents of the German "folkmoot" needs major revision as far as the Black Hills is concerned. The very brevity in point of time that mining codes or vigilance committees were in operation militates against their importance. Moreover, it would appear that eastern precedents for mining laws need further study. Joseph Shafer found that the Iowa and Wisconsin lead miners had established their own mining codes during the 1830's, which were observed until territorial organization occurred. He also found that many of the lead miners had migrated to California in the rush of 1849 and 1850. In tracing the careers of fifty-three distinguished men of the lead region, he discovered that no less than nine of them appeared in California between 1850 and 1851, and that some of them, having been successful in politics in the Galena-Dubuque area, later appeared in California politics holding similar offices.[68]

Another aspect of frontier organization which has been over-

68. Joseph Shafer, *Wisconsin Domesday Book: the Wisconsin Lead Region* (Madison, 1932), pp. 44, 56, 57–73.

looked in the descriptions of mining camp codes and government is represented by the claim association, which flourished in the midwest from 1830 to 1850. Jesse Macy has found that in Iowa claim associations dealing with agricultural land were remarkably similar to those mining codes in the neighboring lead mines of Galena and the Fever River district. One could argue that the miners of California and the Black Hills were engaged in an occupation quite different from that of farming and in such a new pursuit gladly borrowed Spanish mining law and customs; but they also fell back on what they had known in the East. The result was that their extralegal governments and codes were based in part upon agricultural and lead-mining precedents which were applied to a new problem and a new region.[69]

One rather suspects that the frontiersman merely adapted that which he already knew: that Shinn's golden age of mining never existed, that the majority of Bancroft's honest citizens were not conscious of the eyes of their maker being upon them as they organized for justice, or that the "low-type eastern politician" could not be distinguished from the average ambitious miner or settler. The fact remains that the miner was willing to secure wealth outside the law as long as that was practicable, and inside the law when it became safer to secure it that way.

What contributions did the Black Hills settlers make to—and what effect did they have on—territorial politics in Dakota? Clearly the Black Hills preoccupation with establishing law and order to protect property made the offices of sheriff, register of deeds, and judge—whether local or federal—enormously important. The courts, therefore, were by far the most active branch of government, for they had jurisdiction over the mining claims, the water rights, and the trial of criminals. Even before the Hills were settled, the federal court system of Dakota had been notorious for the amount of business which had passed through its hands and for the great cost of the cases involved; yet paradoxically, there had been few litigations the first few years, virtually no serious convictions on the criminal side, and few if any

69. Jesse Macy, "Institutional Beginnings of a Western State," *Johns Hopkins Studies*, 3 (1884), 1–38.

death sentences until the Black Hills were opened.[70] Grand juries
had convened, had investigated and reinvestigated, had pro-
longed the sessions interminably—but had seldom indicted. The
reason was not hard to find: this was another method of earning
hard cash.[71]

The Black Hills citizen, with wealth easily at hand, held the
more traditional view that the courts were a place where justice
in the matter of conflicts over private property could be settled;
and since the value of the property was so great, the judiciary
came to play a primary role in territorial politics. It was not surprising, therefore, that the Republicans of the Hills chose Judge
Granville G. Bennett, of the United States District Court in Deadwood, for delegate to Congress in 1878. Bennett had been assigned to the Hills circuit in 1877. Almost immediately he became one of the key political figures by virtue of his office alone.
His every decision was followed with tremendous interest—for
some of them involved millions of dollars worth of property—
and his ruling that Pennington's county commissioners must resign and allow a general election to be held made him very
popular with the miners and the local politicians.[72]

Judge Bennett's successor on the Black Hills court was Gideon
C. Moody, erstwhile leader of the Broadway faction in Dakota
politics. Some of Judge Moody's decisions also affected mineral
and water rights claims amounting to several million dollars, and
so important a person did he become that he retired from the
bench to accept a position as attorney for the famous Homestake
Mining Company. Moody also assumed the leadership of the Hills
Republicans. With their backing he dominated territorial politics
for the next ten years, and when South Dakota was admitted to
the Union the Hills voters elected Moody to the United States
Senate.[73]

70. The *Dakota Herald* reported on March 3, 1877, that the hanging of Jack
McCall, the Deadwood desperado, was the first to occur in Yankton.

71. *Annual Report of the Attorney-General of the United States for the Year
1872* (Washington, 1873), pp. 4–5. The expenses of the United States marshals
and the federal courts in Dakota totaled $69,474.20 in 1872, when the population
was just over 15,000. The cost was twice as much as that for any other territory.

72. For a brief sketch of Bennett, see *Collections of the State Historical Society
of South Dakota, 3* (1906), 119.

73. See below, Chap. 8.

Besides making the territorial judiciary a major pawn in politics, the Hills virtually transformed the nature of party politics in Dakota. By 1878 the population of the Territory was grouped in three distinct areas: the Southeast, a ribbon of settlements along the Northern Pacific Railroad from the Red River Valley to Bismarck, and the Black Hills. None of these areas had any point of contact with the others except by stagecoach. As late as 1880 it took a stagecoach two days and a half, traveling day and night, to go from Bismarck to the Hills. The trip from Yankton to the Hills took nearly a week. Trips north and south between Bismarck and Yankton were very irregular—unless one traveled by boat—and for all practical purposes Bismarck might have been a thousand miles away from Yankton instead of four hundred.

Each of the three sections possessed a different economy and a distinct political outlook, and the residents of each section had a profound distrust of the residents of the other two. The Southeast, with Yankton as its headquarters, was the most populous region, and until 1878 it maintained an unchallenged control over territorial politics. With the occupation of the Black Hills the situation radically altered. The Southeast suddenly discovered itself reduced to the role of a faction in a three-cornered political game in which the other two sections held the preponderance of power between the sections in a delegate election or in the Assembly. Had each section been safely Republican, the division might not have counted for much, but the Hills and parts of northern Dakota showed indications of being Democratic. The first legal election in the Hills had returned Democratic officers, and Bismarck had a Democratic city government. As the party out of power the Democrats were also more likely to unite in a group effort than the Republicans. "Never before in the history of Dakota did so favorable an opportunity present itself for a grand democratic triumph," wrote the editor of the *Dakota Herald* in 1878. "The political phase of Eastern immigration the last few years, has been essentially democratic." [74]

The Southeast also lost power within the Republican party itself. The Republican Territorial Convention in 1878 confirmed the worst fears of the southeastern oligarchy. A Black Hills dele-

74. *Dakota Herald,* August 3, 1878.

gate was chosen chairman of the convention, and after four nominations were placed before the meeting and ballots taken amidst wildest confusion, the Black Hills and northern Dakota delegations combined to choose Judge Bennett of the Hills over Kidder, Moody, and Surveyor General Dewey.[75] Though Bennett was a very good choice, and some Yankton men preferred him to the other candidates, the hitherto dominant southeastern leaders were considerably shaken.[76]

The practice of sectional voting had been prevalent from the earliest days of the Territory, when Sioux Falls had united against Yankton and the frontier element had united against the federal officers, but the use of the bloc vote by an entire section was something new. The balance-of-power technique, with ever-shifting alliances, was henceforth to be a major characteristic of Dakota politics. Often Yankton and the Black Hills would force a measure or a candidate upon northern Dakota, but since Yankton had everything to lose and the other two much to gain, the alliance was more frequently the Black Hills and the Bismarck areas versus Yankton.[77] The Black Hills simply revived and complicated on a broad scale the old sectionalism based upon geography which had plagued the early assemblies.

While the rumblings of dissatisfaction in the Republican ranks over Bennett's nomination were at their height, the Democratic party leaders convened in the Yankton courthouse fully aware of their good chances to win an election. With great unanimity they chose Dr. C. P. Meyer of Deadwood as the convention president, and without contest the three sections united to nominate Bartlett Tripp, an able, highly respected Yankton lawyer, for delegate. After choosing other nominees for lesser offices, the convention adjourned in high spirits.[78]

Yet the Democratic convention disclosed a major internal change in the rank and file of the party—a change equal in impact to the effect of the new sectional bloc vote. Before 1878 the Democrats had been composed of frontier elements, Easterners

75. Ibid., August 24, 1878.
76. Ibid., September 28, 1878.
77. W. H. H. Beadle, "Memoirs," *Collections of the State Historical Society of South Dakota*, 3 (1906), 119–21.
78. *Dakota Herald*, August 31, 1878.

who had brought party loyalties west with them, Republican
soreheads and bolters, and opportunists. These groups were reflected in the leadership of the party. The leaders of the 1878
convention were with few exceptions neither lawyers nor strong
frontier personalities like Armstrong or Todd, but merchants,
businessmen, and representatives of the so-called saloon element.
One of the Black Hills delegates was Charles S. McKinnis, a
wholesale liquor dealer; Alexander McKenzie and James Emmons
were agents of the saloon faction in Bismarck, and Emmons became one of the secretaries of the convention. Frank Zieback, who
was prominent in Yankton city politics, was supported by the
saloon element in the capital. The merchants were represented
by John W. Turner, the owner of the Bloomingdale Flour Mills,
Harvey W. Bonesteel, of Bon Homme, and other businessmen
from Sioux Falls.[79]

The presence of these men meant that a distinction in the
personnel of the two parties was evolving and that at the same
time a new economic group who were not members of the territorial government or allied with it were becoming the main
source of strength of the Democratic party. The rougher portion
of the population, the poorer and less respectable citizens found
in the new towns of the Hills and northern Dakota, also joined
the Democratic ranks, however, so that two distinct groups within
the party existed.[80] These poorer citizens supported such men as
Turner and Bonesteel—and Bartlett Tripp, who provided a respectable front for the party. The capture of the party by these
two groups was to prove disastrous, for the Republicans could
now claim to represent the "best families" and the agricultural
voter, while the Democrats became the saloon party. There were,
moreover, ethnical and cultural differences, for a number of the
Black Hills Democrats, Bismarck citizens, and the Democrats in
other towns were Irish Catholics, or were laborers in the huge
mining companies. The Scandinavian and German settlers who
were filling up the farm lands of Dakota, on the other hand, were

79. *Dakota Herald*, August 31, September 24, 1878.
80. See an account of Bismarck's population in the *Dakota Herald*, September 7,
1878.

not only Republican but largely Protestant, and the alliance of the Republicans with this segment meant that as long as the Territory remained predominantly rural, the Democratic party, with its large "town element," could never win. After 1878, in fact, it was nearly possible to predict a Dakotan's politics by his occupation or his religion. The *Herald* in a candid post-mortem of the 1878 delegate election, which Judge Bennett had won, took note of the peculiar situation the Democrats were in:

> Political parties in the Territory are of peculiar construction. Considering the native element only, there may be doubt as to where the majority would fall, but most likely it would be Democratic. The old French settlers, and many of the older Germans, who still retain unpleasant memories of the bitter warfare made upon them by the Republican party under a different name, are Democratic; but when we strike the Russian and the Scandinavian elements we find them solidly Republican. They speak little English and read less, and combined they constitute a stone wall in politics against which truth and logic are as impotent as the sea wave against Gibraltar. . . . Their party affiliation is accounted for by the circumstances that their knowledge of American politics is limited to the fact that they came to this country finding the Republican party in control of the national government; they found partisans of this faith in every post office, land office, and Territorial position, and in most instances ready to take advantage of their ignorance to mislead them totally as to the ends and aims of the two parties.[81]

The *Herald* went on to say that the local Democratic party had suffered from weak leadership, with the exception of Armstrong, whereas the Republicans had enjoyed a "constant colonization of Republican officials from the older communities, while the Democrats had been limited to the natural increase which springs from immigration for business purposes." The *Herald* concluded that henceforth the Democrats would probably poll one-third of the

81. Ibid., January 11, 1879.

territorial popular vote, but never more than that without exceptional leadership.[82] Unless the Democrats could win a national election and do some political colonizing of their own, the Democratic party must be resigned to the status of a permanent minority.

Finally, the material prosperity brought by the gold of the Hills and the wheat of the Red River Valley ended any lingering belief in a Great American Desert. Besides gold and wheat, wool production was becoming an important industry in the southeastern counties, and cattle ranching was spreading into the rich grasslands along the Missouri from Pierre to Bismarck. Farming and ranching in the Hills had proven very successful, and Sheriff Seth Bullock himself had introduced alfalfa into the Territory.[83] The long-vaunted visions of empire were fast becoming realities; self-sufficiency in turn caused a considerable shift away from the attitude that government must be an aid to subsidize the economy. From this time on, Dakota entered a new and less colonial stage of political development.

82. Ibid.
83. Robinson, *Encyclopedia of South Dakota*, pp. 101–2.

Chapter 6. The Yankton Oligarchy Fights Back; Rise of

the Division and Statehood Movements: 1877–83

> In the unwritten history of most of the new western States it will probably be found that the change from "Territorial condition to that of a sovereign State" has been effected at the instance, not of the people, but of the politicians—not of the tax payers, but the tax consumers, and we are inclined to think that the people of the present Territories are intelligent enough to profit by their example.
>
> *Dakota Herald, October 29, 1881*

THE GOLD RUSH to the Black Hills meant unparalleled prosperity for the southeastern counties of Dakota. As the chief outfitting center for the Hills, Yankton buzzed with activity. The flour mills of Sioux Falls expanded with the new orders from the Deadwood and Lead City stores. The firm of Bramble and Miner of Yankton shipped merchandise worth hundreds of thousands of dollars into the Hills. General Beadle began the Castle Creek Drain Ditch Company at Deadwood to supply water for mining purposes. H. C. Ash, builder of Yankton's first tavern, now appeared at Deadwood as the proprietor of Delmonico's Restaurant and Hotel. The usual interest in townsite speculation led Yankton men to invest in Hills property.[1] Governor John H. Pennington compensated himself for all his troubles with Black Hills county organization by buying a part of Sheridan City. He persuaded the government to locate a land office there, he used his own power of office to make it the seat of the first district court, and he saw to it that two wagon routes converged upon the paper town. Meanwhile his friend Senator Spencer was laboring in Washington to make Sheridan City the capital of the proposed Territory of Lincoln.[2]

Dr. Burleigh, that indefatigable frontier capitalist, after garner-

1. *Dakota Herald,* March 24, June 23, 1877; Lowe, "The Public Activities of General W. H. H. Beadle," p. 34. See also Briggs, *Frontiers of the Northwest,* pp. 63, 67.

2. *Dakota Herald,* March 24, 1877.

ing a rich harvest from the sale of lots in the boom town of Bismarck, ventured into the greatly stimulated transportation business as the general manager of the triweekly stage line to the Hills over the Fort Pierre route.[3]

The railroads, now much more attracted by the prospects in Dakota, began to extend their lines into the Territory. The Chicago and Northwestern bought up smaller roads leading into central South Dakota, a good ranching and farming region which settlers had previously bypassed. In March 1880 a rival line, the Chicago, Milwaukee, and St. Paul, bought the Dakota Southern and the Sioux City and Pembina lines, thus securing a monopoly on all the roads in southern Dakota.[4] By the end of the year these two roads had advanced across the Territory as far as the Missouri, Fort Pierre being the terminal point of the Chicago and Northwestern, while the new town of Chamberlain became the terminus for the Chicago, Milwaukee, and St. Paul.[5] Both lines began the familiar practice of maintaining lobbyists in Yankton during the Assembly session and exercised considerable influence in the making of political appointments.

Three grasshopper plagues which hit Dakota in 1874, 1875, and 1876 marred this roseate picture somewhat, but the territorial officials were actually more concerned about the unfavorable effect which the news of these visitations might have upon immigration—which had brought the population up to 135,000 according to the 1880 census—than about the hardships suffered by the farming population.[6] Mr. E. B. Clew, leader of the Dakota Grange, was roundly denounced by the local papers when he appeared in Washington to solicit aid from Congress for the hardhit farmers.[7]

Despite the bright economic outlook for the Southeast, however, nearly every prominent political figure of the region was profoundly disturbed over its political future. The business-through-government relationship which they had built over the past fifteen years was threatened with destruction. They had

3. Ibid., April 14, 1877.
4. R. J. Casey and W. A. S. Douglas, *Pioneer Railroad, the Story of the Chicago and North Western System* (New York, 1948), pp. 159 ff. See also the *Dakota Herald*, March 27, 1874.
5. See map, p. 179. Casey and Douglas, *Pioneer Railroad*, p. 164.
6. Hagerty, *The Territory of Dakota*, p. 55.
7. *Dakota Herald*, March 17, 1874.

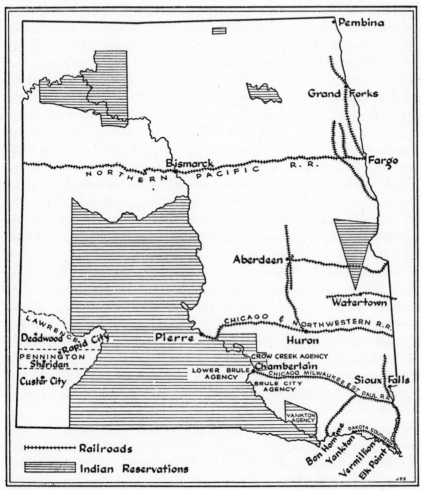

Indices of territorial growth in 1882. Note the Black Hills settlements, the new towns, the rapid advance of railroad building, and the shrinking Indian reservations.

managed to elect Bennett over Tripp by less than 2,000 votes, and that had been because the Russian-Germans and the Scandinavians had remained unquestioningly in the Republican ranks. From 1878 on, in fact, a Pandora's box of political troubles gave the leaders of southeastern Dakota an acute political persecution complex, which caused them to demand a new and smaller territory consisting of the Southeast and the Black Hills, and the admission of this region as a state. When both these attempts met with failure in the early 1880's, the Republican party of southern Dakota promulgated a new states' rights doctrine to justify the extralegal actions that it was to engage in for the next six years.

This sense of persecution did not spring wholly or even primarily from sectional bloc politics as practiced in 1878. Unwittingly the federal government itself provided the first issue in the guise of a reform of the Indian Bureau. It will be remembered that the Dakotans and eastern groups had pressed the federal government to adopt a peace policy toward the Indians in 1866, although each group had different motives.[8] Under Grant an uncertain program was instituted whereby the Departments of War and of the Interior were to have a joint jurisdiction over the Indians, and various religious missionary organizations were to have an important voice in the appointment of local agents and in the program of civilizing and training the Indian. Because the great preponderance of missionaries working among the Sioux of Dakota were Episcopalian, all but two reservations in the Territory were placed under the semi-official jurisdiction of the Episcopal Church. This arrangement, and Grant's whole peace policy, were particularly acceptable to the Dakotans, since the Indian officials sent to Dakota usually joined hands with the local Republican party and the supply merchants to extract the greatest possible profit from the Indian trade. Moreover, a large number of the leading figures in Dakota were Episcopalians, so that by 1875 the Indian bureaucracy, the political bureaucracy, and the missionaries were almost indistinguishable.[9]

This pleasant state of affairs was rudely disturbed by the outbreak of fighting between the Indians and the whites when the

8. See above, pp. 102–7.
9. Kingsbury, *Dakota Territory*, 2, 1038.

latter invaded the Black Hills. The two years of intermittent warfare which followed was climaxed by the Battle of the Little Big Horn and Sitting Bull's shrewd retreat into Canada.[10] An uneasy truce resulted when the Sioux of the Black Hills agreed to enter reservations established along the west bank of the Missouri.[11] The outbreaks started a new debate over Indian policy which revealed the Dakotan's true position. Indian attacks on Hills settlers in 1877 caused the *Daily Press and Dakotaian*, the most influential newspaper in Dakota, to declare that the Indians were "the lazy and useless wards of the nation." "When they have finished their carnival of blood the government will tenderly gather them up, take them into winter quarters, clothe and feed them and tell them not to do so any more." [12] Nor could the paper resist the opportunity to point out that during the strike of 1877 federal troops had taken action against white workers while the Indians were protected by a peace policy.

> In this issue of the *Press and Dakotaian* appears an advertisement calling for proposals for the erection of comfortable homes for the very Indians who are now murdering and mutilating our friends on the western border of the territory. But how is it with the working men of the east who strike for bread instead of blood. The bullets and bayonets of a protecting nation force them to desist and when the work is accomplished they will be gathered up and thrown into dismal prisons as the penalty of their offenses. 'Tis better to be a red handed Indian than a horny handed mechanic.[13]

This honest and indignant outburst, while it reflected the basic hostility of all westerners for the Indians, also reflected something of a change of public opinion in Dakota. This change was most succinctly manifested in new demands for a cession of part of the still sizable Sioux Reservation west of the Missouri.[14] Until

10. See above, p. 151. See also Textor, *Relations between the U.S. and the Sioux Indians*, pp. 119 ff.; Kingsbury, *Dakota Territory*, 1, 938–68.
11. *Daily Press and Dakotaian*, July 27, 1877.
12. Ibid.
13. Ibid.
14. Textor, p. 128.

the Black Hills invasion, the Grant peace policy had been a huge boom. The feeding and clothing of nearly 25,000 Sioux as well as the military troops maintained in the Territory for protection purposes had turned Yankton and other Missouri River towns into quartermaster depots. The letting of Indian contracts created as much interest among the officials and business leaders of Dakota as an election campaign.[15] When Bartlett Tripp, the Democratic candidate for delegate in 1878, proposed to remove the Indians from the Territory completely, the *Press and Dakotaian* replied in horrified tones that "the removal of the Indians from Dakota would prove disastrous to our commercial interests. The products of Dakota's prairies are worth thirty per cent more because of our Indian market than they would be without that market. Our river business is rendered valuable through the location of Indian and military posts above us. The government is a good customer and pays cash for what it receives. No sensible farmer will accept that Indian removal plank of the Tripp platform." [16]

But while Indian lands gradually came to seem more desirable than Indian markets, national Indian policy also entered a new phase when Rutherford B. Hayes was elected President on a Liberal Republican ticket in 1876. Carl Schurz, Secretary of the Interior in the Hayes Cabinet, announced in 1877 that he intended a thorough investigation of Indian affairs and the Indian Bureau. And to aid in "ferreting out the wily expedients resorted to by dishonest contractors or agents," he proposed the formation of a group of special agents who could move "secretly and pounce upon the point to be investigated without premonition." [17]

The leading Republicans of Dakota greeted this announcement with a degree of resentment and bitterness that is almost impossible to imagine, for they had come to feel that Indian affairs in the Territory were something that only they could understand and handle. Their hatred of Schurz and his local representative, Inspector General W. H. Hammond, was so fierce that it brought into high relief the relation of the Indian service· to the territorial

15. See the *Dakota Herald,* December 15, 1877, for an account of a contract award to Dr. Burleigh.
16. *Daily Press and Dakotaian,* October 7, 1878.
17. Kingsbury, *Dakota Territory,* 2, 1040.

economy, its alliance with the Republican party, and the basically anti-Indian view to which this western community unquestioningly subscribed. Democrat and Republican, Hills man and Yanktonian, official and farmer united in their condemnation of any investigation.[18]

The blow did not fall upon the Dakota reservations until 1878, but before then the news that secret agents were interviewing the employees of the various reservations, and the Indians themselves, had leaked out. Inspector Hammond, in anticipation of an unfavorable reaction throughout the West to any investigation, had planted articles in newspapers hinting that a sensational scandal was about to break which would implicate prominent men in both the East and the West.[19] In a preliminary counterattack the territorial press began a campaign to turn the Indians over to the War Department, and the Democratic *Herald* urged that Sherman's extinction policy be followed.[20] The *Press and Dakotaian,* the official Republican paper editorialized:

> If the control and management of the Indians were left to the average western man, he would first capture them, i. e., take all their guns, ponies and feathers, then domicile them on the Missouri River at convenient points and keep them well fed. Such a course would stop all Indian wars, cause to cease all raids and other troubles in the Sioux Country and save millions annually to the Government.
>
> But your scheming sentimentalist will have no such commonsense solution of the Indian question. They want to make little angels of the papooses and big angels of the head chiefs. The flighty head of the interior department proposes to turn the war chiefs into husbandmen, to make farmers of savages and require them to become self sustaining in a country where a New England Yankee would starve.[21]

18. Ibid., pp. 1036 ff. Kingsbury's anti-Schurz and anti-Hammond bias is so great that his presentation is little more than a brief in favor of the local agents, but it is representative of the way nearly every Dakotan felt.

19. Ibid., pp. 1041–2.

20. *Daily Press and Dakotaian,* December 9, 10, 1877.

21. Ibid., March 29, 1878.

And then the blow fell. On March 23, 1878, the *Dakota Herald* reported: "The long-reigning serenity in the Indian Service on the Upper Missouri is being seriously disturbed, though the manifestations have been kept pretty well under control, and the cause and extent of the trouble are not fully known." [22] On the day before, soldiers had marched into four of the Sioux agencies on the Missouri and in the Hills, had announced to the agents that they had been dismissed, and had ordered them to leave the reservations. All the agents' property had been confiscated, as had been the goods of the reservation traders, and depositions had been taken from the various employees and Indians. [23] Inspector Hammond, claiming that he had ample evidence to prove his case, instructed the United States Attorney for Dakota, Hugh J. Campbell, to prosecute the agents for defrauding the federal government, for concealment of goods intended for the Indians, and for forgery. [24]

The chief object of this attack seemed to be Henry F. Livingston, agent to the Sioux at Crow Creek. But this attack actually struck at the very heart of the Yankton oligarchy, for Livingston was none other than the brother-in-law of George H. Hand, the popular and powerful territorial secretary, who was reputed to control the awarding of Indian patronage and supply contracts in Dakota. Unlike many of the federal appointees who came to Dakota with no desire to settle there or to perform their duties well, Hand made Yankton his home and local politics his career. A lawyer and a veteran of the Union army, he had been Governor Edmunds' private secretary in 1865; he had served as United States Attorney General for Dakota in 1867 and as the Register of the United States Land Office in Yankton. In 1874 he became Secretary of Dakota, which position he held for ten years. Not only was he a bona fide popular resident and an able officeholder, but his political connections in the Territory were many. At one time he had been the law partner of both Delegate Spink and Judge Moody. He was also a cousin and close friend of W. S. Bowen, the editor of the *Press and Dakotaian*, and as secretary

22. *Dakota Herald,* March 23, 1878.
23. Ibid., April 13, May 18, May 25, June 29, 1878; *Press and Dakotaian,* March 23 ff.; see especially March 29, 1878.
24. Kingsbury, *Dakota Territory, 2,* 1036 ff.

he had awarded nearly all the public printing to Bowen's firm over the past four years.[25] As the official spokesman for the territorial officials and for the Republican party, the *Press and Dakotaian* sprang to the defense of Livingston and the other agents and traders when Hammond preferred charges against them.[26]

On April 1, 1878, the *Press and Dakotaian* answered Hammond's assertion that the investigation would cause "the greatest commotion ever occasioned in the western country," with the comment: "We greatly fear that by the time these gigantic developments are completed, it will be discovered that Dr. Livingston cut the agency hay in July instead of in October. That he steadfastly refused to resign after committing this offense, and when he knew his place was wanted by another man, that it was necessary to bounce him when the little game of freeze-out failed." [27] Nevertheless, the so-called "Bingham" and "Livingston" cases were tried in 1878 and 1879 at Rapid City and at Yankton respectively. The entire territorial press followed the trials at Rapid City and reported the proceedings with an extremely anti-Schurz and anti-Hammond bias.[28] The Yankton trials, involving Livingston, were not begun until December 1878, when the United States Attorney, Hugh J. Campbell, decided that the evidence against Livingston and the others was so overwhelming that the case would be cut and dried; but since nearly every prominent citizen in southern Dakota had opposed the investigations, it proved very difficult to select an unprejudiced jury.[29] A series of suspicious fires in Yankton occurred during the court session and rumors spread that Inspector Hammond's life had been threatened. Further tension developed when the government brought in Indians to testify against the defendants, for the

25. *Dakota Herald*, March 1, 1879; Professor Pomeroy has found that printing contracts were considered such highly desirable patronage that in every territory they proved to be a major political issue: *The Territories and the United States*, pp. 32 ff.

26. *Press and Dakotaian*, April 15, 1878 ff.

27. Ibid., April 15, 1878.

28. *Dakota Herald*, October 18, November 23, December 7, December 14, 1878; *Press and Dakotaian*, November 20, 21, 22, 29, 1878.

29. See the *Dakota Herald* for December 1878; *Press and Dakotaian*, December 13 ff.; Kingsbury, *Dakota Territory*, 2, 1036 ff.; see also numerous letters concerning Livingston *et al* in OIA, Chron. Files (1878), Dakota.

general feeling was that no Indian should have the right to testify except against another Indian.[30] A reporter, J. N. Rea, from the Chicago *Tribune* and St. Paul *Press,* hovered about Hammond for information and dispatched daily news items which reflected the prosecution's views. In their overzealous efforts, Rea and Hammond printed information about the views of the members of the jury, and Rea became known as the "spy of the jury room." Such action played into the hands of the defense, and Campbell found himself greatly hampered.[31]

When the first Yankton case came up, Major H. E. Gregory, ex-agent at Lower Brulé, and trader E. E. Hudson, of Livingston's agency at Crow Creek, were acquitted.[32] The government saved its case against Livingston until the last in the evident expectation that he would take advantage of the statute of limitations and avoid a trial. This, as Kingsbury has stated, would have been a victory for Washington, Schurz, and Hammond. With public opinion completely on their side, however, the Livingston forces decided to risk the trial, and the prosecution, faced with this change of tactics, entered its own plea that the case was covered by the statute of limitations and proceeded to prepare its case on new grounds.[33] Meanwhile the Livingston forces claimed to have found the real reason for the trials, which William French, a government witness, took note of in a report to the United States Commissioner of Indian Affairs: "There is but one sentiment in Yankton, and it may be said, in the greater portion of Dakota. It is, that Livingston is being persecuted in order to break down the church influence. I was informed by several parties that Livingston was appointed through the influence of a church commission, and being the son-in-law of an Episcopal clergyman has been selected by the government as the one to be victimized." [34] The *Press and Dakotaian* played up this point of

30. Kingsbury, *Dakota Territory,* 2, 1049.
31. Ibid., p. 1045; *Press and Dakotaian,* November 21, 1878; Hugh J. Campbell to Attorney General Charles Devens, July 19, 1878; August 26, 27, 28, 1878, in Marshal's Accounts for Dakota, Department of Justice, Chron. Files, 1878.
32. *Press and Dakotaian,* December 13, 1878.
33. Kingsbury, *Dakota Territory,* 2, 1046-7.
34. William French to the U.S. Commissioner of Indian Affairs, cited in Hugh J. Campbell's report on the Livingston trial to Attorney General Charles Devens, April 5, 1880, OIA, Chron. Files (1880), Dakota (Livingston Report, OIA).

view for all it was worth. In an attack upon Inspector Hammond, Bowen wrote in the spring of 1879:

> Hammond began his work upon the presumption that every'man appointed to a position in the Indian service from the Episcopal church was dishonest. His hatred of the representatives of this religious organization moved him to pursue them with relentless and unceasing vigor to the end that they might not only be removed from the service, but overwhelmed with the odium of complete disgrace. The result was that four of the principal agents along the river, all appointees from the Episcopal church, were summarily dismissed from the service and the personal property of three of them seized by military force.[35]

Not only did the public accept this explanation, but as a token of confidence in his innocence, the citizens of Yankton elected Livingston to the Yankton Board of Education during the middle of his trial! [36]

Livingston's second trial took place in the spring of 1880. It lasted twenty-three days and was, in Campbell's own words, the "most laborious and hotly contested case that has been tried in this territory."[37] The Justice Department supplied Campbell with legal assistants to try the case and rounded up witnesses from the East to testify against the beleaguered ex-agent. This time the prosecution felt on safe ground. Charging that the agent had made a "false, fictitious and fraudulent claim, against the Government," Campbell leveled eight specific counts against him, one of which concerned the concealment beneath a warehouse floor of 5,000 pounds of tobacco designated for the Indians.[38] Campbell had further damaging evidence to present: one of the government witnesses, William French, had been stopped in Sioux City, Iowa, on his way to attend the trial, by Major J. R. Hanson of Yankton, who had hinted that the defendant's counsel could make it "disagreeable" for French if he persisted in testifying. French later stated to the Indian Commissioner that this certainly proved to

35. *Press and Dakotaian,* April 17, 1879.
36. Kingsbury, *Dakota Territory,* 2, 1049.
37. Livingston Report, OIA.
38. Ibid.

be true. Hanson was one of the first settlers of Dakota, had served as agent at Yankton, Crow Creek, and Grand River Reservations, and had been territorial auditor. Naturally he was interested in preserving the existing policy in Dakota Indian administration. As soon as Hanson had dropped his hint to French, the latter was then approached by D. T. Bramble, who as one of the leading supply merchants in Dakota, had engaged in large business dealings with Livingston and other agents. Bramble also pressed French to abandon the trip to Yankton. Finally after French had arrived in Yankton, another "Livingston fan" tried to persuade him to leave town.[39]

Campbell reported that the defense was thunderstruck by all this evidence, but even so the jury acquitted Livingston of all but one count of forgery, which they changed to a misdemeanor charge, and upon trying that fully exonerated him, an outcome which Campbell truthfully said "astonished both parties." [40] When the trial was ended, the jury rose and congratulated Livingston upon his acquittal and the *Press and Dakotaian* announced that twelve months of persecution had been stopped.[41]

The Bingham and the Livingston cases were, from the view of the prosecution, a failure, but the publicity considerably aided the cause of the reformer. The removal of the various agents resulted in a new set of officials. From 1880 to 1890, in fact, the Sioux tribes got their first taste of the training and education which had been promised them for so long.[42] The evidence of Indian frauds in Dakota, a state of affairs peculiarly tolerated by the Sioux Episcopal Church, had been mounting too long for the Indian Bureau or Secretary Schurz to allow it to continue, but the techniques employed by Hammond and his assistants aroused the greatest indignation. Hammond's conduct throughout would indicate that he was much more interested in finding a scapegoat than he was in achieving justice for the Indians.[43]

The significance of the Indian cases does not lie so much in the

39. Ibid.
40. Ibid.
41. *Press and Dakotaian,* April 16, 1879.
42. Textor, *Relations between the U.S. and the Sioux Indians,* pp. 126 ff.
43. Kingsbury, *Dakota Territory,* 2, 1050-1. If the facts presented by Kingsbury about Hammond are true, he was as guilty of as many improprieties as the agents themselves.

fact that an outside force was breaking up a local Indian ring or rings of great complexity and long standing as it does in the average Dakotan's wholehearted sanction and defense of the pattern of Indian relations which the "ring" followed. The Indian question to the Dakotan was clearly a topic about which he had deep emotional feelings that had been shaped out of his own first-hand and unpleasant frontier experience. Flinging aside any moral inquiries about the rights of the Indian, he took the view that it was first of all a question of control; second, one of opportunity for economic profit; and finally, one of education and civilization. In many ways the Indian question was similar to that faced by the South in the post-Civil War period. Both areas were concerned with control over what each considered an inferior and potentially, if not actually, hostile race. Both had felt that these races were to be exploited—although in different ways—and were vital to the economy of each region. Both felt, too, that they had a peculiar understanding of the problem. Influenced by such a pattern of logic, the Dakotan could honestly defend a system of exploitation which the federal government and the East saw as clearly indefensible. And like the South again, the Dakotan developed an acute persecution complex which led in turn to a new and more deliberate awareness of the clash of eastern and western views and to the further rationalization that those ideas and attitudes peculiar to the Territory were good ones that deserved defending. In short, the first organized sentiment for the Dakota way of life had been born, and the first deep reaction against the rule of the federal government had been experienced. The psychological foundations for statehood for southern Dakota had been laid; the colonial mentality was passing.

General Beadle reflected this new attitude in a letter to Secretary Schurz in January 1878. After urging Schurz to appoint a new governor who "comes from the states of our origin" (Governor Pennington was a North Carolinian), he added:

> Under organic laws almost identical we have the most diverse characteristics in our territories, from the miniature republic of Dakota to the plutocracy of New Mexico and the theocracy of Utah. Each of the others also is settled by

a different class of people to a large extent. In selecting officers for Utah, New Mexico or Arizona, regard would naturally be had to special fitness for the peculiar circumstances therein; and why not, for Dakota whose people are peculiar in the same sense that those of Minnesota are, and are as much unlike those of some other territories as Massachusetts is unlike Mississippi.

The inhabitants of Dakota have come here upon the natural lines of migration. It could be guessed in advance what was their nativity, or their nativity being given the cosmopolitan would readily infer the character and tendency of their institutions. Of the native American part nearly one half are from Wisconsin and the remainder from New York, Minnesota, Iowa, and Michigan; while there is a large and excellent element of Scandinavians and Germans, many of whom have resided in the states mentioned. It is therefore natural and the fact [is] that our laws and systems are like those of Wisconsin, New York and Iowa. We have the well-known codes of law common to those states and to California; and after long confusion, we have these now so perfected and locally adapted as to equal the most enlightened states in their orderly arrangement.[44]

Schurz appears to have taken Beadle's advice, for he chose a Michigan man, ex-Senator William Howard, for the new governor, and Beadle, appropriately enough, became his private secretary.[45]

Concurrent with the Indian question, southern Dakota faced the task of adjusting to a new frontier to the north. It has been stated previously that there was little contact between the peoples of the Red River Valley and the Missouri Plateau. The lines of communication, then as now, ran east and west in Dakota, and the Missouri River represented the only major north-south line of communication. Throughout the Territory's history, passengers, mail, and telegraph messages from the greater part of northern

44. W. H. H. Beadle to Secretary of the Interior Schurz, January 26, 1878; Interior Appointment Papers, Dakota (1878), File 135.
45. Lowe, "The Public Activities of General W. H. H. Beadle," pp. 38–9.

Dakota had to go east to St. Paul and then southwest to Sioux Falls and Yankton.

Besides the lack of contact, the Red River Valley—which was the only settled area in the north until after 1873—had its economic ties with Winnipeg to the north and St. Paul to the east; the trapper, the half-breed farmer, the post traders, the customs officers at Pembina, and the officials of the Hudson's Bay and other fur companies were the main inhabitants in this semiwild frontier which drew a livelihood from the fur trade.[46]

Until 1877 northern Dakota was known politically in Yankton through its few representatives in the Assembly. Since they came from the Red River Valley, they were called the Custom House Gang, the ablest of whom was the diminutive Enos Stutsman, perennial president of the Council.[47] With the coming of the Northern Pacific Railroad the situation changed radically. This line, having secured a huge land grant along its right of way from the national government, was to run from St. Paul to the Columbia River basin on the west coast. In 1871 the road invaded the Red River Valley, and by 1874 it had advanced across the windy, open prairie to the roaring "end of track" town of Bismarck on the Missouri River. The Panic of 1873—caused partly by the building of the Northern Pacific—forced the road to seek returns on its investments by placing settlers on its lands and by experimenting with large-scale wheat production. The success of the Dalrymple brothers in this latter venture attracted thousands of Americans and Canadians into northern Dakota to try "bonanza farming" and to produce "Dakota number one hard." These two terms became household words all over the United States and Europe in the next ten years. A boom on the last agricultural frontier in the Northwest had begun.[48]

That northern Dakota had a growing population in 1877 but was still a frontier was well illustrated by its representatives in the Assembly that year. Through new apportionment the North now had seven seats out of a total of thirty-six. Of these seven, the occupants of three were land agents, one was a railroad agent,

46. Briggs, *Frontiers of the Northwest*, pp. 361-3.
47. See above, pp. 82-3.
48. Harold Briggs, "The Settlement and Economic Development of the Territory of Dakota," *South Dakota Historical Review*, 1 (1936), 156-7.

two were merchants (one of these having just graduated from the rank of a post trader), and one, a Norwegian immigrant, was a farmer. Two contestants who were not seated were an ex-trapper turned land agent, and a railroad agent.[49] The birthplaces of these nine men revealed again the predominance of the native American in the frontier politics of Dakota. Three were born in Vermont, one in New Hampshire, two in New York, one in Illinois, one in Ireland, and one in Norway. While it is striking to discover how similar in origin these men were to those pioneers gathering in Yankton in 1862, the combined number of land and railroad agents—six out of nine—was also important, for it meant that these six were in some way connected to the Northern Pacific.[50] The railroad was to be not only colonizer, landholder, speculator, and the means of transportation in northern Dakota, but the chief factor in its politics as well.

As the Custom House Gang gave way to the "Railroad Com-bination," this new and more powerful force in territorial politics created great resentment in Yankton. The Northern Pacific was an uncontrollable absentee power which might ally with other roads in Dakota, for by 1878 out-of-territory companies owned every rail line in Dakota. The Yankton *Press and Dakotaian* began to complain that railroad attorneys were writing the railroad charter laws for the territorial Assembly.[51]

The political representatives of northern Dakota and the North-ern Pacific made their first bid for power when Ansley Gray, a member of the House from Bismarck, introduced a bill in the 1879 session to move the territorial capital to Bismarck.[52] Yankton forces killed the measure, but they recognized that a continuing threat of the most vital sort hung over the heads of every political figure with affiliations to Yankton.

A capital removal bill, the fear of railroad control over political office, and a natural lack of contact made the popularity of a territorial division movement inevitable. The feeling soon de-veloped that the northern and southern settlements were incom-

49. *Press and Dakotaian*, February 22, 1877.
50. Ibid.
51. Ibid., January 23, 1879.
52. Ibid., February 13, 1879.

patible sections. In a sense this sentiment had always existed. As long before as 1858, the half-breeds of Pembina and the Red River Valley had petitioned Congress to make them a separate territory called Chippewa, and as early as 1871 the territorial Assembly had unanimously memorialized Congress to divide Dakota into two territories. Other memorials were passed in 1872, 1874, and 1877, and in 1879 the Assembly took a new tack by passing a memorial to the effect that Dakota should not be admitted to the Union as a single state.[53] Northern Dakota was attracted by the federal patronage which would come to it as a new territory, while southeastern Dakota expected to dominate the Hills in any new southern territory and thus to give the Yankton oligarchy a new lease on life.

The sentiment for division was irrevocably tied to the statehood movement in southern Dakota—a movement that had so many obstacles to overcome that a history of its struggles reads like a minor epic.

The first serious proposals to make Dakota a state came in 1877, after the Black Hills gold rush and the Northern Pacific had brought in enough immigrants so that the Territory could meet the 60,000 population requirement.[54] To this proposal there were grave objections, however. The *Dakota Herald* argued that Dakota, even as a single state, could not support the cost of statehood. It would take $100,000 a year to run the state, the paper estimated, a sum Dakotans could not afford to pay. Nevada had rushed into statehood too quickly and was now in terrible financial straits. "We believe that the great incentive to the agitation of the State movement at this time is to prevent the creation of a new Territory out of the Black Hills country and to take advantage of the large and increasing population that is centering there to form the basis for a claim for the admission of Dakota into the Union." [55]

The advocates of statehood were those persons who hoped to

53. For an excellent summary of the division movement see the Bismarck *Tribune* (Bismarck, D.T.) for December 28, 1887.

54. *Dakota Herald*, April 21, May 5, 1877.

55. Ibid., May 5, 1877.

win office through popular election and who now believed that a state political system promised more advantages in the way of office and patronage than the territorial one.[56] The old "home rule" factions, such as Moody's Broadway Gang had been, were succeeded by "statehood" groups. Even in this limited sense, the mere consideration of statehood indicated how far the Dakotan had moved away from the belief that the Territory was not economically self-sufficient. The conviction that federal support was no longer so vital meant that federal control automatically became less acceptable.

Its psychological foundations having been laid by the persecution of the Indian agents, the new sectionalism in politics, the fear of railroad influence, and the knowledge that a certain level of self-sufficiency had been achieved, the statehood movement expressed itself first in an indirect way. The Assembly, long overshadowed by the delegate and federal officials, assumed a new importance. In 1879 the struggles within the Assembly created more serious interest than ever before; its deliberations affected 135,000 persons, and the Territory was now wealthy enough to levy and collect taxes and build state institutions, such as insane asylums, normal schools, penitentiaries, and a university. There had been battles about the location of such institutions since the first days of territorial organization, but now they were becoming realities. A large new bureaucracy connected with these institutions appeared, looking to the Assembly and not to Washington as its source of existence.[57]

The Assembly revealed its new power in the session of 1881, when the entire Territory was at the crest of a financial and immigration boom. Land agents, lawyers, merchants, and newspapermen from the scores of new towns in Dakota were attempting to get territorial institutions located in their home counties. The Legislature spent every day passing or considering bonding bills, incorporating new towns and street railways, and organizing new counties. The *Dakota Herald* satirically remarked

56. Chicago *Times*, May 12, 1877, quoted in the *Dakota Herald*, May 19, 1877. The *Times* felt that the statehood movement was merely a scheme put forward by a ring of politicians.
57. This change may be noted by a perusal of the House and Council *Journals for the Legislative Assembly of Dakota*, for 1877, 1879, and 1881.

that "the legislature has now bonded everything in the territory but the channel of the Missouri." [58]

Paradoxically, as the Assembly's power increased, its prestige decreased, for the new wealth it could distribute and the new offices it could control caused a new high in logrolling. The opportunities for enrichment through legislation were too available to be ignored. Of the 1883 solons the *Dakota Herald* wrote:

> It is generally conceded that this legislature is the worst with which the Territory was ever afflicted and there can be no doubt but that no Dakota legislature has existed during the past twelve years but what did more harm than good to the public interests. With a great majority of members of the last body there did not appear to lurk a single honest impulse. They came to Yankton imbued with jobs and schemes for private benefit and their exertions during the session have all tended in that direction.[59]

The Elk Point *Coyote* said that the returning legislators should be met with rotten eggs instead of the usual band.[60] Charley Collins, the redoubted Irish editor of the Sioux City *Times*, observed:

> The legislature of Yankton has at last got things fixed to its own personal satisfaction, and the proper division of the spoils and jobbery being effected they have agreed to the removal of the capital at Yankton. We will match Dakota against all the world in ancient or modern times to be able to produce as many official thieves, purchasable legislators, or an equal number of representative men as recreant to their oaths of office, to their constituents, or to justice as the average Dakota legislator.[61]

One cause of the growing sentiment against the territorial system was the excesses of the Assembly; nevertheless, the assemblymen could regain a measure of their popularity by fighting with federal appointees, and especially with the governor. General

58. *Dakota Herald*, March 5, 1881.
59. Ibid., March 10, 1883.
60. Elk Point *Coyote*, quoted in ibid.
61. Sioux City *Times*, quoted in ibid., March 10, 1883.

Beadle observed that after 1879 the "struggles were with the governor and not so much with one another. . . . It seems that from this time members sought special fame at home or generally among the people by being known as pronounced friends of the territory, as against political appointees sent here from other states to govern." [62] After fifteen years of relative unimportance, the Assembly was on its way back into power, and from its ranks came some of the chief advocates of statehood.

Another factor which promoted the desire for statehood was the method of choosing the Republican candidate for delegate in 1880. Delegate Bennett, having turned in a creditable two years of hard work in Washington, wished to run for reelection, but the sectional conflicts which had accompanied his nomination in 1878 had continued to plague him throughout his term, each section claiming that he labored only for the other two. Moreover, a wing of the "home rule" element in the Republican party, led by Richard F. Pettigrew of Sioux Falls, sought the nomination.[63]

In Pettigrew the Territory found a new type of politician. Devoid of humor, puritanical in many respects, but utterly unscrupulous when it came to political double-dealing, Pettigrew was a curious mixture of the demagogue and the sincere man, though he covered his own crooked trail with the dust of so many accusations against his opponents that it was difficult to tell his true nature. When he saw his way opposed in the Assembly, he resorted to trickery and his fists. When he found how popular it was to attack federal appointees, he made statements which would have provoked libel suits in most states. A man of boundless energy and a master in the language of vilification, he was soon a real power in territorial politics. He played up the conflict between the rural elements of the Republican party and the business and professional wings. He allied himself and his Sioux Falls constituents with northern Dakota in order to defeat the Yankton oligarchy, and he attacked the oligarchy itself by exposing Secretary Hand's control of the printing patronage; yet

62. Beadle, "Memoirs," p. 170.
63. Ibid.

Pettigrew's purpose in this fight was to gain control of the printing patronage himself.[64]

At the Republican Territorial Convention, which met at Vermillion in September 1880, Pettigrew traded his own seat in the Assembly for support as delegate, and in a particularly angry session he received the nomination in preference to both Secretary Hand and Delegate Bennett. The *Press and Dakotaian* violently denounced this selection, while the *Herald* termed Pettigrew:

> A political adventurer of the most pronounced type and most unscrupulous character, he is the embodiment of the vulture in politics, simply employing the opportunities which office affords him for his own aggrandizement, with scarcely a pretense to serve the people. Mr. Pettigrew's name, whenever associated with political matters, has been linked with jobs and schemes of self-interest, and if he ever had an unselfish motive in politics he has kept it a profound secret with himself. In well-regulated communities it has been more the custom to send men of his stamp to the penitentiary than to nominate them for office.[65]

Pettigrew was elected by a safe majority, since the Democrats had chosen a weak candidate to oppose him. But the worst was still to come, for Yankton men began to hear ugly rumors that Pettigrew planned to start a campaign to move the capital from Yankton to a more centrally located spot in the Territory, a rumor that made the southeastern oligarchy more determined than ever to separate from northern Dakota and form a state government.

The first advocates of statehood in Dakota had been Yankton politicians. But in 1879 an entirely new element appeared in the

64. *Dakota Herald*, March 1 and 15, 1879. Pettigrew's attacks resulted in a legislative investigation of public printing in Dakota, and when Hand's cousin, W. S. Bowen, appeared as the chief recipient of printing patronage, a press duel began between the Sioux Falls *Times*, a Pettigrew organ, and the *Press and Dakotaian*, the Hand paper.

65. *Dakota Herald*, September 4, 1880; see also the St. Paul *Pioneer Press*, September 4, 1880.

statehood ranks. General W. H. H. Beadle, now the territorial superintendent of public instruction, Dr. Joseph Ward, the founder of Yankton College, United States Attorney Hugh J. Campbell, and Governor William H. Howard met at Ward's home on Thanksgiving Day 1879 and mapped out a nonpartisan statehood movement for southern Dakota.[66] The aims of these men were supposedly nonpolitical. Ward, a product of Andover Theological Seminary and a man of considerable intellect, had developed a great "contempt for the territorial system, and for the graft and misgovernment with which the system was connected." [67] General Beadle, as superintendent of public instruction, was greatly alarmed at the prospects of a new state selling off its school lands for a cheap sum when they could be held until their value was many times increased because of settlement.[68] Hugh Campbell, a restless crusader-type politician saw in the statehood movement a chance to become a founding father and perhaps a United States senator.[69] Governor Howard, successor to Pennington, was aged and ill, and with a career in the Senate behind him he was content to act as the elder statesman who would not hesitate to support a good public cause.[70]

This small group was considerably strengthened when ex-Senator Alonzo J. Edgerton of Minnesota was appointed chief justice of the Dakota supreme court in 1880. Senator William Windom of Minnesota had apparently promised Edgerton that if he would accept this post, he would push the statehood cause in Congress and use his influence to have Edgerton made a senator from the new state. Edgerton came to Dakota, then, with powerful connections and with every inclination to join the statehood forces.

These men, Beadle, Ward, Campbell, Howard, and Edgerton, were five of the most respected figures in Dakota. Although they were members of the Yankton oligarchy, they sincerely dignified the cause of statehood by claiming that the issue was so important

66. Lowe, "The Public Activities of General W. H. H. Beadle," pp. 71–2.
67. Carol Gardner Green, "The Struggle of South Dakota to Become a State," *Collections of the State Historical Society of South Dakota, 13* (1924), 508.
68. Lowe, pp. 56–72.
69. G. H. Durand, *Joseph Ward of Dakota* (Boston, 1913), p. 173.
70. Ibid., p. 151.

that it was above politics. They built up an emotional sentiment for the Dakota way of life so successfully that they deserve to be classed as able propagandists. They were the reformist and intellectual wing of the movement. They gave the statehood cause a rationale; they glorified local rights, and they made the territorial system seem a fetter that signified an inferior citizenry. To their side they drew other reformers, such as the prohibitionists, who were active in Dakota by 1880, as well as the best elements of every town, the lawyers, the ministers, the women's clubs, and some of the politicians themselves.

The division and statehood movements really began in earnest in 1882, when a bipartisan division convention met in Fargo and elected delegates to go to Washington to petition for the creation of a new territory out of northern Dakota.[71] Simultaneously, to the south, a convention met at Sioux Falls to consider statehood and to send a second set of delegates to Washington to present their case. This latter convention represented a fusion of all the elements working for statehood. Ex-Governor Edmunds was the convention's president, under whom the Hand and Pettigrew factions and the Ward-Beadle forces had united to present their case more effectively. The Black Hills also held a meeting to consider the question of statehood.[72]

Shortly thereafter the Ward-Beadle forces joined with Judge Edgerton to exert a fuller influence upon the movement and especially to prevent the school lands from being squandered. They proposed to organize a Citizen's League, with auxiliaries in every county. The members of these leagues were to be considered not as Republicans or Democrats but simply as citizens working for a worthy cause. The *Dakota Herald* predicted that such an organization would bring dismay to the hearts of politicians.[73] By April 1882 the central committee of the League was so impressed with the favorable reports coming in from all parts of the Territory that they called a meeting to consider the advisability of a constitutional convention. This preconvention meeting, which was to take place in June at Canton, Dakota, created a tremendous

71. Fargo *Republican*, October 1881, quoted in the *Dakota Herald*, October 22, 1881. For a fuller report of the convention see the *Dakota Herald*, January 21, 1882.
72. *Dakota Herald*, January 21, February 4, 1882; see also Lowe, p. 76.
73. *Dakota Herald*, February 25, 1882.

interest among the statehood factions. In Yankton the saloon element as well as the "best element" were so anxious to attend that during a public meeting the two groups split, each faction electing a set of delegates. The convention accepted the "best element" representatives, however, for they included many of the leaders of the whole movement, such as Ward, Beadle, Campbell, Edmunds, Kingsbury, Bowen, and many others of the oligarchy.[74]

One hundred and ninety-three members, representing fourteen southern counties, were present in Bedford Hall at Canton when the convention assembled. The "best elements," to use the phrase that the Dakotans themselves often employed, made up the bulk of the membership. The *Herald*, which as the leading Democratic paper had opposed statehood, praised the delegates for their great integrity.[75] Ministers, newspaper editors, and a few of the leading Norwegian and German settlers were there; Turner County alone boasted four ministers in its delegation.[76]

The convention proceeded amidst the greatest excitement and with an almost too great awareness of its own significance. Some of the delegates were as much concerned with reform as with the plan to petition the next Assembly for a constitutional convention. Beadle and Campbell persuaded the convention to include the recommendation in its memorial that the constitution forbid the sale of school lands for less than ten dollars an acre, a very stiff price in a region where homestead claims were still being filed.[77] Other delegates, disgusted by the orgy of spending and bonding that the last Assembly had engaged in, called for elaborate curbs on the taxing and appropriation powers of the future state legislature.[78] The prohibitionists wanted the petition to include a prohibition clause, but the delegates agreed that this issue should be postponed until after statehood had been achieved.[79]

Its petition to the Assembly written, the convention then announced plans for an expanded Citizen's League based on the ideas of Ward, Beadle, and Campbell. They wanted a league in

74. Ibid., April 29, 1882; May 20, 1882.
75. Ibid., June 24 and July 1, 1882.
76. Ibid.
77. Ibid., June 24, 1882.
78. Ibid., July 8, 1882.
79. Ibid., June 24, 1882.

every village, town, and county in the future state. The central committee would direct these local groups and correspond with them on the progress of the movement. In a much cruder way, the Virginians in Ohio had used the same technique when they had founded corresponding societies to agitate for statehood in 1802. Membership in the League was opened to men, women, and children, a policy undoubtedly borrowed from the Dakota Grange. With virtually every person in the Territory eligible for membership and participation, the League directors felt sure that a good constitution would be written and adopted.[80]

After an interim central executive committee had been chosen, the Canton meeting adjourned in a flourish of oratorical self-praise. They had come to Canton "almost in defiance of all party rules, and in many instances with a threat hanging over them of being read out of the party in case they did attend." They compared themselves to the Pilgrim Fathers on the Mayflower and stated that the convention had demonstrated as never before that the people were sovereign. They ended with a call for a constitutional convention of three hundred citizens to meet within the next twelve months.[81] Many of the delegates left Canton with the firm assumption that reform, statehood, and the millennium were right around the corner. Congress had already reported favorably on an enabling bill during the winter of 1881–82, and it was hoped that the bill would soon pass, or at least be acted upon in the December session of 1882. The newspapers in the East, especially in New York, were interested in the movement and were acquainting the rest of the country with the plans of the southern Dakotans.[82]

But disappointment was in store for the Dakotans. In the national elections of November 1882 a Democratic House and a Senate with thirty-seven Republicans and thirty-seven Democrats were returned. It was certain that no Democrat would vote to admit a state that would undoubtedly add two Republicans to the Senate. A second blow came swiftly from the East. In 1880, a suit over the now-famous Yankton County railroad bonds had

80. Ibid.
81. Ibid., July 1, 1882.
82. Green, "The Struggle of South Dakota to Become a State," pp. 510–11.

reached the Supreme Court of the United States. The court declared that Yankton County, which had tried to repudiate the bonds, must pay its creditors. When the county commissioners deliberately failed to do so, the eastern creditors petitioned Congress to admit southern Dakota only after the railroad bond issue had been settled satisfactorily. Their influence proved great enough to ruin the chances for statehood in 1882.[83] The statehood forces had received the first of many rebuffs from Washington.

The final set of circumstances working for statehood came about as the result of the appointment of Nehemiah G. Ordway to the governorship after Governor Howard's death in April 1880. The southeastern Republican rank and file, and particularly the Yankton oligarchy, urged that George H. Hand, the popular territorial secretary, be appointed Howard's successor. Petitions from every side poured in to President Hayes and Secretary Schurz. But Hand's name had been so linked to the Indian ring and to the Livingston case that he was not chosen. Several officials on the spot warned Washington, in fact, that if Hand were made governor, all the efforts to reform the Indian service in Dakota would be nullified.[84] The refusal to elevate Hand caused a new grievance against federal control.

To replace Howard, Nehemiah G. Ordway, a tall, distinguished-looking New Hampshire politician was appointed. Ordway had been sergeant-at-arms in the House of Representatives for many years, after which he had returned to New Hampshire, where he served in the state legislature both as representative and as senator. He was a state senator when President Hayes tendered him the governorship of Dakota in 1880.[85] Ordway's sanctimonious, dignified manner, which impressed such leaders of the oligarchy as Edmunds, Bowen, and Secretary Hand himself, hid an able, scheming, ambitious mind. The new governor came to Dakota, in fact, with the most far-reaching plans to organize a

83. Ibid., pp. 511–12.
84. See petitions and letters concerning Hand in Interior Appointment Papers, Dakota (1879–82), Files 164 and 170, George H. Hand.
85. Nehemiah G. Ordway in the *DAB*.

Nehemiah G. Ordway: governor of
Dakota Territory (1880–84),
advocate of capital removal, and of
the single-state plan

Two Leaders in the Capital Removal and Statehood Struggles

Arthur C. Mellette: U.S. land agent,
advocate of statehood for
Southern Dakota, last governor of
Dakota Territory (1889), and
first governor of South Dakota

vast political machine. These plans suddenly became apparent in the fall of 1882, when the Yankton politicians realized that by controlling federal patronage, Ordway had built up a powerful alliance with northern Dakota leaders, such as Alexander Mc-Kenzie, and a large part of the territorial press, which he supported with the printing patronage from land office sales.[86] Ordway even tried to control the federal patronage that normally fell to the jurisdiction of the delegate, but there he ran into the ambitious incumbent, Pettigrew. Thinking it best to cooperate with Pettigrew rather than to fight him, Ordway proposed an alliance of forces. "They would become so strong and influential as to be able to elect each other to the United States Senate when the Territory of Dakota was admitted as a state," Ordway explained. Pettigrew declined, declaring, "I will never have anything to do with you but will fight you so long as you remain in the territory." [87]

The governor's scheme to share the delegate's patronage having failed, Ordway secretly determined to remove the capital from Yankton to Pierre, where his son, George Ordway, was the railroad agent for the Chicago and Northwestern Railroad Company. And if this plan did not work, the governor had property in Bismarck upon which a capital could be located.[88] In either case, he could count upon the backing of the railroad and stood to make a handsome profit through the sale of town lots.

Ordway had laid his plans well, for when the Assembly convened in 1883 in Yankton, *one-third* of the members of the Council were newspaper editors who had received patronage from the governor in some form! [89] Lobbyists also frequented Yankton as never before. General C. E. Simmons, the land commissioner of the Chicago and Northwestern appeared at the capital and two

86. Lois Malvina Drake, "The Influence of the Newspapers of Dakota Territory upon the Administration of Nehemiah G. Ordway, Governor from 1880 to 1884" (Master's thesis, Department of Journalism, University of Missouri, Columbia, Missouri, 1941), pp. 1–51. Unpublished copy deposited in State Department of History, Pierre, South Dakota. See also below, pp. 217 ff.

87. Ibid., pp. 6–7.

88. Ibid., pp. 32, 37; see also Bruce Nelson, *Land of the Dacotahs* (Minneapolis, 1946), pp. 130 ff.

89. Drake, p. 42.

trusted agents of the Northern Pacific, Judson LaMoure, and Alexander McKenzie, were in town.[90] The time was ripe to bring a capital removal bill upon the unsuspecting Yanktonians.

The Ordway forces realized that Yankton would never permit an outright removal bill to pass the Assembly, so they at first proposed a bill locating the capital at Huron, a small town in central southern Dakota, an area as yet sparsely populated. So surprised and flattered were the citizens of Huron by this consideration that they were immediately converted, along with all of central Dakota, to the support of any capital removal plan. This bill failing, however, the Ordway factions, backed by the northern Dakota members, pushed through a bill creating a capital removal commission which was to meet in Yankton within thirty days of their appointment, organize, and visit various Dakota towns thought to be suitable for a capital. From the moment Yankton learned of this bill, its citizens were in arms. They had to keep the capital at Yankton, and they were willing to employ desperate measures. Their bitterness increased still more when they learned that Ordway had vetoed a bill calling for a constitutional convention for southern Dakota on the grounds that the cost of such a convention would have to be borne by the entire Territory and that would be an unfair burden on the northern section.[91] This veto had the full approval of the railroad lobbyists, who openly preferred the more lenient territorial railroad laws to those which a state legislature might be expected to pass.[92]

Despite every effort to prevent its passage, the bill establishing a capital commission passed the Assembly. Since the commission had to organize in Yankton within thirty days, however, the Yankton citizens still had hopes of halting the entire scheme by preventing the commission from meeting within the city limits. This the Yanktonians set out to do. The three members of the commission from Yankton were carefully watched; any suspicious gathering was reported, and the local members of the commission were openly threatened with violence. The *Dakota Herald* pre-

90. *Dakota Herald*, February 17 and 24, 1883.
91. Drake, pp. 45 ff.
92. Ibid.

dicted that the commission would organize on March 30 and advised the Yanktonians "to place their hen roosts under lock and key and to clear their clothes lines before dark, in anticipation of the visit." [93] But the days passed and no meeting occurred. The Yankton citizens began to breathe more easily; perhaps they had called the governor's bluff. And then at 6:00 A.M. one morning an inconspicuous train rolled very slowly into the railroad yards of Yankton and continued through the town westward at a leisurely speed. No one thought it was important, but inside one of its coaches the capital commission, with the wily Alexander McKenzie of Bismarck as its head, quickly and legally organized. The oligarchy had been outsmarted.[94]

With its new population, its new prosperity, and its new sections, Dakota underwent violent political transformations between 1877 and 1883. The two new frontiers in the Hills and in northern Dakota had challenged the domination of the older, and now more conservative, Missouri Valley settlements. The combination of circumstances gave the older region a persecution complex out of which arose a statehood movement. The movement began as a political maneuver to regain lost power, but it soon took on a crusading, reformist nature; it developed a dislike of outside control; it clothed the naked economic motivations which had characterized early Dakota politics with a respectable rationale about "home rule." As early as 1877 the *Press and Dakotaian* could exclaim: "We are so heartily disgusted with our dependent condition, with being snubbed at every turn in life, with having all our interest subjected to the whims and corrupt acts of persons in power that we feel very much as the thirteen colonies felt when they flung away their dependent condition and asserted their position among nations." [95] The advocates of home rule stimulated a new pride in Dakota as a region, as a particular way of life that deserved praise. Such an attitude naturally enhanced the worth and prestige of local institutions and gave a new purpose to the popularly elected legislature.

With the rapidly disappearing frontier the parties themselves

93. *Dakota Herald,* March 17, 1883.
94. Ibid., April 7, 1883.
95. *Press and Dakotaian,* April 30, 1877.

took on new forms: they were much better organized, more distinct. A party machine could command the loyalty once given only to strong, vigorous personalities like Burleigh or Armstrong. When the Bon Homme *Citizen* declared in 1877 that it would henceforth be an "independent paper so far as politics were concerned," the *Dakota Herald* replied that this was impossible. The political parties were so well defined, the *Herald* stated, that there was no middle ground on which to stand.[96] The parties, moreover, now revealed interesting class distinctions. As the open-range ranchman, the fur trapper, and the frontiersman vanished from the scene, the Democrats became the party of the town population, the workman in the Black Hills mines, the saloon elements, and a group of merchants. At the same time the Republicans, constantly colonizing with leaders from the East, always in control of the patronage, and allied to the native and immigrant rural vote, had become both the majority party and the respectable party by virtue of Republican dominance in Washington. Yet the local party had undergone an internal revolution of its own. The federal faction, though still powerful, found that its club of patronage could no longer be wielded with terrifying effect. The home rule faction, made up of such diverse elements as the Ward-Beadle group and the Pettigrew group, had assumed preeminence in direct proportion to the increasing self-sufficiency of the Territory. The local voter's support had at last become more valuable than influence at Washington.

The first phase of the statehood movement ended in 1883 with the capital removal fight, but the nonpartisan appeal of "home rule" had stirred the sleeping giant of democracy. By its use of the Grange system of enrolling entire families in its organization, the Dakota Citizen's League had unwittingly persuaded the average citizen and the farmer, whether immigrant or native, that he held the reins of government in his hands, that he was the true sovereign. The League, then, laid the psychological groundwork not only for statehood but for a people's movement as well. For the League, though drawing some techniques from the Grange, was the training ground for the future leaders of the Farmers' Alliance in Dakota. The meetings of the League in every village

96. *Dakota Herald,* May 26, 1877.

and hamlet brought to the forefront new men who were to grasp the control of government from the very group who had called them into action. This fact has been completely overlooked by historians, who have stressed the national economic causes behind the Alliance movement: the conviction on the part of the rural population that the territorial system was inadequate and corrupt was actually a strong stimulus to the Alliance movement when it appeared there in the middle 1880's.

Chapter 7. Capital Removal and the Statehood

Movement, Second Phase: 1883–85

> There is no inherent right in the people of any territory to be consti-
> tuted into a state.
>
> *Senator George Franklin Edmunds, 1866*

> . . . organize the state government, divide up the offices and then ask
> Congress what it is going to do about it.
>
> *Frank Washabaugh to the Dakota Council, 1883*

AFTER a perfunctory set of visits to a dozen Dakota towns, in 1883 the capital commission chose Bismarck as the new capital of the Territory. This decision began a six-year political struggle which soon included so many other issues and groups that the final outcome amounted to a political and social revolution in Dakota. At first it seemed to be the old story of a new geographic area—northern Dakota—coming into political prominence by virtue of its increased voting power. Such a development had occurred throughout the history of the United States when a new region was settled. The piedmont farmers of Virginia had moved their statehouse from Williamsburg to Richmond; Charleston surrendered the position of capital city to Columbia; in Ohio enterprising Yankees lost out for a time to Virginia and Kentucky settlers, who placed the capital at Chillicothe.

In Dakota the capital location issue quickly burgeoned into a contest between those factions who for selfish reasons took the colonial view that Dakota should remain a ward of the United States, and those who for equally selfish reasons believed that the Territory was ready for self-government. The former faction naturally included the governor and the federal officers; the latter group contained the Dakota Citizen's League, a strange amalgamation of practical politicians, prohibitionists, and many so-called nonpolitical reformers.

Nor should the scope and importance of this fight be underestimated. Powerful outside interests like the railroads preferred a territorial system of government, for through their influence in Washington they could better control appointments to territorial office. Governor Howard was a land commissioner for the Northern Pacific, and after 1884 that same line maintained an active lobby in Washington headed by ex-Governor Ordway—who was removed from office in 1884—to prevent by any means possible the achievement of statehood.[1] It appears that the last five territorial governors were men picked and approved by the Northern Pacific; the Chicago, St. Paul, and Milwaukee; or the Chicago and Northwestern Company.[2]

Senators and congressmen with the patronage of a Territory at their command, as well as that of their own state, were loath to surrender this wealth to the representatives of a new state. Minnesota politicians in particular felt that Dakota was a neighboring province to be ruled at their pleasure and to which surplus party hacks might be sent.[3] At the same time the Democratic party in Congress clearly intended to prevent the admission of any state that would send two Republican senators to Congress and several Republican votes to the electoral college.

The outside interest in continuing territorial status did not end here, for between 1880 and 1890 Dakota attracted millions of dollars in eastern and foreign investments. With interest rates often running as high as 20 per cent expanding Dakota, with its bonanza farms, its burgeoning cattle and sheep industries, and the demand for farm machinery and supplies, was the investor's paradise. The Territory could boast that it had more banks within its borders (299) than the total number of banks in eight other states combined![4] New Hampshire banks alone sank $25,000,000 into western lands and businesses in this decade, and much of it found its way to Dakota.[5] It was perfectly natural, therefore, that

1. See the account of Ordway's activities in Washington in the *Bismarck Tribune*, January 4, 1888.
2. The correspondence of Governors Gilbert A. Pierce (1884–85), Louis K. Church (1885–89) and Arthur C. Mellette (1889) in the Governor's File, Bismarck, indicates but does not completely prove this statement.
3. Pomeroy, *The Territories and the United States*, p. 67.
4. Kingsbury, *Dakota Territory*, 2, 1832. In 1887 Dakota had 62 national and 232 private banks.
5. Edward C. Kirkland, *A History of American Economic Life* (New York, 1940), p. 507.

the eastern investor should be anxious to prevent state control of loans and interest rates.

To oppose this increasingly onerous colonial status, the Dakota Citizen's League did not hesitate to use the discontent created over capital removal as a means to launch its statehood campaign. But when it became evident that Yankton would never retrieve the capital and that this was an issue with annually decreasing popular appeal, a wing of the League sought to renovate a body of states' rights arguments as a weapon to fit its needs. The revival of such heretical doctrine as a practical political issue only twenty years after the Civil War is a fact that deserves much study and explanation. Why should the average picayune Dakota politician attempt to invoke the outmoded principles of his father's generation? His efforts to break into the Union by brandishing the cudgel of states' rights was to prove an interesting and often amusing story.

At the same time that the Dakota version of Calhounian and Jeffersonian principles was being broadcast, the ideas of social reform that were stirring every state in the Union had penetrated the small towns of the Upper Missouri Valley. Prohibitionists, women suffragists, minority representationists, and advocates of the initiative and referendum could be found there. The frontier technique of conquering the plains had been so highly developed between 1876 and 1886 that the average American immigrant went through the settlement phase too rapidly to allow his social and moral views and activities to suffer from real neglect. After a year's passing, the midwestern Yankee usually had prospered enough to devote leisure time to other than purely economic pursuits. This was particularly the case for town residents who ran a store, practiced law, or sold real estate. It was much less the case for the average dirt farmer.[6]

All these characteristics made the statehood cause appear to be a broad, many faceted movement. Yet a closer scrutiny of the statehood movement reveals that many of its leaders feared all

6. A perusal of the social columns of several Dakota newspapers, the *Dakota Herald*, the Yankton *Press*, the Yankton *Press and Dakotaian*, and the Bismarck *Tribune*, with their accounts of lectures, church socials, W.C.T.U. meetings, appeals for overseas missions, and on the lighter side, accounts of baseball clubs, lends great support to this conclusion.

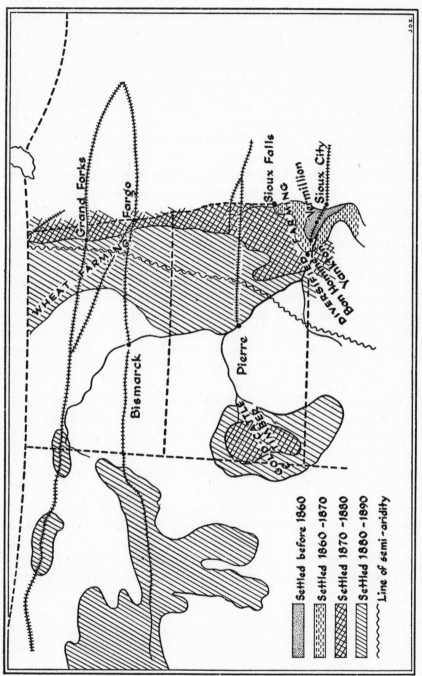

Agricultural regions and lines of settlement in Dakota Territory, 1860–90.

radical reforms, that they were the uneasy and often unwilling allies of the sincere reformers. Furthermore, they were frightened by the rural voter's increasing interest in politics, for they were determined that the only true change to be accomplished by statehood was the substitution of local control of patronage for federal control. But the statehood leaders reckoned without the factors in the national economy which produced a depression in agricultural prices after 1875, and without the series of droughts and severe winters that were to plague the Great Plains for a decade after 1886. Angry and bewildered, the Dakota farmer sought aid first through the territorial Assembly, by asking for a railroad commission to regulate rates and for a fair system of grading wheat at the elevators.[7] Although a railroad commission was established and a grading law passed, both were singularly ineffective.[8] The Citizen's League told the farmer that statehood was the solution to his problems, but the latter soon realized that many of the statehood leaders were the same brand of men who ran the territorial government, who were his assemblymen, who held a mortgage on his farm, who had sold him farm machinery, and who had bought his wheat at starvation prices. Thus it was that the farmer sought relief in his own organization, that of the Farmers' Alliance.

What had begun as a protest over the removal of the capital soon broadened into three movements operating simultaneously: a statehood movement, a crusade by social reformers, and a farmers' revolt. The general view has been that all three were reform minded, that all three held the same aim. Yet when it came to a showdown, the statehood men found their deadliest enemies to be the agrarians, for the farmer was revolting against the professional political and businessman. The uniqueness of the Dakota situation lay in the fact that the farmer was not trying to recapture control of local government as the Grangers had tried to do in Illinois and Ohio—he was attempting to capture

7. *First Annual Report of the Board of Railroad Commissioners of the Territory of Dakota* (Fargo, D.T., 1886), pp. 7–13.

8. *Second, Third and Fourth Annual Reports of the Board of Railroad Commissioners of the Territory of Dakota* (Grand Forks and Bismarck, D.T., 1886–88), introduction of each report.

it for the first time! The conditions which led to the coming of this upheaval will be discussed in the next two chapters.

The struggle to prevent the removal of the capital from Yankton in 1883 precipitated the most violent and sustained political agitation that Dakota had ever experienced. From the moment the capital commission secretly met and organized on the slow-moving train, the southern part of the Territory was aflame. Yet the significance of the removal issue was not so much in the indignation it aroused as in the manner in which Governor Ordway and his associates carried out their plans. Before Ordway's term, nearly every governor or federal official had personally led a clique or a faction whose members were known to the greater majority of the territorial citizens. It was difficult, because of the smallness and intimacy of the population, to make a political deal without having it general rumor soon after consummation, and the deal itself was usually with intraterritorial factions and not with outside parties, unless it happened to be with officials in Washington. But now the settled portion of Dakota was so large, its population so scattered, and its attitudes so sectionalized that a certain amount of anonymity in politics was possible for the first time. The "rings" or "combinations" could better hide their actions, the true leader could remain unknown, or, if he were a key political figure such as Ordway was, he could keep his many connections a secret from the rank and file. The sudden appearance of the capital commission in the Yankton railroad yards —nine men from all parts of Dakota—with no one having been apprised that they had rendezvoused in Sioux Falls for several days before the organization trip, indicates the degree of secrecy with which the schemers could operate. The politician could now use the telegraph, for by 1883 lines were threading most of the Territory. He could make a quick trip to St. Paul on any one of four railroads, and there, with his colleagues, decide the next political move in a room at the Merchants Hotel—which became known, in fact, as the unofficial capital of Dakota.[9]

9. Nelson, *Land of the Dacotahs*, p. 253; see also Bismarck *Tribune*, April 9, 1889. Note, too, F. A. Gale to L. K. Church, February 7, 1888, Governor's File, Bismarck. In this letter Gale chastised Governor Church for holding a meeting of

There was also the new factor of the absentee railroad companies who owned every main line in Dakota. A perusal of the names of the directors and high officials of very important roads running through Dakota reveals not a single Dakotan.[10] Dakotans were to discover that political policy was often ready-made for them by the managers of the Northern Pacific, the Chicago, Milwaukee, and St. Paul, and the Northwestern railroads. An example of this policy may be seen in a letter written by B. C. Cook, an official of the Chicago and Northwestern, to Governor Howard of Dakota. Cook informed Howard that he was sending Charles E. Simmons, the Chicago and Northwestern's land officer, to represent the road's interests in Yankton during the meeting of the legislature, and that he had also sent along a general railroad law which the Assembly was to adopt.[11]

All this meant that henceforth Dakota politics would have its anonymous ringleaders as well as the western equivalent of the boss in the smoke-filled room. In short, the factions led by vigorous personalities were being replaced by more complicated and impersonal party machinery, and the politician who possessed a knowledge of this machinery had a distinct advantage.

No more appropriate person to introduce machine politics to Dakota could have been found than Governor Nehemiah Ordway. This pious-sounding, white-headed New Hampshire lawyer was a master of both secret manipulation and the use of open and virulent press campaigns to achieve his ends. He came to Dakota with perhaps the most ambitious and well-formulated political plans that any federal official in Dakota had ever had. His activities were to make the railroad speculations of Governor Burbank and the townsite grabbing of Governor Pennington seem puny by comparison. Moreover, Ordway, since he had served twelve years as sergeant-at-arms of the House of Representatives,

---

the northern Dakota Democratic party in Sioux Falls. It should have been held in St. Paul, so that the southern wing of the party would not have been able to find out the details, Gale advised.

10. *Annual Reports of the Board of Railroad Commissioners of the Territory of Dakota*, 1886–89. The *Reports* list the officers, board of directors, and the local agents of every road in Dakota.

11. B. C. Cook to Governor William Howard, January 9, 1879, Governor's File, Bismarck.

had made valuable contacts before coming to Dakota.[12] Although
there is no documentary proof, he was doubtless appointed at the
suggestion of various New Hampshire businessmen who had investments in the Territory. Furthermore, when Ordway appeared
in Yankton to take up his duties, he brought with him a ring of
associates. His secretary, L. G. Johnson, soon became a county
commissioner, townsite boomer, and newspaper editor. Ordway's
own son, George, conveniently became territorial auditor; a young
ward of the Governor's also became county commissioner, and
another New Hampshire friend secured a fat contract from Ordway to build a territorial penitentiary at Sioux Falls.[13] To these
men should be added the local followers who joined his ranks
after he came to Dakota.

At first Ordway was so cautious in his maneuvers that he convinced the Yankton oligarchy he was in their camp during his
first two years in office. Secretary Hand was friendly with the
governor, as was Attorney General Hugh Campbell. Ex-Governor
Edmunds had urged Ordway's reappointment in 1882 when the
question arose.[14] And although the oligarchy began to suspect the
Governor's motives by the fall of 1883, they had little idea of the
degree of control which he had assumed over the 1883 Assembly;
consequently the passage of the capital removal bill came as a
great shock to them. At the same time Ordway, once his motives
were known, acted boldly in carrying out his removal project.
He agreed to approve bills for the erection of normal schools or
prisons in the home towns of some of the legislators only if they
would vote for removal and accept the appointment of his son as
territorial auditor.[15]

While the venal Ordway exerted a powerful influence in Dakota politics until 1890, his chief colleague in the capital removal
scheme was even more important. This was Alexander McKenzie
of Bismarck, the wily sheriff of Burleigh County and trusted agent

12. Nelson, *Land of the Dacotahs*, pp. 129–30.
13. See the "Ordway Reply to Malfeasance in Office," a sixty-three page manuscript deposited in the Governor's File, Bismarck, for some account of the Governor's
relations with Johnson and others.
14. Petition urging Ordway's reappointment (*ca.* March 1882), signed by ex-
Governors Edmunds, Faulk, and Pennington and other Dakota citizens; Governor's
File, Bismarck.
15. Drake, "Influence of the Newspapers," p. 96.

of the Northern Pacific Railroad. Many contemporaries called him Alexander the Great, Boss of northern Dakota. "Tall, handsome, and possessed of unbounded physical courage, yet quiet and soft-spoken, he was a natural leader of men and an adroit practical psychologist; he knew how and where to dispense gifts and favors to the best advantage—a quality which gave him a reputation somewhat of the Robin Hood type." [16] McKenzie had come to Bismarck with the railroad; he had gone into the saloon business and thence into local politics as the lobbyist of the Northern Pacific. His type could be found in nearly every large eastern city between 1870 and 1900, for he was a party boss who did favors for private interests such as the railroad. Under his reign Bismarck gained a rightfully deserved reputation as one of the most corrupt towns in the United States.[17] In the 1890's he drifted on to the Alaskan gold fields, where his political manipulations resulted in his arrest by the federal government. He was convicted and served a term in a California prison.

McKenzie remained the silent, shrewd enigma to the very end. After his prison term he returned to North Dakota, and when he died he provided the Dakotans with a final scandal to savor, for two widows came forward to claim the estate. Alexander McKenzie, it seemed, had been a bigamist for some twenty years.[18] Such a career has not been allowed to go unappreciated, for Rex Beach used McKenzie as one of the central figures—his fictional name is Alex McNamara—in his novel about northern Alaska called *The Spoilers.*[19]

As the boss of northern Dakota politics, McKenzie was invaluable to Ordway's removal plans, and indeed it may have been

16. Nelson, *Land of the Dacotahs*, p. 128.

17. Ibid., p. 253. This corruption became known only after North Dakota became a state, since the McKenzie ring lasted into the twentieth century, but it was functioning in the 1880's as well.

18. Interview with Thomas Hall, Secretary of State of North Dakota, August 20, 1948. Mr. Hall knew McKenzie personally.

19. Nelson, *Land of the Dacotahs*, p. 127. A Dakota pioneer and contemporary of McKenzie, Dan Scott, has described McKenzie in less romantic terms than Nelson. "Mentally McKenzie was a greatly overrated man," Scott wrote, "but he possessed a natural cunning in placing political corruption funds which in time made him an indispensable factor in conventions and elections. . . . He was never anything but one of those 'necessary political evils!'" "Reminiscences of Dan Scott," clipping from *Black Hills Journal* (no date) deposited in State Department of History, Pierre, South Dakota.

McKenzie who first suggested that the capital be moved to a spot which could benefit northern Dakota and the Northern Pacific. He came to Yankton during the Assembly session of 1880 on the excuse that he had to bring a prisoner down to the Yankton court. When he left a few days later, Ordway had agreed to make him a member of the capital commission, and together they had probably chosen Bismarck for the new territorial capital.[20]

Ordway, McKenzie, and others like them represented the officials and the combinations with whom the Yankton oligarchy and the statehood men had to do battle. The struggle involved two fairly complex organizations, each with several leaders and each using several fairly advanced methods of political strategy more common to the East than to the frontier. The whole removal fight indicated a use of Eastern political techniques to deal with what was basically a frontier question, the location of the seat of government.

In still another way Ordway and McKenzie used a frontier situation to their advantage when they tried to gain control of the extensive territorial press. It should be remembered that hundreds of newspapers existed in Dakota during the 1880's, most of which depended for their support almost wholly on public land sale notices, records of sale, and other types of public printing. Since they drew a livelihood from the dispensation of a public official, the newspapers took an economic interest in politics that can scarcely be exaggerated.[21] What Ordway proposed to do was to bring the editors of all these tiny publications into a political alliance that would appear to the public only as an innocuous "press association." The weapon of coercion was to be public

20. Bruce Nelson in his *Land of the Dacotahs*, pp. 130–2, suggests that Mc-Kenzie double-crossed Ordway when he secretly persuaded the commission to choose Bismarck over the paper town of Ordway, which the governor owned, and over the small town of Pierre, most of which Ordway and his son owned. But while the governor owned land in Pierre, he also held lots in Bismarck and he was later a lobbyist for the Northern Pacific; after the capital was settled in Bismarck, Ordway, McKenzie, and two others of the capital removal commissioners joined forces to open a bank there. It seems likely that this would not have been the case had Ordway been double-crossed. See statement by Burleigh F. Spaulding, member of the Capital Removal Commission, in the Grand Forks (N.D.) *Herald*, September 19, 1932.

21. Pomeroy, *The Territories and the United States*, p. 32; see also Ruth E. Bergman, "Printing in South Dakota during the Territorial Period," MS, State Department of History, Pierre, South Dakota.

printing patronage, and if the scheme worked, Ordway knew that the most vocal group in Dakota would be forced to voice only Ordway sentiments.[22]

Ordway first established a newspaper of his own in Yankton, which he named the *Dakota Outlook*. His secretary, L. G. Johnson, assumed the editorship. The *Outlook* failed, however, and so Ordway secretly suggested to Maris Taylor, editor of the Democratic *Dakota Herald,* that it would be worth his while for this to become the administration paper. Taylor declined the offer, which was then made to E. W. Caldwell, editor of the powerful Sioux Falls *Press*. Caldwell also refused, so that in the fall of 1880 Ordway again established his own newspaper, but this time it was published in Pierre, where his son George exercised a large political and economic influence over the town and the surrounding county.[23]

By 1882 Ordway had managed to enlist a number of editors to support his objectives, and together they formed the Dakota Press Association. It was no accident in the 1883 Assembly that the unusual percentage of the Assemblymen were editors from northern Dakota who joined with the governor to push through the removal bill.[24]

The chief Ordway papers were his own *Dakota Outlook;* the Fargo *Argus*, whose editor, A. W. Edwards, was one of the most conspicuous lobbyists for capital removal in 1883; and the Bismarck *Tribune,* owned by C. A. Lounsberry, a politically ambitious editor who, as a good friend of McKenzie, always defended the Northern Pacific. Still others were the Jamestown *Alert* and the Grand Forks *Plaindealer,* whose founder, George H. Walsh— known as the "boss of the number one hard counties"—had first introduced the Huron bill to mislead the Yanktonians.[25] Finally there was N. C. Nash, editor of the *Sioux Valley News* in Canton, who was described by his enemies as a "leading mouthpiece of the capital commission swindle and the infamous Ordway." [26] Many others in or connected with the 1883 Assembly as its hired

22. Drake, "Influence of the Newspapers," p. 1.
23. Ibid., pp. 29–33.
24. Ibid., p. 42.
25. Ibid.
26. Ibid., p. 44.

officers were newspaper men. J. O'Brien Scobey, president of the Council in 1883, was a close friend of George A. Hopp, editor of three central Dakota newspapers. J. W. Shannon, a lobbyist from Huron, was a partner of Hopp's in the newspaper business. And while Ordway received little support from the Black Hills papers, he did secure the allegiance of the St. Paul *Pioneer Press* —which reflected Northern Pacific Railroad views—and the Sioux City *Journal*.[27]

To fight Ordway and his nefarious press ring, the antiremoval-ists used three means: they organized their own press campaign, they exerted pressure locally and in Washington to secure state-hood for southern Dakota, and finally, they questioned the legality of his actions in court. These three attacks were carried on simul-taneously for two years, until Ordway was removed from office by President Arthur in 1884.[28]

The leader of the anti-Ordway press was W. S. Bowen, editor and owner of the Yankton *Press and Dakotaian*. With Secretary Hand's help, Bowen had made the *Press and Dakotaian* the most powerful newspaper in Dakota and virtually the official organ for the local Republican party. A small, energetic man, he, too, knew how to work behind the scenes or to use the press in a slashing exposé campaign of his own. His able partner, George W. Kings-bury, a member of the inner circle of the Yankton Republicans, aided him at every step. Together, Bowen and Kingsbury adopted the method of printing complete articles from all other news-papers opposing Ordway while carrying on editorial attacks of their own.[29] This system gave an illusion of universality to the condemnation of the governor when ten or twenty articles were quoted at once, all of them denouncing the governor.

The general tone of this press war is very obvious in an edi-torial from the Elk Point *Coyote:* "Not a single paper in Dakota, with the exception of those directly controlled by the rascals engineering the great steal, or those whose editors hope for a suck at some of the trickling streams of swag, support the mon-strous scheme. Every daily in southern Dakota, and twenty-four

27. Ibid., pp. 45–7.
28. Ibid., pp. 190–1.
29. Ibid., pp. 53–6.

out of twenty-five of the weeklies, are vigorously lashing the shameless crew. . . . All honor to Dakota's honest editors." [30]

Bowen and Kingsbury were joined by F. M. Ziebach, many time Democratic mayor of Yankton, who was now editor of the Scotland *Citizen;* by E. W. Caldwell of the Sioux Falls *Press;* and by J. H. King of the Chamberlain *Register.* Bowen's hand was considerably strengthened by a surprise alliance with his former enemy, Delegate R. F. Pettigrew of Sioux Falls, who felt that Ordway was such a threat to the delegate's control of part of the federal patronage that all sections of southern Dakota must fight together. When Pettigrew secured the appointment of Bowen as postmaster for Yankton, the alliance between the two was truly cemented.[31]

Besides name calling, the *Press and Dakotaian* undertook to retrace the history of the 1883 Assembly in an effort to ferret out examples of bribery or corrupt bargains. Within a few days it found that a Walsh County assemblyman, George P. Harvey, had been a friend of Ordway's back in New Hampshire. This same Harvey had introduced a bill in the session to tax the railroads heavily, which action he took, it later appeared, to quell the opposition of both the Northwestern and the Milwaukee Railroads, which were fighting removal of the capital because their lines ran to or near Yankton. Furthermore, the railroad tax bill went to a committee of "grangers" who had expressed a dislike of railroads. As soon as this was done, the managers of the Milwaukee and Northwestern were informed by telegram that the attitude of their Yankton lobbyists (General Lawler and Colonel Simmons) on the capital question had "provoked the granger element and legislation hostile to the railroads had already been introduced." [32] The two lobbyists, Lawler and Simmons, received immediate instructions to take a neutral position, and the "railroad tax bill was never reported . . . nor did Mr. Harvey manifest the slightest anxiety regarding its fate." [33]

30. The Elk Point *Coyote* was quoted in the *Press and Dakotaian* of April 4, 1883, and the quote is cited in turn in Drake's "Influence of the Newspapers," p. 59.
31. Drake, "Influence of the Newspapers," p. 53.
32. *Dakota Herald,* March 17, 1883.
33. Ibid., April 21, 1883.

For the next two years the anti-Ordway press hurled scores of accusations against the unpopular governor. The *Press and Dakotaian* in scrutinizing Ordway's early career discovered that he had engaged in some very questionable business ventures while he was sergeant-at-arms in Washington. The papers did not hesitate to report the details of these ventures over and over again.[34] Such attacks and inquiries so enraged the governor that he published equally long and detailed defenses of his entire career. His voluminous file in the Dakota Territorial Papers in the National Archives consists largely of copies of these defenses which he sent to the Secretary of the Interior.[35]

In April 1883 the political phase of the campaign against Ordway began when the antiremovalists called a protest meeting in Sioux Falls. In a building packed to capacity, the Yankton old guard—Edmunds, Faulk, Beadle, DeWitt, Miner and Kingsbury, Moody, and others—joined with the Pettigrew forces to denounce the governor and the removal scheme. They succeeded in forming an executive committee for each county whose function it would be to gather facts on Ordway and present them to the president. If this did not secure his dismissal, the committees would then request that he be impeached before Congress.[36]

Ordway immediately threw down his own editorial gauntlet in a press dispatch and in a telegram to the president: "A delegation of Yankton county bond repudiators, headed by Newton Edmunds, held a meeting today with the Pettigrew ring at Sioux Falls to put forth an attack upon the governor and the legislative Assembly on account of the passage of the capital removal bill. The executive and legislative accept the issue and will meet those and all other rings before the people of the territory and vindicate their action." [37]

On April 20, before an audience overflowing into the aisles, Pettigrew spoke at Turner Hall in Yankton about the iniquitous commission and the governor.[38] Within the week, however, Ord-

34. Drake, "Influence of the Newspapers," pp. 8–15.

35. The Ordway file is to be found in the Interior Appointment Papers, Dakota, Files, 165, 200, 201, N. G. Ordway.

36. *Dakota Herald*, April 7, 1883.

37. Ibid., April 14, 1883.

38. Ibid., April 21, 1883.

way struck back when a meeting was called at Canton to denounce the capital commission. The ubiquitous McKenzie descended upon the town and "circulated the report that if the meeting should be controlled by them, the commission would make Canton its headquarters, and as a result the town would profit in many ways." Canton citizens, impressed by McKenzie's promise, packed the meeting with Ordway men, who passed a resolution, under conditions approaching that of a riot, approving the removal scheme.[39]

Protests and resolutions were not enough, however. On April 3, 1883, Attorney General Hugh J. Campbell held a meeting on the Yankton Citizen's League in his law office to consider the feasibility of calling a constitutional convention for southern Dakota. A month later most of southern Dakota sent four hundred delegates to a preconstitutional convention at Huron, where they were to map out a program that would result in statehood. While many of the delegates were the same persons who had attended the Canton convention the year before, this time they were not so smug as to think that statehood could be easily attained.[40] They realized that a simple appeal to the public to rid itself of Ordway by declaring for statehood would not work, so they decided to justify the statehood cause by an appeal to their constitutional rights as interpreted by Attorney General Campbell.

Campbell maintained that since southern Dakota had fulfilled the traditional requirements for statehood, it had a perfect right to organize as a state and to declare itself a member of the Union without waiting for Congress to pass an enabling act: "the peoples of Southern Dakota could by united popular action, separate at a stroke the councils of the north and south, destroy the power of the political combination which opposed division, and begin as a separate state organization." [41]

To support his argument, Campbell noted that Michigan had possessed a functioning state government for fourteen months before it had entered the Union in 1834.[42] Campbell also claimed

39. Drake, "Influence of the Newspapers," pp. 78–9.
40. Kingsbury, *Dakota Territory*, 2, 1657–68.
41. Durand, *Joseph Ward of Dakota*, p. 157.
42. *Dakota Herald*, June 2, 1883.

that both the Northwest Ordinance and the Louisiana Treaty of Cession had intended that the territory therein included was to be organized into states as soon as possible.[43] Then Campbell made what he thought was his strongest point: he cited Justice Roger Taney's remarks on the rights of citizens in a territory, which Taney had made in connection with the Dred Scott case. Taney had stated: "There is certainly no power given by the Constitution to the Federal Government to establish or maintain Colonies bordering on the United States or at a distance, to be ruled and governed at its own pleasure; nor to enlarge its territorial limits in any way, except by the admission of new States. That power is plainly given. . . . But no power is given to acquire a Territory to be held and governed permanently in that character."[44] Taney had concluded that Congress clearly had the power to expand the territory of the United States by acquiring lands, but each was to become a state "as soon as its population and situation would entitle it to admission. It is acquired to become a State, and not to be held as a colony and governed by Congress with absolute authority . . ."[45]

From this opinion Campbell drew five overlapping conclusions to be used in the Dakota fight for statehood:

1. That the federal government has no power to maintain colonies to be ruled and governed at its own pleasure.

2. It has no power to hold and govern a territory permanently.

3. A territory must be admitted as soon as its population and situation entitle it to admission.

4. A territory is acquired to become a state, and must not be prohibited from becoming one.

5. The Congress has power to hold possession of the territory and govern it only until it is settled and inhabited by a civilized community and is capable of self-government, then it is to be admitted on equal terms with other states as a member of the union.[46]

A Dakotan spouting political theory, which went into the constitutional aspects of the territorial question, produced amaze-

43. Ibid., June 2 and June 9, 1883.
44. Dred Scott v. Sanford, 19 Howard 393, 446 (1857).
45. Ibid.
46. *Dakota Herald*, June 2 and 9, 1883.

ment, horror, and amusement in the press. Campbell's appeal to the Dred Scott case left much to be desired, yet from there he wandered further afield into the question of states' rights, for after asserting that a territory had an inherent right to become a state, he had to maintain that state's rights and privileges as a member of the Union. Jefferson's and Madison's Kentucky and Virginia Resolutions, Calhoun's disquisitions on states' rights, and the entire states' rights leadership, in fact, were employed by Campbell and his followers to prove that southern Dakota could not be kept out of the Union by Congress. Thirty years before, they had been used to prove that no state could be forced to stay in the Union. It was truly one of the great ironies of American history that Calhoun's arguments were used for state admission to, as well as for state secession from, the Union.[47]

Actually, the conditions producing the "we are a state" doctrine —for that is what the public called Campbell's claims—bore some similarity to those producing the nullification doctrine. Dakota's theory of admission was a means of destroying the hated territorial system which in the hands of Ordway, the northern Dakota politicians like McKenzie, and the railroad lobbies had become an outside political tyranny. The persecution complex brought on by a dozen factors had reached the level where principles of justification, however weak they might be, and however small the number of persons subscribing to them, were being posed. The southern Dakotans were actually more interested in seceding from the Territory and regaining their lost power than they were in becoming a state. Statehood was at bottom only the instrument for self-rule.

At the risk of drawing a parallel too far, we might say that the statehood advocates were actually secessionists of a sort, and their use of states' rights and secession doctrine makes the coincidence too great to ignore. They were conscious themselves that they

47. Dr. Joseph Ward, President of Yankton College and a close friend of Campbell's, justified the appeal to states' rights in the following manner: "Because some States have insisted on an excessive exercise of their sovereignty, using to the full powers that have once been formally abdicated in favor of the general government, it is no just cause for refusing other States rights that are fundamental, that are essential to their very existence. . . . It is the Union that exists by consent of the States." Joseph Ward, "The Territorial System of the United States," *Andover Review* (1888), p. 56.

were basing their case on discredited political concepts, so they were always careful to point out that they were citing only those sections of Calhoun or Taney or others that continued to be acceptable American political theory.[48] The fact that the political ideas of the Dakotans were so much those of the older sections, that under similar conditions similar reactions took place and traditional theories and concepts were called back into action, suggests that Dakota "theorists" were citing those arguments which they had heard in their youth and that they had not developed any indigenous ones of their own since coming to Dakota. They were guilty, one might even assert, of a singular lack of political originality.

Before the Huron Convention adjourned and its four hundred members returned to their homes, Campbell's doctrine was incorporated into the convention resolutions, and by way of implementing them the delegates agreed to call for a state constitutional convention of one hundred fifty delegates to meet in September 1883. They also established the voting machinery in each southern county, for they did not trust the regularly constituted election officials.[49]

That summer, politicians and Citizen's Leaguers kept the interest in the coming convention at a high pitch. The statehood forces, recognizing the need for publicity and favorable public opinion, bombarded eastern newspapers with articles on the statehood plan. Campbell printed his theory in pamphlet form to be distributed over the Territory. Lauren Dunlap, the Dakota Commissioner of Immigration, who also doubled as a correspondent for the Chicago *Inter-Ocean*, a newspaper with a large circulation in Dakota, wrote in July: "Dakota today is ripe for action and open rebellion as was Virginia when the convention of '98 passed the Madison resolution of defiance." [50] Dunlap declared that he had traveled in every southern state before the Civil War but that he had never before heard such statements as were being

48. Ward, "The Territorial System of the United States," p. 56, warned his readers that Campbell's theory did not mean nullification, secession, or even treason, but that it did mean that "supremacy of the Union and States rights exist side by side."

49. The constitutional delegates were to be paid three dollars a day in scrip, later to be redeemed by the future state legislature.

50. Quoted in the *Dakota Herald*, August 4, 1883.

made in Dakota against the national government: "We shall not recognize Gov. Ordway, because we shall have a governor of our own, which we have elected. We shall fail to elect a territorial legislature, but choose a state legislature instead, but we shall repeal every law passed during the existence of the territory. The territorial governor, secretary, auditor, treasurer, and the courts will have no laws to execute." [51]

Such statements were accompanied by the most optimistic reports that every citizen was on the side of the statehood forces. In early August Delegate Pettigrew claimed that every group in Dakota—the merchants, the bankers, and the farmers—were behind the movement. Even the press was on their side, Pettigrew insisted, although he was willing to admit that three rascally papers preferred to support Ordway rather than statehood. [52]

These assertions were the sheerest propaganda. Not only was the contest largely between two sets of politicians, but it failed to excite the average citizen. There is evidence, in fact, that if the average Dakotan had chosen to participate in the movement, it would have embarrassed the statehood leaders themselves. Of the score of conventions held by the statehood forces during the next six years, the majority of them met at the height of the harvesting season or during the spring planting season when the rural population was too busy to choose convention delegates or to go themselves as delegates to the various meetings. [53]

Not only was there general apathy among the rank and file of voters, but opposition also came from many sources other than Ordway, McKenzie, and their followers. The Black Hills manifested only a casual interest in division and statehood, according to the St. Paul *Pioneer Press*. [54] Many of the Democrats opposed the convention, and the rumor that the prohibitionists would dominate the session was so persistent that several delegates were elected by the saloon elements to protect their livelihood. [55]

51. Ibid.
52. Ibid., August 4, 1883.
53. Robert Dollard, a member of the Constitutional Convention of 1885, called attention to this fact during a debate on methods of popularizing statehood: *Dakota Constitutional Convention, 1885* (Huron, S.D., 1907), *1*, 644–7.
54. *Dakota Herald*, August 11, 1883. The *Herald* was quoting the St. Paul *Pioneer Press*.
55. *Dakota Herald*, August 4, 1883.

Outside the Territory the Chicago *Times* attacked the convention when it insisted that the delegates had been fraudulently elected.[56]

The "we are a state" concept came in for its share of attacks during the summer of 1883, when lawyers began to question the validity of the constitutional arguments that Campbell had presented. Peter G. Shannon, an elderly lawyer who had served as chief justice of Dakota from 1873 to 1881, devastated Campbell's logic in a series of articles printed in the *Herald*. While Shannon admitted that Dakota should be divided and the southern half made a state, he found that by Campbell's definition northern Dakota was also a state, and that by this type of reasoning Utah could organize as a state immediately.[57]

Turning to the question of Congress' power over a territory, Shannon asserted that this issue had long been decided by the Civil War. For support he relied largely upon Judge Cooley's opinion of territorial powers and rights as given in his popular *Constitutional Limitations*, a book that was rapidly becoming the bible of constitutional lawyers in the 1880's.[58] With a particular relish Shannon cited Chief Justice Waite's opinion in the case of the Yankton bond repudiators—a case that the oligarchy knew all too well—in which Waite had specifically asserted Congress' power to rule the territories in the following words: *"Congress may not only abrogate the laws of the territorial legislature, but it may itself legislate directly for the local government."* [59] Shannon further observed that: "Consequently the constitution of the United States being the sovereign law of the territories, no person or persons inhabiting the territories can lawfully do anything which is in opposition to this fundamental law; not even the aggregate body of the people of a territory—to say nothing of a majority." [60]

Just as the constitutional convention was about to meet in

56. Chicago *Times*, August 5, 1883, quoted in the *Dakota Herald*, August 18, 1883.
57. Peter C. Shannon, "The State of Dakota," *Dakota Herald*, August 25, 1883.
58. Ibid.
59. *Dakota Herald*, September 1, 1883; italics are Shannon's.
60. Ibid. Shannon made particular use of the Senate debates on reconstruction during the 1866–67 session of Congress. See especially Senator Edmunds' remarks, *Cong. Globe*, 39th Cong., 2d sess., p. 215.

Sioux Falls, Shannon printed his third article attacking Campbell's theory. This time he concentrated on the Michigan precedent that Campbell had made so much of. When the Michigan state government was organized, Shannon explained to his readers, Calhoun and South Carolina had just drawn attention to states' rights by the nullification doctrine. Moreover, the governor of the "state" of Michigan was twenty-three year old Steven T. Mason of Virginia and Kentucky who had been trained, Shannon suggested, in the principles of the famous resolutions of 1798–99, and was the one who had started the statehood movement in Michigan. Mason had taken the view that Congress had neglected them and they must assert their "equal rights," by taking a census, calling a "convention for the institution of a State government, and the election of a representative and senators to congress." Although Mason's plan was carried out and Congress accepted Michigan's state government, Shannon denied that Michigan had set a true precedent, for when the Senate and House of Representatives of the State of Michigan presented a memorial to Congress, that body had accepted it only as coming from a body of private citizens. Even Calhoun had agreed that this was the only proper procedure. This fact alone, Shannon concluded, defeated the whole "airy fabric" of Campbell's logic.[61]

Shannon's arguments left much to be desired, but when compared with Campbell's briefs on statehood, they appeared to be impeccable. Even so, the pragmatic approach to the problem of statehood was still so predominant in Dakota that the Sioux Falls Constitutional Convention could assemble largely unmoved by Shannon's cutting remarks.

Some twenty-six years after the extralegal "squatter legislature" had met in Sioux Falls in 1857, a second extralegal group convened to write a constitution for the "State of Dakota." Some of the legislators of 1857—Brookings and Kidder—were delegates to the 1883 meeting, and despite many differences, both groups had the same aim: to secure political control of an entire region. The men of 1857 had acted boldly; they had a clear plan of economic and political exploitation; they had unhesitatingly voted

61. *Dakota Herald*, September 8, 1883.

the names of dead relatives to make their electoral statistics seem more impressive; they had filed fraudulent land claims with inspired imagination. The Constitutional Convention of 1883 could not get away with such tactics, and it was to take up three measures which the earlier assemblage would never have considered: a prohibition clause, a clause preventing the exploitation and cheap sale of the public school lands, and a clause permitting woman suffrage. These topics were undoubtedly symbols of the passing political frontier, and certainly they showed the influence of eastern reform movements and liberal ideas upon the "best elements" in Dakota. Yet out of the 125 delegates that gathered in Sioux Falls during those sunny September harvest days, eleven were real estate dealers—a euphemistic name for land speculator. Led by a promising young land agent from Indiana, Arthur C. Mellette, they successfully opposed a memorial to Congress which asked for permission to open more Sioux Reservation lands for settlement. The boom that Dakota was enjoying had so raised land prices that every agent was making money; moreover, more lands were being bought or preempted than homesteaded. But if new lands were thrown on the market, they would cause an immediate drop in all land prices, something the land agents did not wish to happen.[62]

The similarity to earlier legislatures and to the "squatter legislature" itself was illustrated by the occupations and nativity of the Sioux Falls delegates. Forty-two were lawyers, thirty-one were farmers, thirteen were newspaper editors, eleven were land agents, and the remaining twenty-eight were in various businesses and professions. Only seventeen of 125 were foreign born, but all but two of the native born were from the northern United States. Their average age was thirty-five, which is one year younger than the average age of the so-called youthful California delegates who convened in June 1849 to write a state constitution. The most prominent men in the convention were again the Yankton oligarchy and the "old guard" from the remainder of southern

62. Drake, "Influence of the Newspapers," pp. 84–5. Miss Drake has very painstakingly garnered information about each of the delegates to the 1883 Constitutional Convention; see also *Dakota Herald*, September 8, 1883, for an account of the convention debates over the wisdom of opening the Sioux Reservation to settlers.

Dakota. Campbell, Bowen, Kingsbury, Beadle, Ward, and ex-Governor Faulk all were there. Gideon C. Moody, one-time leader of the Broadway Gang and now attorney for the Homestake Mining Company, was there along with his ex-enemy, W. W. Brookings of the Capital Street Gang. Ex-office holders like Edmunds, Pennington, and Barney Caulfield (an ex-Congressman from Illinois) were in evidence.[63]

In addition to these older politicians, a new group of young men led by Mellette, the real estate agent, were there. And still another group consisted of the out-and-out reformers who were more interested in securing prohibition or woman suffrage than they were in regaining control of Dakota politics. The prohibition forces under the auspices of the territorial W.C.T.U. actually held their annual meeting in Sioux Falls at the same time that the Constitutional Convention was in session, so that their influence might be felt the more strongly. The conjunction of the two groups naturally embarrassed the political leaders, who were afraid that the public would believe that the whole statehood cause was a cloak for prohibitionists and impractical crusaders.[64]

Despite the much heralded "we are a state" theory and the popular belief that western political conventions usually expressed radical ideas, the delegates were generally conservative and proposed no radical innovations in the constitution they drew up. There were, as John Hicks has noted, almost uniformly good and able men with a "disinclination to experiment," for "the frontier, with even greater ignorance of the outside world, consciously and intentionally copied the ideas of the older states." [65]

The proceedings themselves appear to have been cut and dried except for the issues of school lands, prohibition, and woman suffrage. The situation was so well in hand, in fact, that Bartlett Tripp, the leader of the Democratic party in Dakota, but a safe and conservative lawyer by profession, was named president of the convention by acclamation. His choice stressed the bipartisan nature of the meeting, and it was hoped that it would persuade

63. Ibid.; see also *Dakota Herald,* September 8, 1883. For the names of the delegates to the Sioux Falls Constitutional Convention see the *Dakota Constitutional Convention* (1885), *1,* 6–8.

64. *Dakota Herald,* August 4, 1883.

65. John D. Hicks, "The Constitution of the Northwest States," *University of Nebraska Studies,* 23 (1923), 33.

the Democratic House in Washington that the statehood movement was a people's movement and above politics. Nevertheless,
Tripp was a trusted member of the Yankton oligarchy, one of the
wealthiest men in the Territory, and as an attorney for the Chicago, Milwaukee, and St. Paul Railroad he naturally harbored no
"granger" ideas.[66]

The constitution itself, while wholly traditional in form, did
reflect the political passions of the hour. The document provided
for the usual bicameral legislature, but the lavish spending of the
1883 session of the Assembly—some $4,000,000 through bonding
bills and appropriations—so alarmed the delegates that they
placed elaborate restrictions upon the future state legislature's
taxing and appropriation powers.[67] Likewise, the powers of the
governor were curbed and his veto power reduced.[68] The judiciary, in many ways the weakest branch of the territorial system,
received a thorough overhauling; the number of appointive officials was drastically cut. The grand jury system had curbs placed
upon it, and a three-fourths majority decision by a jury was made
binding.[69]

The most notable part of the constitution was Beadle's school
lands clause, in which the future state agreed not to sell its
school lands for less than ten dollars an acre. The proceeds of
sale were to go into a perpetual fund, the interest on which would
in turn be used to support the school system.[70]

In a sense Beadle was putting into practical use the theory of
increasing land values presented by Henry George in *Progress
and Poverty* only four years before. The excellent "Dakota system"
for school lands eventually was adopted not only by South Dakota
but by every western state coming into the Union under the
Omnibus Bill of 1889.[71]

The two other controversial issues, prohibition and woman

66. Bismarck *Tribune*, November 24, 1885.
67. The proceedings of the convention may be found in the *Dakota Herald*,
September 8, 1883 ff., and in the *Press and Dakotaian*, September 8, 1883 ff. There
is no official report of the proceedings.
68. Kingsbury, *Dakota Territory*, 2, 1884 ff. Kingsbury had access to the records
of the debates and has partially recorded them in ibid., pp. 1669–1716.
69. For a discussion of the jury system see ibid., pp. 1693 ff.
70. Hicks, "The Constitution of the Northwest States," pp. 84–5.
71. Ibid., pp. 76–80; see also John L. Coulter, "The Public Land Policy of
Dakota Territory and North and South Dakota," 1909 (MS in the Carnegie Institute Papers, Yale University Library), for a laudatory analysis.

suffrage, were postponed for reasons of political expediency, because their advocates were not yet strong enough to force the issue. The Sioux Falls constitution was a solid, praiseworthy document which fairly represented the conservative wishes of a majority of the Dakota citizens. But it was interesting too, for what it omitted. Restrictions on banking, on monopolies, and on railroads were receiving national attention in the 1880's. Granger laws had been passed in some midwestern states for nearly a decade, and the specter of a granger-inspired railroad law had played an important part in the capital removal intrigue.[72] Yet the conservative nature of the delegates, the fact that more were lawyers and business men with interests in banks and railroads resulted in their proposing only the mildest regulations in these fields.[73]

The convention adjourned on September 19 with the announcement that the constitution would be submitted for popular approval in October. But again the statehood forces ran into powerful opposition. While the constitutional convention was still in session, a north Dakota group, undoubtedly backed by McKenzie and Ordway, met in Fargo to protest the South's appropriation of the name "Dakota," which the Fargo delegates vehemently asserted had been made famous through north Dakota's production of "Dakota number one hard wheat." They also censured the southern convention for refusing to discuss apportionment and settlement of the territorial debt.[74]

At this point the Democrats, speaking through the *Dakota Herald*, suddenly changed from a neutral position on the statehood question to one of opposition. The *Herald* predicted that the constitution had so many objectionable features that it would be defeated.[75] And with a weather eye on the farm vote, the paper asked why the convention had left the question of railroad taxation and legislation up to the Legislature, which obviously could not be trusted. "It is only necessary to take a glance at what has been going on in New Jersey, Pennsylvania and other eastern states, to say nothing of the west—to ascertain the deep

72. See above, p. 220.
73. *Dakota Herald,* September 29, 1883.
74. Green, "The Struggle of South Dakota to Become a State," p. 518.
75. *Dakota Herald,* September 22, 1883.

and wily danger to which the people have been groaningly doomed." [76]

With great glee the *Herald* pointed out that the clause allowing the railroads to be taxed upon their gross earnings had been written by an attorney for the Northwestern Railroad. The newspaper also found great fault with the more general tax law, which provided that corporate property would be taxed at a "uniform rate" with other property.[77]

Later, the incorrigible Dr. Burleigh took up this same theme in a more general way when he published a series of letters in the *Herald* claiming that the constitution did not provide nearly enough guarantees against the "prejudice, caprice or venality of the legislature. . . . Who, I ask, with the experience of the past before their eyes—with the betrayal of sacred interest, fresh in their memories—will for a moment claim that the legislatures, unbridled by the most positive and unmistakable constitutional inhibitions, is a safe repository of the people's dearest rights." [78]

Burleigh feared that the control of taxation was a dangerous thing to leave in the hands of the Legislature, which was "just where the moneyed corporations of the country want it left." He concluded with the accusation that the Sioux Falls document was a railroad constitution.[79] The shrewd doctor, with as black a record as the most unbridled Legislature could boast, knew that the time was near in Dakota when the farmer would demand curbs on the railroads and the political officials, and he was simply laying the foundations for a possible political comeback of his own.

Nor would the prohibition forces remain in line. The *Herald* spread the report that the saloon element had won out at the convention when the delegates postponed the liquor question. On September 28 six counties met in a prohibition convention at Huron to register their opposition to any constitution without a prohibition clause.[80]

Just before the vote was taken on the constitution, Judge Shan-

76. Ibid., September 29, 1883.
77. Ibid.
78. Ibid., October 6, 1883.
79. Ibid.
80. Ibid., September 29, 1883.

non again appeared in print to denounce the proposed constitution and the entire statehood cause. There is some evidence that
Shannon was being considered in Washington to replace Ordway
as governor, so naturally Shannon objected to statehood.[81] Then
upon voting day the *Herald* distributed five thousand broadside
leaflets containing arguments for the rejection of the document,
and in its editorial columns the paper declared: "the corporation
agents, attorneys and sponsors of the Sioux Falls constitution
. . . have conspired to keep Governor Ordway in office for the
purpose of intimidating voters, who neither read nor reason, into
casting their ballots for that infamous document as an avenue of
escape from his misrule." [82] No proconstitution official, the *Herald*
shrewdly observed, had filed a complaint against Ordway in
Washington, so that their scapegoat would be sure to remain in
evidence until the election was over.[83]

When the constitution was submitted to the people of southern
Dakota, 12,336 voters approved the document and 6814 opposed
it. The Citizen's League forces, despite the favorable vote, were
left in great gloom, for some 30,000 voters had stayed at home.
As a result Congress failed to be impressed and refused to grant
statehood on the basis of so small a vote. The Minneapolis
Tribune reported that the whole affair attracted no more attention
than a footrace, and the Minneapolis *Evening Journal* pointed
out: "The most sensible portion of the population of south Dakota
has virtually defeated the revolutionary movement by staying
home and refusing to vote." [84]

A combination of circumstances conspired to prevent the ratification of the constitution by a large vote. Not only was there
opposition in the form of Ordway, McKenzie, and others of their
ilk, but their rings of newspaper editors and office holders were
both strong and articulate. There was also the unexpected element
of unrest among the territorial farming population because of the
low prices being paid by the grain elevators in the fall of 1883,
a condition which had distracted the farmers from any interest
in a constitution. During the weeks when the campaign over

81. *Ibid.*, October 20, 1883.
82. *Ibid.*
83. *Ibid.*
84. These papers were quoted in the *Dakota Herald*, November 17, 1883.

the constitution was at its height, mass protest meetings were taking place in Watertown, Dakota, to condemn the Chicago, Milwaukee, and St. Paul's new policy of refusing grain cars to individual farmers, and of taking only that grain which they would sell to an elevator company. This "existing combination between the railway company and the elevator companies" led the farmers of Spink County to call it an "oppressive and out-rageous monopoly." [85] This unrest was undoubtedly the real reason for the *Herald's* sudden claim that the Sioux Falls document was a railroad constitution.

Newspapers gave still other reasons for the constitution's de facto defeat. The Flandrau *Enterprise* observed that many people were lukewarm on the subject of admission when it was coupled with division. Many others felt that it was a hopeless effort without federal sanction and that many distrusted the politicians connected with the statehood movement as much as they did Ordway. The coincidence of the antiremoval campaign and the statehood movement was too obvious for some of the voters to ignore; thus they thought that the whole statehood clique was more interested in retaining the capital at Yankton than it was in statehood itself. The *Dakota Huronite* reflected this view when it said that the support of the entire territorial press could not quell the distrust of the statehood politicians, of the ambiguous clauses on taxation, the location of the capital, and the evasiveness with which the liquor issue was treated.[86] The final taunt to the downcast Citizen's League came when the *Brookings Press* squibbed, "Hugh J. Campbell will please rise and inform us just how many of us are a state." [87]

This extralegal phase of the statehood movement revealed several important developments in territorial politics: the loss of control of the public which the oligarchy had once had; the presence of a new unorganized mass of settlers; and the decline in importance of government office and government patronage to the average Dakota citizen during the boom agricultural period from 1878 to 1884. Further, it exhibited the professional and

85. Mellette *Tribune*, September 29, 1883, quoted in the *Dakota Herald*, November 3, 1883.
86. *Dakota Huronite*, quoted in the *Dakota Herald*, November 24, 1883.
87. *Brookings Press*, quoted in the *Dakota Herald*, November 24, 1883.

distinct nature of the minority that had launched the statehood movement, for it was the friends and the associates of the statehood leaders who had voted in favor of the constitution on October 20. In short, the best elements had voted for the best elements; the Citizen's League had not yet made its cause the people's cause.

While the press and the politicians labored to dismiss Ordway, to prevent capital removal, and to advance the causes of division and statehood, Ordway's opponents took legal action against the governor and his "Syndicate," as the *Press and Dakotaian* came to call the capital commission and the Ordwayites.[88]

Almost as soon as the capital removal bill had passed, in fact, the *Press and Dakotaian* printed the rumor that the City of Huron had paid $27,000 to get the capital. Other newspapers took up the cry of bribery during the spring of 1883, but they were able to garner only one specific instance of corruption when a council member confessed that he had been offered $15,000 to vote for the bill. The evidence stopped with his statement, nonetheless, so that the press had to concentrate upon the matter of Ordway's signing bills for the erection of nine normal schools in as many towns, in return for which the Assembly members from the nine towns were to vote "yes" on the capital removal bill. There was evidence, moreover, that the governor had actually vetoed bills favored by antiremovalists until they had come around to his point of view. If they proved tractable, he had usually approved a substitute bill granting their wants.[89]

In May 1883 the Yankton grand jury undertook to investigate irregularities in the governor's organization of new counties and in the appointment of county commissioners. Ordway was accused of selling county commissions to the highest bidder and the grand jury called him in to defend himself. The jury was so packed with Ordway enemies and was so in sympathy with the views of Attorney General Campbell, who was in charge of the investigation, that they refused to ask the Governor questions, thus leaving the task of proving his innocence to Ordway himself. When he did not do so, the grand jury censured Ordway for his

88. *Press and Dakotaian*, June 11, 1883.
89. Drake, "Influence of the Newspapers," p. 92.

interference in the organization of Douglas County. Then they issued three indictments against certain members of the 1883 Council and its messengers for attempted bribery, but no warrants were ever issued for the arrest of these men.[90]

In May 1883 a second legal effort to control Ordway and prevent capital removal began when four Yankton citizens brought a *quo warranto* suit against six of the capital commissioners, alleging that since the Organic Act of Dakota specified that the capital was to be located by the Legislature, the commissioners were an illegal body.[91] The case was tried on July 25 before Judge Edgerton, a leader of the statehood forces who was naturally sympathetic to the plaintiffs. He decided in their favor on September 15, just as the Sioux Falls Constitutional Convention was in the midst of its deliberations. The Yankton press felt that justice had at last been done, and the *Herald* commented: "The scoundrels have been brought to a halt and the carnival of corruption in which they have revelled is cut short." [92]

Such jubilation was both premature and unwarranted, for the commission by this time had already located the capital at Bismarck, and Ordway and his son, the territorial auditor, had moved their offices to that city. Further, the commissioners appealed their case to the territorial supreme court, where, because of the sudden death of one of the judges, the Ordway men outnumbered the antiremovalists, and Edgerton's decision was reversed.[93]

Hitherto Ordway appears to have kept Washington convinced, by his elaborate reports of explanation and his long denials, that he was not acting improperly or incorrectly. He consistently pointed out that the Yankton antiremovalists were the same persons who had been the Yankton bond repudiators. He referred to the Pettigrew faction upon all occasions as the members of a corrupt real estate ring. The county organization fights, he explained, were due to the rapidity with which Dakota was being settled, for it was impossible to establish an adequate local government quickly enough to prevent disorders. He was always confident that the only opposition to his administration came from

90. Ibid., pp. 94-101.
91. Ibid., pp. 102-6.
92. *Dakota Herald*, September 15, 1883.
93. Drake, "Influence of the Newspapers," pp. 105-7.

a bunch of soreheads intent upon regaining office or profiting by the organization of a county at a particular time.[94]

After the fall of 1883, explanations were not so easy. Several of the territorial officers, among them the treasurer, refused to move their offices to Bismarck.[95] The territorial supreme court refused to budge, and most important of all, the territorial secretary, James H. Teller, brother to the incumbent Secretary of the Interior, H. M. Teller, declined to change his seat of office.[96] Teller claimed that Ordway could not order him to move; since Teller received his appointment from Washington, an order must come through the federal government. This meant that Ordway would be forced to appeal to Teller's own brother to remove the secretary. The Dakota Territory files in the National Archives also reveal that the Yankton antiremovalists had secretly recommended Secretary Teller as the next territorial governor if statehood was not forthcoming. Thus they gave the secretary a powerful incentive to join the fight against Ordway.[97]

With Dakota's government located in two cities over four hundred miles from one another, Ordway's star was soon in decline. The Secretary of the Interior refused to order his brother to Bismarck, and furthermore, he received specific evidence of Ordway's speculation in county organizations in the early part of 1884. It is interesting to note that Bartlett Tripp, president of the constitutional convention, was the one to prepare this brief against Ordway, a brief which despite its prejudice was both eloquent and damning.[98]

94. Ibid., pp. 115–33; see also the Yankton *Press and Dakotaian,* March 24, 1884. For Ordway's defense of himself see his "Reply," MS, Governor's Files, Bismarck.

95. Drake, p. 105.

96. James H. Teller to H. M. Teller, September 24, 1883; James H. Teller to H. M. Teller, October 2, 1883; Interior Appointment Papers, Dakota (1883), File 200.

97. Application of James H. Teller for the governorship of Dakota, endorsed by Hugh J. Campbell, George H. Hand, John L. Pennington, Alonzo J. Edgerton, Bartlett Tripp, and W. S. Bowen, in Interior Appointment Papers, Dakota (1883), File 164.

98. Tripp's evidence showed that Ordway had turned over county commissions to his son for sale to the highest bidder while the governor was out of the Territory so as not to be involved in the sale directly. Tripp also cited case after case where Ordway had appointed his son as commissioner, or had directed his private secretary to live in a county for two weeks so that he could qualify as a county commissioner. In one instance Ordway made his law partner in Yankton, L. E.

Meanwhile the Citizen's League made an effort to dramatize the injustice of Ordway's methods of county organization by proposing that each new county elect its own commissioners and send their names to the Sioux Falls Constitutional Convention, or to its Executive Committee, which would legalize the action. In July 1883 the *Press and Dakotaian* sought to capitalize on this discontent by announcing, "let every county which has been blackmailed send to the *Press and Dakotaian* written and sworn statements of any corrupt transaction in its organization, and we will print them and see that they also go before the constitutional convention with the proofs in your possession, and Ordway will be punished as well as removed." [99]

While this scheme was not carried out, the evidence mounted steadily against Ordway throughout the winter of 1883–84, and on April 1, 1884, a grand jury again convened in Yankton to consider evidence of irregularities in the organization of Faulk and Hyde counties. The information presented there secured Ordway's indictment for corrupt practices while in office. When the trial began in June, however, Ordway, backed by four lawyers as counsel, moved to quash the indictment on the basis that a federal employee could not be tried by a territorial court. Judge Edgerton, although sympathetic to the indictors, granted this motion and Ordway escaped. [100]

Edgerton's unpopular ruling was still being discussed when the Governor launched his counterattack against Hugh J. Campbell, the wheelhorse of the Citizen's League and the one whom Ordway held personally responsible for his indictment. Ordway wrote

---

Whitcher of New Hampshire, a county commissioner for Hyde County. Tripp also explained how Ordway had refused to permit the residents of Faulk County to organize until they had met his terms. It should be remembered that the governor was under great pressure from townsite boomers who wanted their infant village to become a county seat and who were not above shouting fraud when he refused to cooperate with them to enhance land and town lot prices. Thus some charges against Ordway were probably unfair. Bartlett Tripp to President Chester A. Arthur, received February 25, 1884, Interior Appointment Papers, Dakota (1883), File 164, Nehemiah G. Ordway.

99. Drake, "Influence of the Newspapers," p. 117. Miss Drake is quoting an editorial from the *Press and Dakotaian*, July 24, 1883.

100. A federal investigation later revealed that George Hand, sworn enemy of Ordway, had supplied the grand jury with the evidence that secured his indictment. See above, p. 103 n.

President Arthur: "Hugh J. Campbell, United States Attorney for Dakota Territory, is a malignant personal enemy of Governor Ordway and has maligned and defamed him in the public press and on the stump for more than a year past." [101] Ordway recited no less than twenty charges against Campbell, most of them concerning Campbell's public statements about the governor, a typical one of these being that Ordway had received $30,000 in cash for removing the capital to Bismarck.[102] When the Justice Department investigated the charges, it found that Campbell was indeed guilty of acts based upon enmity and that he had neglected his work as attorney for Dakota Territory in order to prosecute the governor. The investigators also discovered that Campbell was employed in a private capacity by the Chicago and Northwestern Railroad Company, a road which was anxious to defeat the capital removal bill.[103] A favorable jury cleared Campbell of these charges, but the fact remains that he had acted in a highly irregular manner. Meanwhile, the continual flow of protests to Washington finally penetrated the consciousness of enough officials to cause Ordway's removal. On June 25, 1884, President Arthur named Gilbert A. Pierce, a debonair journalist and playwright from Chicago, to succeed him.[104] But the anti-removalists and the statehood forces suffered a defeat too, for Campbell was relieved of his duties as United States Attorney General for Dakota.[105]

The pernicious influence of Ordway was too great to be ended by simply removing him; indeed, the fight against him was to last for six more years. Upon his removal he settled in Bismarck, where he had considerable investments in land and buildings as well as in his Capital National Bank.[106] He was still popular

101. N. G. Ordway to President Arthur, May 12, 1884, Justice Appointment Papers, Dakota (1884), N. G. Ordway File.

102. Ibid.

103. The Justice Department sent two examiners, Alexander Boteler and William Haight, to investigate the charges against Campbell. Their findings were contained in a report submitted to the Attorney General, August 28, 1884, Justice Appointment Papers (1884), Dakota, H. J. Campbell File.

104. Kingsbury, *Dakota Territory*, 2, 1345.

105. Drake, "Influence of the Newspapers," pp. 140–3. Miss Drake has stated that Campbell was guilty of none of Ordway's charges. The Dakota Territorial Papers in Washington indicate that he was guilty of all the charges. See above, n. 103.

106. Grand Forks *Herald*, September 19, 1932.

in northern Dakota political circles, and he kept up his valuable contacts in Washington, where he appeared from time to time as a lobbyist for the Northern Pacific. Like ex-Governors Pennington, Faulk, and Edmunds, he had invested so heavily in Dakota that he decided to make it his home.

The conclusion is inescapable that Ordway was one of the most corrupt officials ever to appear in Dakota. He was an excellent example of the cynical post-Civil War politician who brought the political morality of the country to such a low level between 1865 and 1900.

Just as Ordway had organized a press association for political purposes, the anti-Ordway press was now so organized that after the governor's removal it sought to defeat every legislator from southern Dakota who had voted for capital removal when the campaign for the election of the 1885 Assembly took place. Not only were they successful in this—every removalist but one from southern Dakota was turned out of office—but the 1885 Assembly held up the appropriations for the building of the new capital at Bismarck and they refused to accept the report by the capital commission which placed the capital at Bismarck. The 1885 Assembly, bent upon complete revenge, passed a bill locating the capital at Pierre, but Governor Pierce, who was suspected throughout his term of office as a secret minion of the Northern Pacific, vetoed the Pierre bill, and the question rested there for a time.[107]

The capital removal fight was not actually settled until the legislative session of 1887 agreed to leave the capital at Bismarck and appropriate funds to relieve the considerably embarrassed commissioners. Thus virtual anarchy among the territorial offices was ended. Ordway's enemies, the Yankton men, had lost the battle, but by making the territorial system seem corrupt, they bettered their own prospects in the political field: for from 1883 until statehood came in 1889 the southern Dakotans controlled the office of delegate and, in large measure, the Assembly.[108]

Out of the chaotic state of politics during the boom years of 1880–83 the ultimate dislike of the territorial system in Dakota developed, and the final forging of a disciplined professional

107. Drake, pp. 151–64.
108. Ibid.

group of politicians, acting unquestioningly within the Republican party's ranks, took place. The party had come to be more than a large faction; it had, such as it was, an ideology; it had a policy toward such questions as railroad regulations or banking laws and school lands. Its members discussed, albeit reluctantly, the social issues of the day, such as prohibition, woman suffrage, and minority party representation.

Ironically, the territorial system, which the local Republican party was now pledged to end, had furnished nearly every leader of the statehood forces; the system had been, in fact, responsible for the party's success in Dakota's tempestuous political history. The American territorial system was deliberately designed to carry in itself the seeds of its own eventual destruction, and had certainly done just this in Dakota. The obviously corrupt Ordway regime, fattening upon the political and speculative schemes which could be foisted upon a rapidly expanding region whose institutions were still physically mobile, helped to produce this hatred of colonial status, but the distaste was furthered by the old guard who had been removed from office, by the reformer who wanted new laws, and by the intellectual wing of the statehood movement, who felt a sincere political and inferiority complex and who deliberately strove to make this feeling general so that the cause of statehood would be advanced.

The fierceness of the fight, the largeness of the stakes, and the nature of the issues, i.e. the physical location of institutions, whether they were capital or normal school, insane asylum or old soldiers' home, the organization of a county or the control of patronage, indicated that Dakota was still a political frontier in many ways. Yet characteristics of the East were coming in. The Ordway-McKenzie ring with its efficient political machine, its powerful out-of-territory connections, and its dangerous press organizations employed the same methods that Ordway had known and used in his Washington jobberies and in New Hampshire, while the reformers reflected the same techniques and approaches to the issues of prohibition and woman suffrage that had been used in the East.

Perhaps the most impressive fact was that both sides, whether corrupt or honest, were traditional in their political efforts, and most classic of all, the Yankton oligarchy, reduced to a political minority by the geography of an expanding political and economic frontier, resorted to that familiar pattern of asserting states' rights and secession of a sort just as so many other sections of the nation had threatened to do throughout the whole of American history, when they had felt that they suffered from supposed or true federal tyranny. The political originality of the Dakotans lay in the logic that they would escape federal tyranny by entering the federal union, not by getting out of it!

Chapter 8. Attempted Revolution; the Statehood

Movement: 1885–89

> *Gjermund:* The Republicans are arming to the teeth, they got a sly
> old fox for leader, and they're going to put on a campaign the
> like of which you've never seen before. For them its a question
> of life or death; they're ready to spend no end of money. Doubt-
> less they'll win. . . . Tell me, just where do you stand?
>
> *Peder:* Of all the parties, the Populists are advocating the most sweep-
> ing reforms; they've a great program. For that reason—
>
> *Gjermund:* For that reason you should stay clear of them! . . . The
> great progressive ideas never win out overnight; they must fight
> long-drawn-out battles. It is always that way, for the masses are
> too slow-moving; among them new ideas germinate slowly. When
> a progressive measure wins out it is usually being pushed through
> by the conservative cud-chewers; by that time the idea is nc
> longer new. *Ole Rölvaag* [1]

It would be a conservative estimate to say that less than two
hundred men achieved statehood for North and South Dakota in
1889, and that of these two hundred only a dozen possessed any
true political popularity. What is more, the twelve were all from
southern Dakota, all of them were in the Republican party, and
with few exceptions they lacked any altruistic motives in their
struggle for statehood. They hid their motives, in fact, and in
such a way as to suggest that they had little faith in the electorate.
Many of the statehood leaders were undoubtedly honest men,
and it is true that reformers such as General Beadle, the Reverend
Joseph Ward, and the Socialist Catholic priest Father Robert
Haire supported the statehood men in their cause. But the fact
remains that most of the leaders were peculiarly untouched or
unimpressed by any radical political ideas or any program of
social reform which were being considered throughout the
country between 1880 and 1900.

The one great exception among the leaders of this small group

1. *Their Fathers' God* (New York, 1931), p. 294. By permission of Harper and
Brothers.

was Hugh J. Campbell, the author of the "we are a state" hypothesis, prosecutor of the Dakota Indian rings and arch opponent of Governor Ordway. It was Campbell's theory which has given the above-mentioned two hundred men the reputation of being political rebels who harbored new ideas about state sovereignty and who were prepared to defy Congress by establishing a squatter state government. A close scrutiny of the facts will reveal that none of these things was true. Campbell himself eventually discovered that both he and his theory (which he passionately believed in) had been used by the statehood forces without either ever having been taken seriously. And when the man and his idea had served their purpose, they were abandoned without so much as a vote of thanks.

Campbell's genuine indignation over the injustice of 500,000 Americans being forced to live under the territorial system in Dakota was useful because he could sway the voter. The Bismarck *Tribune* correctly called him the "wheel horse" of the whole statehood movement. Possessing some of the zeal and fervor which one might attribute to an Old Testament prophet, Campbell could tongue lash the most unenthusiastic audience into a frenzy over the supposed tyranny of territorial government. Although his first great ambition was to be one of the first senators from South Dakota, this was not the only motive behind his ceaseless efforts to achieve statehood. It is little wonder that he grew bitter and joined the Farmers' Alliance movement in 1890 when his own party passed him by.[2]

The small group who brought about statehood has been mentioned at various times previously as the Yankton oligarchy, the professional politicians either in or out of office, and the business and professional men of the Territory. By 1885 they were almost as distinct as an economic, social, and political class, and they considered themselves so. They spoke of themselves as being the 20 per cent of the Dakota population who were not the farmers. Most of them had migrated from the northern tier of the United States, with the majority perhaps being from New England, New York, and the Old Northwest. Socially, morally, and intellectually they were middle class in their beliefs and habits. Ethnically

2. Kingsbury, *Dakota Territory*, 2, 1883–4.

they were Old American, religiously they were Protestant, and with a few major exceptions they were Republican. They were family men who lived in the scores of small towns in Dakota. Some of them worked for the railroads, some owned grain elevators. Many of them were bankers, for Dakota at this time was an investor's paradise. Quite a few were editors, for Dakota had over 350 newspapers during the 1880's.[3] A large majority, however, were lawyers interested in a half-dozen businesses other than that of law. A great number were members of the G.A.R., an organization very active in Dakota politics during the late 1880's.[4] Needless to say, all of these men were interested in politics. The statement, "the business of government is business" explains most aptly their political philosophy, for long after the conviction had disappeared that Dakota needed government subsidy to exist, businessmen continued to see government as a wing of the business structure of the Territory.

Politically, these two hundred or so men were ubiquitous. They were in the territorial Assembly; they held local county offices; they controlled the office of delegate during the last four years before statehood by sending Oscar S. Gifford, a Yankton lawyer and wholesale liquor dealer to Congress for two terms.[5] These men dominated the Republican party conventions; they wrote the Sioux Falls Constitution of 1883 and its successors in 1885 and 1889. In the scores of business and political conventions and in the G.A.R. encampments their names appear as constants between 1880 and 1890. When it is recalled that the Territory was undergoing a fabulous population growth—from 135,000 to 500,000 during these ten years—the fact that the oligarchy managed to retain political and economic control of part of the Territory is a remarkable tribute to their ability. In this highly unstable decade they also managed to hold the rapidly increasing number of German and Scandinavian voters in line without sacrificing any major office to them.

One of the major figures of this statehood group was Judge

3. O. S. Gifford, statement to House Committee on Territories, February 1, 1888, in *Admission of Dakota* (Washington, 1888), pp. 4–5.

4. St. Paul *Pioneer Press*, March 30, 1889. At a G.A.R. convention held in Dakota in 1889 Governor Mellette, Representative Kanouse, Senator Moody, Judge Edgerton, ex-Delegate Gifford, and many other prominent officials attended.

5. Robinson, *Encyclopedia of South Dakota*, p. 323.

Alonzo J. Edgerton, formerly a United States Senator from Minnesota. Like Campbell, Edgerton aspired to be a senator from southern Dakota. He represented the conservative branch of the Yankton oligarchy in the statehood movement, and his connections in Washington with Senator Windom of Minnesota made him a valuable man for the cause. As chief justice of the Territory between 1881 and 1885 he lent the needed prestige of his office to the statehood forces.

More capable than Edgerton but equally conservative was the veteran politician Colonel Gideon C. Moody, the vigorous ex-leader of the Broadway Gang, formerly a member of the territorial supreme court and now a successful lawyer for the giant Homestake Mining Company in the Black Hills. Backed by his employer, Senator George Hearst of California, and retaining his political connections, Moody had become the political boss of the Black Hills as well as one of the central figures in Dakota politics for a decade. Like Edgerton, however, his goal was the United States Senate.[6]

The most elusive of the leaders of the statehood cause was Arthur C. Mellette, a relative newcomer from Indiana. Mellette, it appears, was a friend of Senator Benjamin Harrison and the representative of several Indiana investors who were interested in Dakota as a field for profitable speculation. To carry out these schemes, Harrison secured Mellette's appointment as United States land officer in the newly settled town of Watertown, Dakota. Harrison's sudden interest in the cause of statehood for Dakota coincided with Mellette's arrival in Watertown.[7] It is interesting to note, too, that Harrison's Senate fight for Dakota's admission kept his name before the nation in the years preceding his election to the presidency, while Mellette's espousal of the same cause in Dakota netted him the position of territorial governor when Harrison became president in 1889. When South Dakota was admitted in the fall of 1889, Mellette became its first governor.[8]

6. See sketch of Moody in Kingsbury, *Dakota Territory*, 2, 1919 ff.

7. The most complete source of information on Mellette is his personal correspondence between 1886 and 1893, which is deposited in the State Department of History, Pierre, South Dakota. This remarkable collection consists of some 5,000 or more letters, most of them dealing with political matters (Mellette Papers).

8. Robinson, *Encyclopedia of South Dakota*, p. 514.

Mellette, like his colleagues, had a hand in a half-dozen businesses. He soon resigned from the land office to establish a private land business of his own, which proved to be prosperous. Later, he became president of a Watertown bank and of a local railroad as well.[9]

Mellette's political genius seemed to lie in party organization and in secret manipulation. He kept tabs on every part of the Territory for some five years before he became governor. Some five thousand letters in his personal correspondence tell an eloquent inside story of the fractious Republican party machine between 1886 and 1891, and Mellette's success in keeping the most bumptious small-town politicians in line is impressive. From these letters it is also apparent that Mellette had important connections in Washington besides those with Harrison and the Indiana delegation.[10] Yet from this pile of first-hand material, little can be gleaned about Mellette as a personality, for while he was very popular during the statehood agitation and possessed a reputation for honesty, he still remains a sphinxlike politician who, like McKenzie, preferred the secret maneuver to the public one.

A description of the vanguard of the statehood forces would not be complete without new mention of Richard F. Pettigrew, Republican boss of the Big Sioux Valley, chief boomer of the prosperous town of Sioux Falls, and owner of perhaps the largest real estate business in Dakota. More open than Mellette or Edgerton, Pettigrew had contributed materially to Governor Ordway's political downfall by joining forces with the Yankton oligarchy to fight for statehood and for his own election to the United States Senate. His virulent invective and his savage attacks upon any political opponent were to help the statehood forces in vote getting.[11]

These five men, Campbell, Moody, Edgerton, Mellette, and Pettigrew, with their personal following secured statehood for North and South Dakota and office for themselves. That Moody

9. See letter of Perry S. Heath, resident correspondent of the Indianapolis *Journal* in Washington, to Mellette, 1886–93, in which Heath discusses land speculation projects with the Governor. See especially, Heath to Mellette, May 12, 1890, Mellette Papers.

10. Mellette Papers.

11. See sketch of Pettigrew in Robinson, *Encyclopedia of South Dakota*, p. 584.

and Pettigrew were the first senators from South Dakota, that Mellette was the first governor, and that Edgerton was given a consolation prize by being appointed judge of the United States Circuit Court for South Dakota, is not surprising. Only Campbell failed to secure a just reward for his work.

The fight for statehood was a stirring one. Its telling contributes substantially to an understanding of Dakota politics as well as to a better comprehension of some facets of national politics between 1880 and 1890. The statehood fight explains, too, many things about the great unrest that shook the Plains Northwest and the whole nation in the form of the later Alliance and Populist movements. The Dakota struggle also reflected similar struggles in Montana, Utah, Washington, New Mexico, and Wyoming for statehood; consequently, Dakota serves as a valuable case study of a political agitation that extended over the whole trans-Mississippi West. Finally, the statehood fight was to exhibit to the nation the first post-Civil War practice of states' rights principles as weapons to fight the federal government.

Governor Ordway had been removed only six months when a new obstacle appeared to block the path to statehood: the Democratic party, which came into power for the first time in twenty-five years with Cleveland's election in 1884. The Democratic Congress of 1885 naturally opposed the admission of southern Dakota as a state, since it would undoubtedly send two Republican senators to Washington. And should the Territory be divided into two states—which is what the southern Dakotans wanted fully as much as statehood—that would mean a possible four Republican senators plus several new Republican votes in the House and in the electoral college. The most ringing appeal to patriotic duty could not erase these statistics from the Democrats' minds.

While President Cleveland tried to avoid the appointment of spoilsmen and unpopular hacks to the major territorial positions, it is true that Democratic congressmen were enjoying the pleasure of placing Democrats in territorial offices. The possibility of creating federally subsidized Democratic machines in the territories was soon under consideration, for it is an often overlooked fact that Congress, by virtue of the territorial system, had direct control over one-half of the trans-Mississippi West from 1860 to 1890 and that they dispersed patronage for no less than nine territories during these years.[12]

In Dakota the change in administration brought many repudiated figures back into prominence along with the patronage-starved local Democrats. Ex-Governor Ordway appeared in Washington as a Democratic lobbyist for various Bismarck political and business interests and for the Northern Pacific Railroad. He was particularly anxious to hinder the statehood movement, since Bismarck wished to remain the territorial capital of a large Dakota. His position was supported by the Northern Pacific for the obvious reason that railroads possessed greater freedom under the territorial system.[13]

There was the chance that a few more years of Democratic rule would place northern Dakota in the Democratic column politically. Not only was Ordway and nearly every ex-member of his administration willing to cross party lines, but a sizable portion of the northern Dakota wheat farmers were Canadians who had joined the Democratic party because it, like Canada, advocated low tariff and free trade principles.[14] The Bismarck ring, led by McKenzie, had never been organized on a party basis, so that it was particularly free to join the Democratic ranks.

To the above factions could be added the regular Democrats in Dakota who for the first time since Andrew Johnson were tasting the sweet fruits of appointive office. It was natural that these men, guided by the Cleveland appointees, Governor Louis Kossuth Church, a New York lawyer and friend of James J. Hill of the Great Northern, and Secretary Michael L. McCormack, a member of the Bismarck ring, should not favor statehood. On the other hand, the newly appointed chief justice, Bartlett Tripp; M. H.

12. Pomeroy, *The Territories and the United States*, pp. 70-2.
13. Ibid., p. 105. See also Kingsbury, *Dakota Territory*, 2, 1404.
14. H. C. Hansbrough to Mellette, Devil's Lake, Dakota, May 21, 1889, Mellette Papers: "I am told that the Democratic National Committee is already engaged in sending large quantities of free trade literature to this region, and they are using the Democratic Postmasters and other Democratic office holders as agents to circulate this obnoxious and dangerous political pabulum. The northern portion of this half of Dakota is thickly settled by Canadians who brought their free trade ideas with them and who continue to sing 'God Save the Queen.' "

Day, Democratic leader of the Black Hills; and Maris Taylor, the outspoken editor of the *Dakota Herald* led another wing of the party which felt it had so little in common with its northern colleagues that it joined the Republicans in advocating statehood for southern Dakota.[15] This split was an indication, incidentally, that geographic sectionalism in Dakota was still a stronger sentiment than loyalty to party. But while a split existed in the local Democratic party, the statehood forces nevertheless had to deal with the united hostility of the national Democratic party in Congress.

The new strategy of the statehood forces took the form of a petition to the Assembly of 1885 which asked for a new state constitutional convention for southern Dakota. The Citizen's League (which changed its name to the Statehood League in 1886) wrote the petition and gathered an impressive list of signers, including the chairmen of both major parties. The Assembly lost no time in providing for the new convention, and Governor Pierce, who had not yet been replaced by Church, approved the measure.[16]

Sioux Falls, which seemed destined to be the cradle for new governments in Dakota, was the scene of the second constitutional convention. It met in September at the height of the harvesting season, so that few of the rural population could afford to be there, a fact that one of the delegates pointed out during a debate over methods of creating a favorable sentiment for the new document.[17] The delegates were in many cases the same men who had appeared at the extralegal convention of 1883.[18] The controlling forces were also the same, and the election of Judge Edgerton to the chair assured the inner circle that their leadership was unchallenged.[19]

The 1885 convention was more concerned with methods to assure the popular ratification of their handiwork than they were with writing a new constitution. They fully approved of retaining

15. Kingsbury, *Dakota Territory*, 2, 1404.
16. Ibid., pp. 1727–31.
17. *Dakota Constitutional Convention, 1885, 1,* 647.
18. For a list of the 1883 delegates see ibid., pp. 7–8, and for a list of the 1885 delegates, see pp. 45–46 and p. 58.
19. Ibid., p. 58.

their 1883 document, with only a few minor changes. Thus their work as a constitution-making body was virtually complete before they met. The two problems they faced were to find a method which would force Congress to grant statehood, and to find some way for handling the touchy issues dragged in by the reformers.

The first of these issues to arise was that of prohibition. Theodore Kanouse, John A. Owen, and the Reverend Joseph Ward, the secular and religious leaders of the antiliquor forces, had been elected to the convention with the object of including a prohibition clause in the proposed constitution or at least securing a territorial vote upon the question. As in 1883, the convention voted overwhelmingly to submit the question to the voters separately from the constitution itself.[20]

The delegates also gave short shrift to a Democratic proposal that provisions for minority representation be included in the 1885 document, but to capture the Democratic voter they agreed to submit this issue separately. The woman suffragists and the advocates of the initiative and referendum got only a hearing, however.[21]

Actually the members of the convention were conservative in their treatment of nearly every new question. In a blast at woman suffrage Colonel Moody, the dominant figure at the session, set the general tone of the debates when he said, "We have got to pass the gauntlet of all criticism of our enemies, powerful here, but still more powerful out of this commonwealth. Let us be prudent; let us be conservative; let us make liberal provision for submitting all these provisions to the people when the time comes. But let us try no new untried experiments now." [22]

Moody's outburst boded ill for the Campbellites who had come to Sioux Falls prepared to force Congress to make them a state by having the convention declare southern Dakota to be a state, to elect a state government, and to have it assume the attributes of a sovereign state within the Union. The Campbellites would set this

20. Ibid., pp. 194, 326.
21. Hicks, "The Constitution of the Northwest States," pp. 48–9; *Dakota Constitutional Convention, 1885, 1,* 382. An excellent summary of the initiative and referendum exists in B. E. Tiffany, "The Initiative and Referendum in South Dakota," *Collections of the State Historical Society of South Dakota, 12* (1924), 331–71.
22. *Dakota Constitutional Convention, 1885, 1,* 403.

STATEHOOD!

Ex-Chief Justice Shannon and Hon. W. A. Burleigh of Yankton, will address the people of Lincoln county at Bedford hall on Saturday, Oct. 27th 1883 afternoon and evening. Come and hear these eminent gentlemen expose the RAILROAD CONSTITUTION of the Sioux Falls convention.

—— ALL ARE INVITED. ——

Announcement of a rally of the anti-statehood forces in Southern Dakota in 1883

new governmental machinery in motion alongside the territorial government. Only then, Campbell declared, would Congress listen to reason. Campbell's ability to sway the delegates with his oratory hung like a pall of fear over the Moody-Edgerton faction throughout the session, but the debates reached their only tense moment when the two groups met in basic disagreement over the preamble to the constitution. Campbell wanted the preamble to include as one of the fundamental privileges of the people of the future state the right to "alter, reform or abolish their form of government in such a manner as they may think proper." [23]

To prevent the inclusion of such a radical statement, President Edgerton himself descended from the chair to oppose it.[24] Dakotans, he exclaimed, did not wish to enter the Union as rebels. But fire-eating speeches from Campbell so aroused the delegates that at first they refused to change the wording, and Delegate McCallum, an outspoken suffragist, protested in a moving speech that "if we have to go into the Union on our knees, let us stay out." [25] Under the influence of Campbell's oratory the convention voted to keep in the offending word "abolish" in the preamble. Yet before adjournment the conservatives somehow managed to secure its removal.[26]

The second phase of the Campbell-conservative struggle came over the feasibility of electing a state government when the voters went to the polls to approve the 1885 constitution. The conservatives agreed that it would be a dramatic move which would appeal to the voter. They also believed that a people's mandate would be the best method of persuading Congress to admit the state. But they did not agree with Campbell that unless a "real" state government were elected and statehood granted, "revolution" would occur. Again the conservatives compromised by allowing a state roster of officers to be elected, but made only vague provision for their function.[27] What they aimed to do was to assert Campbell's principles without ever practicing them. More than anything else, the debate over the use of Campbell's plan clearly

23. Ibid., pp. 347 ff.
24. Kingsbury, *Dakota Territory*, 2, 1739.
25. Ibid., p. 1741.
26. Ibid., p. 1742.
27. *Dakota Constitutional Convention, 1885, 1,* 634 ff.

revealed the true nature of the statehood movement. When Delegate Dollard rose to deny that Dakotans were on the "verge of revolution," it was evident that he was right. "It is a fact that they have taken so little interest in this movement that not to exceed one in ten, as I am informed, have cast their votes for the Delegates to this Convention, and that a great majority of them do not know now that the Convention is in session. Is that evidence that the people are on the verge of revolution?" [28] Delegate Owen, a prohibition chief, rose to concur, and added, "Why you could not arouse the people of these prairies to revolution any more than you could lift a ten-ton pile-driver with a knitting needle." [29] Asserting only the principles of Campbell's theories, the Convention adjourned in good spirits after the sergeant-at-arms, a good baritone, had sung "Marching Through Georgia" to the pleased delegates.[30]

A month later the same delegates met again, but this time in the guise of the "State Republican Party Convention." They nominated a complete roster of candidates for state and congressional office. In most instances the candidates coincided with the delegates, and it was not surprising to find that Arthur C. Mellette was their choice for governor.[31]

In November 1885 the Dakota voters south of the forty-sixth parallel went to the polls to approve a state constitution for the second time. On this occasion they also elected a state government, barely approved of prohibition, and roundly defeated minority representation. As in 1883, nevertheless, the vote was too light to be called a people's mandate, for only 31,000 had voted and nearly 7,000 of these had been cast against the constitution and statehood.[32]

The slight vote did not stop the statehood forces from convening the "State Legislature" in December 1885 at Huron, the new "state capital." "Governor" Mellette, who had been elected without opposition, addressed the body on the justice of their

28. Ibid., p. 647.
29. Ibid., p. 653.
30. Ibid., p. 658.
31. For a list of the candidates for office in 1885, see ibid., p. 45; see also the Bismarck *Tribune*, October 22 and 23, 1885, for more details about the election and the platform proposed by the statehood forces.
32. Kingsbury, *Dakota Territory*, 2, 1752–3.

actions. While arguing that the state must be recognized, Mellette labored heavily to distinguish between their act of sovereignty and that of the secessionists in 1861.

> The only possible argument against the case we present to Congress is that the Civil War materially changed the construction of the Constitution and modified the traditions of American law as to the relation sustained by the states to the Federal Government. It is urged that every precedent upon which we predicate our case is antebellum construction of our unwritten Constitution obliterated by the blood of that awful sacrifice. Upon careful examination, however, we discover that our issue is not involved in or related to the questions settled by the Civil War.[33]

As weak as Mellette's defense was, the legislators of the "State of Dakota" were undoubtedly reassured that they were not rebels, for they promptly elected Edgerton and Moody to the United States Senate. It was ironic that after defending Campbell's theory, Mellette, Moody, Edgerton, and the conservatives joined forces to prevent Campbell's election as a senator because they feared that his outspoken nature would harm the cause in Washington.[34] And now, having gone as far as they dared, the "State of Dakota" left the next move up to Congress.

The same week that the "Legislature of the State of Dakota" met, the Senate took up the question of admission. The senators were soon divided along party and sectional lines. Already a candidate for the Republican nomination for the presidency in 1888, the dignified senator from Indiana, Benjamin Harrison, rose to introduce a bill for the admission of Dakota on the basis of the Sioux Falls Constitution.[35] When the Senate got around to considering the bill in January 1886, Mathew C. Butler of South Carolina and G. G. Vest of Missouri, both members of the Senate Committee on Territories, voiced their opposition. Vest manifested a particular interest in the Campbell theory of states' rights. Was not this the same Campbell who had been instrumental in

33. Ibid., p. 1759.
34. Ibid., pp. 1759 ff.; see also the Bismarck *Tribune*, December 22, 1885.
35. *Cong. Record*, 49th Cong., 1st sess. (December 15, 1885), p. 179.

swinging the Louisiana electoral votes to the Republican side in the Hayes-Tilden contest of 1876, asked the Missouri senator? Was not Campbell now occupied at another task of a dubious and obviously partisan nature? Was not the election of senators by the Dakota state legislature without congressional permission an expression of state sovereignty? [36]

These questions launched a debate which lasted into February 1886 and produced only one tangible result: a Democratically sponsored bill to make Dakota Territory a single state. Butler of South Carolina introduced this Democratic answer to the Dakotans and the Cleveland administration did not materially deviate from it for the next four years. There is some evidence that ex-Governor Ordway was a friend of Senator Butler's and had drawn the one-state bill for the South Carolinian. There is evidence, too, indicating that Ordway had filled Butler with hopes that four years of well-placed patronage in Dakota might change the color of the Territory's politics.[37]

The Butler bill received small support, however, and on February 6 Harrison's admission bill passed the Senate by a vote of thirty-two to twenty-two. Despite the fact that only one Democrat had voted for the Harrison proposal, and oblivious to the fact that it had run the gauntlet of a Democratic House, the statehood forces in Dakota became intensely optimistic. Edgerton, Moody, Kanouse, and Mellette journeyed to Washington to impress President Cleveland with the justice of their cause. Cleveland's noncommittal attitude appears to have made them even more optimistic, and anxious to put the best construction on their actions they confided to the president that they were not Campbellite states' righters. Cleveland seemed to react favorably to this piece of information, so that the Moody-Edgerton faction returned to Dakota with glowing reports of impending success.[38]

Then their optimism began to wane. The House Committee on Territories refused to report the Harrison bill; a number of northern Dakota politicians, undoubtedly inspired by McKenzie, held a convention at Fargo to endorse Senator Butler's one-state bill;

36. Ibid. (December 18, 1885), pp. 302 ff. It is true that Campbell had been involved in the Louisiana election disputes in 1876.

37. Kingsbury, *Dakota Territory*, 2, 1765 ff.

38. Ibid., pp. 1778 ff.

the expected appointment of F. M. Ziebach, a territorial resident, a divisionist, and a statehood Democrat, as territorial governor did not occur.[39] Instead, Cleveland chose Louis Kossuth Church, a one-state proponent who had close connections with the Bismarck ring.[40] Bitterness and indecision arose in the ranks of the statehood men. In May the constitutional convention reconvened, and in a furious session the Campbell and Edgerton wings accused one another of ruining the chances for success. This time the Campbellites won out when the convention agreed to continue the existence of the provisional state government.[41]

From Washington, however, came danger signals. Delegate Gifford wrote Mellette that the action of the convention was playing into the hands of the Democrats. "Senators Harrison and Edmunds are a good deal exercised over the late and prospective action of our constitutional convention. They say that this course if persisted in and carried out will certainly defeat division. They can't stand it and that is the whole story. . . . Vest, Butler et al . . . . claimed we would take these very steps."[42]

From Campbell, Mellette heard another version of where the danger lay. Dakota had not presented a firm enough front to Congress, Campbell wrote, for

> . . . when Edgerton made his pompous windy speech to Cleveland and took occasion to assure him that we would do nothing of the kind, he gave away the whole case. The —— vanity of the man, is only excelled by his mountainous imbecility. He is the best Falstaff both in belly, wind and cowardice I have ever seen off the stage. He is unlike Falstaff, however, in his utter poverty of ideas.[43]

39. Ibid., p. 1783; for an account of the Fargo convention, see pp. 1776–8. Ziebach was a tremendously popular figure in Dakota, and had he been made governor, Dakota might have consented to come in as a single state with the Democratic party in power. See his huge file of endorsements in Interior Appointment Papers, Dakota (1885), File 235, F. M. Ziebach.

40. Kingsbury, *Dakota Territory*, 2, 1458.

41. Ibid., pp. 1783–4.

42. O. S. Gifford to A. C. Mellette, Washington, May 17, 1886; Mellette Papers.

43. H. J. Campbell to A. C. Mellette, Yankton, February 16, 1886; Mellette Papers.

As angry as he was, Campbell was correct in his analysis of the Washington situation. The Dakotans in protesting privately to Cleveland—and undoubtedly to leading Democratic senators —that they would not carry out Campbell's plan but would only espouse it, gave away the game. The House Committee on Territories therefore did not trouble to report the Harrison bill until just before adjournment in June 1886, and even then it was reported adversely.[44]

It was a chastened and unenthusiastic state Legislature that met in Huron the following December to hear Mellette speak again on the difference between secession and admission principles, for the congressional debates had returned again and again to the similarity between the two. Still fearing to pass laws or to activate their paper government in any way, the legislators began to slip away from Huron, and within a few days, no quorum being present, adjournment was necessary.[45] This lack of spirit greatly depressed Campbell, who had wanted Mellette to persuade the legislature to pass laws and defy the territorial officials. Only by these acts, he said, could Dakotans "startle the Democratic party into action and revive the Kansas fight."[46] But the statehood men had no stomach for such talk. The Democrats in Congress, it seemed, had won the second round.

The statehood forces began their third campaign in February 1887 when they persuaded the territorial Assembly to call for a ballot on division of the Territory in November of that year.[47] The suggestion for this new approach appears to have come from W. S. Bowen, whose paper, the Yankton *Press and Dakotaian* was wholeheartedly devoted to the Campbellite wing of the statehood movement. In a letter to a statehood supporter, Bowen urged that all the latent northern Dakota sentiment for division be developed. Fight the influence of the Northern Pacific, he

44. Kingsbury, *Dakota Territory,* 2, 1768.
45. Ibid., pp. 1788 ff.
46. H. J. Campbell to Augustine Davis, December 26, 1886, MS letters concerning statehood deposited in the State Department of History, Pierre, South Dakota (Statehood Papers).
47. For a history of the entire division movement in Dakota up to 1888 see the Bismarck *Tribune,* December 28, 1887.

declared, by persuading the Manitoba Railroad (the Great Northern) that division would be a blow at the power of its rival, the
Northern Pacific. The Statehood League must print and scatter
pamphlets by the "thousands and tens of thousands," Bowen
wrote.

> The foreign element need attention. A simple demonstra-
> tion of economy of our proposed statehood over the large
> state and the economy of statehood over territorial govern-
> ment, together with an explanation of the designs of the
> Northern Pacific printed in Scandinavian, German, and
> Bohemian, and well circulated would gain us thousands of
> votes. These people believe that the big state or the terri-
> tory costs less than the small state and are impervious to
> any other argument. I have urged this upon Campbell, but
> it has no fruits. We need to prepare to vote down a consti-
> tution of the whole.[48]

The division convention which met in June 1887 was controlled
by Campbell, Ward, Mellette, Edgerton, Pettigrew, and Kanouse,
but they had consented to follow Bowen's proposals of the preceding year, and as a result new faces dotted the convention hall.
M. H. Day, a leading Democratic divisionist from the Black Hills,
was there. Father Robert Haire, the radical Catholic priest who
advocated socialism, was a delegate. T. H. Conniff, a member of
the fast-growing Farmers' Alliance, had come. Representatives
of the foreign segments of the population were included.[49] With
Campbell at its head, the convention planned a thorough campaign. Northern Dakota political leaders were to be urged to
turn out the vote in their section for division, and unlike the
statehood vote of 1885, which was cast only in counties below
the forty-sixth parallel, this ballot would be territory wide.[50]

The vote on the division question in November 1887 gave the
statehood leaders the shock of their lives. Northern Dakota voted
18,000 to 8,000 against division, and though the majority for division in southern Dakota was over 14,000, 15,000 had declared

48. W. S. Bowen to Augustine Davis, June 1886, Statehood Papers.
49. Kingsbury, *Dakota Territory*, 2, 1801–8.
50. See the report of the "Committee on Plan of Campaign" quoted in Kingsbury, *Dakota Territory*, 2, 1803–4.

for no division.[51] This unexpected turn of events led the divisionist leaders to vehement outbursts against the treacherous Northern Pacific and the incumbent Democrats, but to no avail. Bowen wrote disconsolately to a fellow editor, "The opposition of the democracy is considerable and almost every democratic office holder is an agent of Church and the N.P. [Northern Pacific] in their admission as a whole efforts." [52] "It is time the Divisionists were moving," wailed Charles T. Hackett, editor of the Turner County *New Era.* "They slept all over the territory on election day while the Edwards, the McKenzies and Johnsons and Sheafes and Boyntons were stealthily fixing an anti-vote." [53]

The single-state advocates took so much heart at the vote, in fact, that they promptly called a convention of their own at Aberdeen, Dakota, to oppose division and to back the Butler bill in Congress. Supported by Governor Church and all the Democratic officials, by ex-Governors Pennington and Ordway, and by Ordway's secretary, L. G. Johnson, as well as by all of the Ordway editors, the single staters presented a powerful block to any divisionist or two-state plans.[54] Once again the statehood forces had been checked on the home front and once again the scene of action moved to Washington.

To combat the growth of any more sentiment for the one-state idea, Delegate Gifford presented bills for the organization of two states out of Dakota Territory at the next session of Congress. The idea of urging statehood only for southern Dakota had at last been abandoned in favor of a two-state admission fight. The

51. Ibid., pp. 1809-10.
52. W. S. Bowen to Augustine Davis, November 23, 1887, Statehood Papers.
53. Charles T. Hackett to Augustine Davis, November 23, 1887, Statehood Papers. "Where are Mellete, Davis, Miller, Ward, Diggs, Campbell, Edgerton, et al?" Hackett asked. "I tell you I am a Divisionist from the ground up—division is the apple of my eye. I'd rather live ten years longer in a territory than go in as one state. But—

"But the people here even are tired of territorialhood. They are growing uneasy. Some are talking of accepting one state if we can get nothing better. They are being bluffed. They want Division as badly as we do. But you know noise and blare have attractions! The people like a bold leadership. The only bold leadership just now is the brassy one-state move." Ibid.

54. Bismarck *Tribune,* December 16, 1887. Campbell welcomed an active move on the part of the opposition. "As an organized development of the elements opposed to Division viz—the old Ordway gang, the N. P. RR., the McKenzie-Edwards outfit, the Democratic office-holders, and the Aberdeen local interests, I rather welcome it." Campbell to Augustine Davis, December 1, 1887, Statehood Papers.

same forces were again drawn into conflict, however, Senators Butler and Vest leading the fight against a two-state plan, while Harrison, now joined by Platt of Connecticut, backed the Gifford bills.[55]

It was in the course of these debates that the Senate first heard a public explanation of the motives of the single-staters in Dakota. Cushman Davis of Minnesota correctly exposed Ordway's reasons for opposing the two-state idea. He also explained the true purpose of the Aberdeen convention and by these statements impugned the validity of the administration's arguments against admission. Even so, 1888 was a presidential election year, and neither party expected to force action on the Dakota question until after the November results were known. The issue played a part in the election itself, however, for the Republicans included as one of the national platform planks the admission of North and South Dakota and any other eligible territories as soon as possible. The Democrats renewed their support of the increasingly suspect one-state plan.[56]

In Dakota hopes were again rising. The country was now interested in the admission question as it had never been before. Eastern newspapers carried stories of the struggle.[57] The "we are a state" idea of Campbell's had attracted the attention of at least one prominent scholar, John W. Burgess of Columbia University, who wrote after reading a speech by Mellette:

> The fundamental error which your pseudo-governor makes in his political science and constitutional law is this: He has no clear conception, or rather he has a completely erroneous conception as to who the sovereign people are in our political system. They are the enfranchised citizens of the United States resident within the states. He evidently thinks they are the population, resident or squatting,

55. *Cong. Record*, 50th Cong., 1st sess. (April 9, 1888), pp. 2803 ff.; (April 19, 1888), pp. 3124 ff. See also Senator O. H. Platt's speech on admission in *Admission of Dakota, April 19, 1888* (Washington, 1888), pp. 1–15.

56. Thomas H. McKee, *The National Conventions and Platforms of All Political Parties, 1789–1905* (Baltimore, 1906), pp. 236, 241–2.

57. Two Chicago papers, the *Tribune* and the *Inter-Ocean*, had followed the course of the statehood agitation since 1883. After 1885, New York papers, especially the *Tribune*, expressed a sympathetic interest.

in a district subject by the constitution to the exclusive control of the congress. He has gotten into this confusion of ideas through that vicious theory of natural rights, which is a legal and political jack-o-lantern that will lead any man who follows it into the meshes and bogs of a baseless speculation. These acts of his and his followers are nearly up to the ragged line which separates braggadocio from treason. You may allow them to amuse themselves by strutting around in the purple as we are accustomed to see men and women do upon the boards of a theater, but if they undertake to do any governmental act, then it is the duty of the regularly constituted territorial government, or if there be none (a hypothesis), of the government at Washington to put them under arrest.[58]

Professor Burgess' blast, while an interesting point of view, did not reflect the sentiment either of the country or of the Dakotans. The latter were becoming increasingly absorbed in the statehood cause, in fact, which indicated that the more broadly based type of appeals suggested by Bowen were having their effect. The statehood forces were so encouraged by the new show of interest that they tried a new approach by dividing their numbers along professional lines, and by urging each profession to hold a convention in which they would petition Congress for statehood. With a fanatic's energy Campbell organized a convention of statehood leagues. Pettigrew, Mellette, and others organized a lawyers' auxiliary convention. W. S. Bowen, of the *Press and Dakotaian,* and Theodore Kanouse called an editors' convention, while Dr. Ward and the Reverend E. E. Clough, two very politically minded ministers, held a clergyman's convention. A farmers' and businessman's convention also met to endorse statehood.[59]

Meanwhile within the Republican party ranks Campbell labored mightily to make admission the only issue in the territorial elections of that year. We must "break the solid North," he wrote Augustine Davis, and defeat the one-state plan. "I look

58. The Burgess letter was printed in the Bismarck *Tribune,* January 5, 1887.
59. Kingsbury, *Dakota Territory,* 2, 1836, 1842.

upon the plan to carry this fight into active politics as our sole resource. . . . If we allow the elections to go off on some other issue, then two whole years are lost." [60]

To the pugnacious Campbell all this activity was highly pleasing. He spoke almost daily before conventions or small village meetings. His prestige was never greater and the "we are a state" idea was never more popular. Campbell himself became so carried away by his own crusading that he began to hint to various party leaders that he should be their choice for territorial delegate in the fall of 1888. Only *he* had the force to push an admission bill through Congress, he somewhat immodestly asserted.[61] So great was the alarm of the conservatives that this stormy petrel would succeed in his ambitions that they persuaded John R. Gamble, a prominent Yankton lawyer and eloquent public speaker, to turn his Fourth of July address for 1888 into a closely reasoned attack on Campbell's thesis.[62] This public split on what seemed to be the eve of success would have enormously weakened the whole statehood cause had it not been for Harrison's election to the presidency in November of that year. After six years of constant struggle, statehood was at last a certainty.

Again the scene of action shifted to Washington, where the Lame Duck Congress of 1888–89 renewed its consideration of the admission of the Dakotas, and that of Montana, Washington, and New Mexico as well. The sudden appearance of New Mexico as a suppliant for admission was explained by the Democrats' desire to admit a state that would send Democratic senators to Washington. New Mexico would also cancel the effect of Dakota's admission if the latter could be forced to come in as one state. Of the other two territories, it was hoped that Washington would go Democratic in the future, but it was clear that Montana would not. Thus if the Democratic scheme worked, four new states would be admitted, two of them probably Democratic in their politics and two of them Republican. Under this plan the Senate

60. H. J. Campbell to Augustine Davis, April 14, 1888, Statehood Papers. See also the Bismarck *Tribune*, May 16, and 29, July 12, 1888.

61. H. J. Campbell to Augustine Davis, April 14, 1888, Statehood Papers.

62. Bismarck *Tribune*, July 11, 1888. For the speech itself see Kingsbury, *Dakota Territory, 2, 1846–52.*

would remain virtually unchanged in its political make-up.[63]

Congressman William Springer of Illinois made the final Democratic effort to admit Dakota as a single state. As chairman of the House Committee on Territories, Springer was in a powerful position to forward his views. The one-state bill, originally submitted by Butler, was now revised and called the Springer bill.[64] Its author soon discovered, however, that his tactics of counterbalancing Dakota and New Mexico would not succeed, nor would it be wise. The sentiment of the nation was overwhelmingly for admission of the northwestern tier of territories, while the idea of admitting New Mexico, with its large Spanish-speaking Mexican population, was not popular. Meanwhile Dakotans were becoming more vocal daily, and the local Democratic party, fearing the wrath of the aroused voter, repudiated the Springer bill.[65] Ex-Governor Ordway himself appears to have decided that the one-state idea was doomed, and the old opportunist tried to disassociate himself from the Springer bill.[66] The Democrats were also faced with the possibility that Harrison would use the admission issue as an excuse to call a special session of Congress in the spring of 1889 if the Lame Duck session should refuse to grant statehood. After a series of conferences, the so-called Omnibus Bill, largely shaped by Springer in the House and Butler, Platt, and Cullom in the Senate, proved acceptable to both Houses, and on February 22, 1889, the Democrats and Republicans joined to pass the bill which created four new states. Cleveland signed the act a few days before he left office.[67] Exactly twenty-eight years before, a repudiated Democratic administration had helped the Republicans create Dakota Territory on the very eve of the Civil War. Now a second out-going Democratic

63. See Senator Benjamin Harrison's discussion of "mating" the states in his speech to Congress, January 27, 1886, quoted in *Dakota, Her Claims to Admission as a State* (Washington, 1886), pp. 9–10.

64. Kingsbury, *Dakota Territory*, 2, 1857–8.

65. Not only did the Democrats repudiate the one-state bill, but at their annual territorial convention they chose a pronounced divisionist, John W. Harden, as their candidate for delegate in 1888. Bismarck *Tribune*, July 12, 1888.

66. Bismarck *Tribune*, March 12, 1889.

67. Kingsbury has printed nearly every House and Senate report on the Dakota section of the Omnibus Bill, as well as newspaper accounts, resolutions, and the Omnibus Bill itself. See his *Dakota Territory*, 2, 1868–78.

administration, the first to control the government since Dakota's creation, repeated the process by allowing Dakota to enter the Union as two new states.

South Dakota, the area where the entire impulse for statehood and division had centered, came into the Union preoccupied with other issues. Drought, depression of farm prices, high interest rates, mortgage foreclosures, and discrimination by railroads had provoked the farming population of those rich prairie lands to furious activity. Farmers' Alliance conventions, which had been meeting in the Territory annually for five years, suddenly became political conventions, and the horny-handed farmer, so recently held in contempt by the statehood men, abruptly emerged as an irrepressible political power. Farmers' newspapers, farmers' grain elevators, and farmers' cooperative insurance societies everywhere became important. After a decade of struggle with their enemy in Washington, that is, the federal government, the statehood men, and the oligarchy discovered a new and more dangerous opponent in their own back yard!

The danger signals of this new threat had been apparent for a long time, for as early as 1885 the farmers had pushed a railroad commission law through the Assembly. But the immediacy of the threat became obvious when a new constitutional convention met in Sioux Falls in July 1889 to reapprove the 1885 document and establish the machinery for entering the Union required by the Omnibus Bill. Judge Edgerton, who was slated to become the president of the convention, found that a combination of delegates representing the Democrats, the Alliance, and the prohibitionists were prepared to elect their own candidate. Only by a great effort did Edgerton and Moody prevent this revolt.[68] Fortunately for them, the conservatives had been able to persuade Congress to allow South Dakota to enter the Union on the basis of their 1885 constitution, so that the violent discontent expressed by Alliance men could not find any outlet in constitutional changes.[69]

While the old guard held an unsteady grip on the convention in South Dakota, the long-growing hostility to absentee govern-

68. *South Dakota Constitutional Convention* (Huron, S.D., 1907), 2, 70 ff.
69. Hicks, "The Constitution of the Northwest States," p. 24.

ment, boss rule, and corruption in northern Dakota had resulted in the complete capture of the North Dakota constitutional convention by the Alliance forces. Fred B. Fancher, president of the North Dakota Farmers' Alliance became president of the constitutional convention when it met in Bismarck.[70] And so great was the passion for reform that nearly every radical constitutional measure in vogue at the time—minority representation; the initiative, referendum, and recall; a unicameral legislature, a system whereby the constitution would be revised by a new convention every few years—all were considered.[71]

At the first Republican state convention, in both North and South Dakota, the Alliance men, most of whom preferred to act within the party ranks rather than as a third party, demanded their share of offices in the new states. In North Dakota, Fancher went so far as to list the specific offices which he and his farmers wished to control.[72] A beleaguered and irate Republican party leadership was forced to meet Fancher's demands.[73] In South Dakota, where the Alliance was not so strong, the old statehood leaders managed to elect Mellette as governor and Moody and Pettigrew as United States Senators, to repudiate Campbell, and to find a United States Circuit Judgeship for aging Judge Edgerton. Moreover, nearly every delegate to the past statehood conventions was given an office. But no one rested easily, for the harsh voice of the farmer was being heard in politics. The oligarchy, the businessmen, the editors, and the lawyers wrote angry letters to one another about the "cranks" who wanted to run the state. Mellette's correspondence after 1888 dealt with little else but the problem of controlling the farmers, and it is damaging revelation of the small vision of these men that they were never once prepared to grant that the farmer had any right to enter the political forum as an equal.[74] Their chief reaction was anger;

70. Bismarck *Tribune*, July 5, 1889. For an account of the North Dakota convention see *Journal of the Constitutional Convention of North Dakota*, Bismarck, 1889. See also Hicks, "The Constitution of the Northwest States," pp. 41–5.
71. Bismarck *Tribune*, July 10–31, 1889.
72. Ibid., August 20, 1889.
73. Kingsbury, *Dakota Territory*, 2, 1930–1.
74. The following letter from J. L. Lockhart to A. C. Mellette, Milbank, Dakota, May 16, 1889, Mellette Papers, is fairly typical of the letters which passed between the statehood Republicans for three years. The writer was describing a county convention of the Republican party:

their constant question was: what is their price? Only a few saw the situation in the larger sense as a social and economic problem created by national and international rather than by local factors, and these few did not control the party.[75]

Several important features stand out in the successful six-year crusade for statehood for North and South Dakota. Most prominent was the constant evidence that while the people liked the idea, it was never a people's movement. Four times, in 1883, 1885, 1887, and 1889, the voters were called to the polls to approve a constitution or to vote on statehood or division. In every instance except the last, the vote was extremely light. In regular elections, such as that of the Assembly or of the delegate, the number of votes cast in southern Dakota was over double those cast for the constitution.[76]

Many of the most ardent statehood men, Campbell, Bowen, and Ward excepted, preferred a "quiet revolution" in which the public would endorse their cause without taking any great in-

---

"We held our convention today; had a hard fight, but got there. Our crank Alliance men run in democrats to these caucuses; they best Col. Smedley in his own town with democrats and Mugwump votes, but the Col. aint to be downed. He came with a contesting delegation and although it looked dark this forenoon we got mad and made the sun to pour its glorious upon us. Their plan was to have a farmers' caucus; they held one; would not let us in, but—Mr. Hartwell at our solicitations went in and raised cane with them. They adjourned for dinner. Col. Smedly, S. S. Lockhart, D. W. Diggs, and myself hustled and seen all delegates when they came out—and told them that the cranks were deceiving them, that they were fighting you, but they went to the caucus again. Col. Smedly proposed to go into the adjoining room and hold a caucus. I proposed it be a strictly Mellette caucus. Col. called [for] Mellette men to come this way; they commenced deserting the cranks and rushed to us; then the cranks came out saying for God Sake come with us and hold a general caucus. That is what we wanted; we went and made things sing and were not in their caucus five minutes till we had them balloting for a Governor. Only five votes were cast against you but these five were going to deceive the poor innocent farmer. . . . I wished I could talk to you longer but I have not slept for two nights nor done anything for four days but work after what we have accomplished. Governor, dont forget A. B. Smedly, S. S. Lockhart, D. W. Diggs and those that stood by us in this fight. Do all you can for Diggs for Treas. He is a dandy. (signed) J. L. Lockhart."

75. The South Dakota Republicans went through the most intense period of self-examination during the years 1889–92, but their conclusions were always that they were opposed by cranks and that the weakness of the party was due to a laxity in internal discipline and the lack of an efficient party machine. Never did they admit that the issues were more basic than this.

76. The average total vote on the constitution in 1883 and 1885 was somewhere between thirty and forty thousand. The vote in 1889 was seventy-eight thousand. *South Dakota Legislative Manual, 1947* (Pierre, S.D., 1947.), p. 234.

terest in it, but by following this course they faced the insoluble dilemma of securing a peoples' mandate without telling the people the reason for the mandate. That this plan was characteristic of the earlier phases of the movement Congress readily perceived, and correctly felt little obligation to act until 1888. By this time, however, the statehood issue had transcended party lines in Dakota, it was becoming a peoples' movement, and the nation was in sympathy with the statehood agitation. But before 1888 the whole tone of the Congressional debates was set by the well-founded suspicion that political jobbers, more interested in retaining the capital at Yankton, curbing the political influence of the Northern Pacific, or controlling the patronage than in self-rule, were behind the statehood cause.

The Dakota historians, the most prominent and voluminous of whom is George W. Kingsbury, a member of the inner circle of the Yankton political leaders who began the whole statehood agitation, have tried earnestly to make the statehood movement a broad, popular issue stemming jointly from a local and national impulse to reform. Kingsbury, G. H. Durand, and Barrett Lowe have particularly stressed the reformist roles of W. H. H. Beadle with his school lands clauses and Ward with his prohibitionist ideas.[77] As a result, Beadle, Ward, and a few others, all of them from Yankton, have been made the heroes of the movement, which they undoubtedly are. But their importance and influence, which was far from negligible, it must be admitted, has nevertheless been so overemphasized that a somewhat incorrect version of the movement is now accepted as being accurate. Almost the entire central core of the statehood figures has been sacrificed for adulation of the more peripheral reformist element, which after 1885 never controlled a single Dakota convention that met in the cause of division and statehood. Nor did they ever control an important office in the new state government. This is not to say that the reformers failed. Rather, by the submission of their causes to the public to vote upon, they were sustained, particularly in the case of prohibition and school lands.

77. See Kingsbury, *History of Dakota Territory;* G. H. Durand, *Joseph Ward of Dakota,* Boston, 1913; Barrett Lowe, *Heroes and Hero Tales of South Dakota,* 1931.

The interesting thing here is that the statehood forces avoided responsibility for most of the reform planks by keeping them out of the constitution and by letting the public decide at the polls by a separate vote on each. In this way they attracted the reform voter to the polls without committing themselves to any reform measure.

The mistaken belief has also developed that the Farmers' Alliance movement with its liberal legislative program of reform worked hand in glove with the statehood forces, and that Alliance radicalism was synonymous with statehood radicalism. Nothing could be less true. The two movements occurred at the same time, but their aims were as divergent as it is possible for aims to be. One asked for control of the new states and little else; the other requested political and economic reforms of the most basic sort. One represented the businessman and the lawyer, the other represented the farmer. The history of the first years of statehood in both states stands as a monument to the fact that statehood leaders and Alliance leaders were seldom synonymous.

While the statehood cause was not the people's cause or a broad reform movement, it does point up the fact that in twenty-eight years' time a specific and distinct segment of the population had developed the technique of controlling local government for its benefit alone. Very few of their actions smacked of a desire to democratize government on this the last of the settlement frontiers. This attitude would suggest that Dakota politics only reflected the bankruptcy of principles which characterized both major national parties between 1880 and 1896. It would imply, too, that Lord Bryce's famous conclusion that no great difference existed between the two parties certainly applied to Dakota, where the territorial officials and the statehood men, though bitter enemies, belonged for the most part to the same party and held the same views. The point at issue was that one group was in office and the other was not.

The fact that a large majority of Dakotans were Republicans and that their political fights were intraparty and not interparty ones reveals in still another way how Washington could impose itself on Dakota through the territorial system. Twenty-eight years of Washington domination could hardly fail to mold the basic political patterns and attitudes of the sections which had been settled for the longest period, so that it is hardly surprising that South Dakota has been overwhelmingly in the Republican column in nearly every national and local election since 1889. The state today has what is virtually a one-party system which, though perpetuated by many factors, is still due partly to one-party domination during the state's formative years.

Absence of true principles in the statehood fight, outside of those presented by Campbell and certain reformers, does not mean that discontent did not exist. No region settled by several hundred thousand intelligent citizens would stomach appointed officials of Ordway's stripe for any length of time. In all probability had Congress refused to admit South Dakota in 1889, the Campbell plan would have been carried out by the Farmers' Alliance, who would have used it as a vehicle to obtain justice from the railroads and economic relief from depressed conditions caused by drought and low prices. The true significance of the use of the states' rights body of ideas, however, is that the Dakotans employed only the set of constitutional tricks which was already familiar to them. They voiced what were the most traditional and time worn of constitutional arguments to express political discontent. States'-rights principles had received what many considered to be a death blow in 1865. Now, twenty years later, the Dakotans were merely asserting them in a new way in order to get into the Union. While such a lack of originality is indeed striking, what is even more impressive is that Campbell and his followers had also borrowed freely from another supposedly outmoded complex of ideas, that of popular sovereignty. In their public speeches Dakotans compared their attempts to govern themselves to the struggle of the antislavery Kansans in 1857. Senator Butler's and Congressman Springer's one-state bills, it was asserted, would force a "LeCompton Constitution" on the free citizens of Dakota.[78] Campbell's own comment to Augustine

78. Harrison to Senate, January 27, 1886, in *Dakota, Her Claims to Admission as a State*, p. 7; see also Harrison to Senate, February 4, 1886, in *Dakota, Reply to Senators Vest and Morgan* (Washington, 1886), p. 5.

Davis on one occasion that they should "revive the Kansas fight" was more than an isolated analogy. Dr. Joseph Ward wrote in 1888 that if Dakotans were not given their own government, a new Kansas would develop. He warned the Democrats: "The people took the matter in hand then, as they will again, when they take the pains to understand the situation, and for twenty-four years put another party in charge of the government." [79]

The Senate debates literally bristled with references to Kansas, popular sovereignty, and states' rights. Senator Vest more than once declared that the Dakotans should be barred from admission, for they were arguing repudiated secessionist principles, and the Senate had the unique experience of hearing a senator from South Carolina (Butler) agreeing with Vest. [80] On the other side the Republicans, while they never supported any of Campbell's theories and indeed were rather embarrassed by them, did not hesitate to accuse the Southerners in Congress of keeping Dakota out of the Union because so many Union veterans lived there. [81]

The hint of sectional prejudice in the Dakota debates was more than a passing one. While the Democrats opposed the entry of the territories of Dakota, Montana, Washington, and Wyoming on political grounds, the discussion revealed a latent Southern aversion to the admission of a purely Northern tier of new states. Southern senators such as John T. Morgan of Alabama and Butler of South Carolina saw New Mexico as a sectional counterbalance as well as a political counterbalance to Dakota. Harrison himself asked at one point in the debates, "Can we not get rid of this old and disreputable mating business? It grew out of slavery." [82]

Of course it would be absurd to presume that the Dakota statehood issue or the entire trans-Mississippi West territorial problem could have burgeoned into prominence in the form of a revival of constitutional questions unless Campbell's plans had been activated. Suffice it to say that echoes of the earlier conflicts and the serious employment of earlier constitutional arguments dis-

79. Ward, "The Territorial System of the United States," p. 55.
80. *Cong. Record*, 50th Cong., 1st sess. (April 9, 1888), pp. 2803 ff.; (April 19, 1888), pp. 3124 ff. See also Kingsbury, *Dakota Territory*, 2, 1818–30.
81. Green, "The Struggle of South Dakota to Become a State," p. 528.
82. Harrison to Senate, January 27, 1886, *Dakota, Her Claims to Admission as a State*, p. 9.

closed that after three decades of quiet, these basic problems could still arise to haunt Congress. But Congress forestalled the threatened Campbellian revolution by the Omnibus Bill. The true revolution, a true "peoples' revolution" in Dakota, came ironically enough, in the revolt of the farmer against the statehood forces.

Chapter 9. True Revolution; the Revolt of the

Dakota Farmers: 1885–89

I never seen the time before but what I could sooth the boys down
and make them feel good but seemingly this fall they are not to be
"comforted." I hope they are not so bad in other counties as they are
in this.   *J. L. Lockhart to Governor Mellette*
of South Dakota, July 13, 1890 [1]

THE FARMERS' ALLIANCE of Dakota Territory has received short
shrift from Dakota historians, who are inclined to assert that
many of its members were cranks. It must be admitted that a
number of strange characters wandered onto the Dakota political
stage between 1888 and 1896. Actually the Alliance was the
second political training ground—the Republican party being the
first—for the Scandinavian and German immigrants who had
settled in Dakota; it served as the first sounding board for the
angry, drought-stricken Dakota farmers of the late 1880's, and
it seemed to offer them the greatest hopes for relief. The Alliance
also became the means to political office in both Dakotas between
1889 and 1896. It was the motivating force behind the first large-
scale demands for reform in local government during the last
days of the Territory and the first years of statehood. Thirdly, the
Alliance was the true predecessor to the famous Non-Partisan
League of North Dakota.

The underlying causes of this agrarian protest, which took on
national proportions in the form of the Alliance and Populist
parties during the 1890's, are too well known to warrant more
than a brief repetition here. Suffice it to say that with the expansion of the agricultural domain into the trans-Mississippi West,
and with the application of machinery and scientific farming
techniques, the American farmer after 1860 was able to bring
more land into cultivation in thirty years than in the entire pre-

1. Mellette Papers. Lockhart's complaint was that the Independents, a political
party formed by the South Dakota Alliance, had disrupted the local party machine
and had stolen their best men.

vious history of the nation. The stimulus for such an expansion
was the railroad, which gave the western farmer an easy access
to a world market for the first time. Misled by a wet-weather cycle
in the plains region from 1878 to 1886, lured on by highly exaggerated immigration propaganda issued by state and territorial
governments, railroads, and private land agencies, and disre-
garding the fact that they had to buy in a protected market and
sell in a free market, hundreds of thousands of farmers opti-
mistically marched onto the windy, treeless plains of the Dakotas,
Nebraska, and Kansas to make their fortunes in wheat, corn, and
livestock.

The overproduction of farm goods and overexpansion of farming regions which occurred between 1880 and 1900 came at a
time of falling prices and appreciating production costs, and one
of the most common results was that the farmer became hopelessly enmeshed in debts. Land and crops had to be mortgaged;
often he lost his farm and had to remain on it as a mere tenant.
This depressing situation was vastly complicated when railroads
and elevator companies sought to exact exorbitant tariffs from
the farmer for services rendered. To complicate matters still
further, a dry-weather cycle began in 1885 which was so devastating to crops in some regions of Dakota and Kansas that even
wheat for seed was not available in certain years. An extremely
severe winter in 1887 and 1888 also killed thousands of cattle
on the northern ranges; yet drought and cold promised little relief
through scarcity, for Dakota alone in 1889 produced a record
wheat crop at the same time that portions of the Territory were
suffering from extreme drought.[2]

What had been the dream of a prosperous future had turned
into a nightmare of present poverty which the farmer sought
desperately to end by joining the Farmers' Alliance movement.
It is beyond the scope of this study to treat the Dakota Alliance
in its entirety. Rather the aim is to point out that certain so-called
radical ideas and characteristics of the whole Alliance movement,
national and local, had been known and practiced on the Dakota

2. Frank H. Hagerty, *Territory of Dakota; the State of North Dakota; the State
of South Dakota; an Official Statistical, Historical and Political Abstract* (Aberdeen,
S.D., 1889), p. 80.

political frontier for a generation. Political techniques, and ideas about the role and nature of government in the economy which had been forged in the rough school of Dakota politics, served as important precedents to guide future Alliance leaders. The Alliance man was, after all, a pragmatist who was quite willing to imitate his predecessors in political office and in business itself.

Several factors unique to the Dakota scene and closely bound up with the Alliance agitation must be considered in order to understand the final phase of political development which the Territory underwent in the late 1880's.

First, it should be remembered that the Dakota farmers revolted not to *regain* control of the local government in 1889 but to *gain* control for the first time. The scramble for office which the farmers engaged in that year sprang from a desire for the reward of the office itself as much as from a desire to use the office to relieve economic distress. The hearty emoluments enjoyed by the territorial officials proved to be as attractive to the farmer as they were to the oligarchy. It may safely be said that the Alliance was a political organization in Dakota from the first day it began to function, and that the great antagonism of the statehood men and the Yankton oligarchy was founded upon the correct belief that the farmer and the statehood men had the same ends in mind. There is every evidence that the Alliance leaders, Henry L. Loucks, Alonzo Wardell, John W. Harden, and A. D. Chase in South Dakota, and Walsh, Fancher, and Miller in North Dakota, had all the interest of professional politicians in the spoils of office.[3] The old fight against federal office holders was simply transformed into a new fight against the interests and against the statehood men.

In a stricken economy the old Dakota attitude that government itself was an important paying business operated as a strong factor in turning the Alliance men toward politics. Once again

3. No Alliance leaders in the two Dakotas appear to have been men of exceptional ability; like the statehood forces they took refuge in group organization. The most prominent was Henry L. Loucks of Watertown, who later became president of the National Alliance. John W. Harden, A. D. Chase, Alonzo Wardell, all were professional politicians. In North Dakota, Fred B. Fancher and John Miller later served as governors.

the suspicion that agriculture in Dakota might not be practicable
—there are hints of the revival of the American Desert legend
here—led men to see the government as a prop to the economy
and a source of wealth. The Alliance had ample precedent for
holding such a view in the history of the Dakota "starving time"
from 1862 to 1868, and it may well be that such a precedent could
be found in the earlier histories of all the plains states in which
the Alliance and Populist movements thrived. If this should prove
to be the case, the histories of these agrarian movements need
significant revision.

The political debut of the Dakota Alliance occurred in the
last territorial Assembly, which met in 1889. The Alliance had
campaigned for two years in order to capture a majority of the
seats in both houses. They secured twenty-eight out of forty-
eight seats in the lower house and seven out of a possible twenty-
four in the Council.[4] They elected the presiding officers of both
houses and they held political caucuses throughout the legislative
proceedings.[5]

Assuming a semilegislative character themselves, they presented the Assembly with a long list of thirty-one requests, rang-
ing from a demand that the Territory grant loans to farmers for
purchasing seed, to a suggestion that Dakota change its county
system of local government to that of a township system. They
urged abolition of the immigration bureau; they asked that the
territorial government take steps to destroy the Russian thistle,
and they suggested that the Australian ballot system be adopted
at Dakota elections.[6]

With an arrogance born of true zeal, the Alliance went so far
as to propose a resolution in the lower house that any bill "which
has been introduced in the house at the request of the Territorial
Farmers' Alliance may be called upon at any time, out of its
regular order, for any purpose, by a majority vote of the house;

4. Bismarck *Tribune*, January 6, 1889. Both the president of the Council and
the speaker of the House were farmer-picked men, according to the *Tribune*,
January 9, 1889.
5. Ibid., January 10, 1889.
6. Jamestown *Alert*, December 12, 1888, quoted in the Bismarck *Tribune*,
December 15, 1888.

that the statement of the member introducing the bill shall be taken as evidence of the fact that such bill has been introduced at the request of said Alliance." [7]

The spirit of the resolution was typical of the farmers' actions throughout the sessions. In a healthy reaction to misrule they managed to enact a new railroad commission law, to curb interest rates, to pass new corporate tax laws, and to get the needed loans for seed wheat purchases.[8] Yet much of their energy was misdirected; they passed a mediocre railroad law simply because they did not trust the writers of the better proposals.[9] They introduced no less than 692 bills, of which 128 became law. Governor Church, in a lavish exercise of the veto, prevented forty-three more from taking effect.[10] Fully one-third of these bills were administrative in their nature or of a temporary character, which indicated the farmer's readiness to use law to correct immediate abuses and to aid him in what was considered to be a temporary period of distress.[11] In view of the fact that statehood was an assured certainty within the year and that these laws would have to be reenacted in the form of state statutes, their energy was particularly impressive.

The Dakota Assembly had played a secondary role in politics throughout most of the territorial period. Now in this last session, the farmer returned it to a place of primary importance as the one electoral medium given him by the territorial system to voice his complaints. The spirit of reform that was evident all over the nation had produced an effect even in the territories.

While the farmer reflected the new spirit of reform, he retained the traditional Dakota view that government was an important economic institution. The government had sold or given him his land; it had aided him in the construction of the railroads, either by federal land grant or by sale of county territorial bonds. Government, in the form of Indian agencies and army post quartermasters, had been the farmers' and the merchants' steady customer throughout the first years of settlement and indeed to the

7. Bismarck *Tribune*, January 10, 1889.
8. Ibid., January 30, 1889.
9. Ibid., March 3, 1889.
10. Ibid., March 10, 1889.
11. Ibid.

end of the territorial apprenticeship. Government in the form of land sale notices and public printing had supplied over three hundred newspapers with funds to operate. Now, in a second period of distress, it was highly logical for the farmer to look again to the territorial government as a source of aid, whether in the form of patronage, usury laws, loans to purchase wheat, or destruction of the Russian thistle.

In 1889 the Alliance resurrected still another political concept from the recent experience of the past when it urged that the territorial immigration bureau be abolished. The idea behind this request was that Dakota could support only a limited number of inhabitants. The conviction was rapidly growing that the saturation point in population had already been reached. Here again the legend that Dakota was part of the Great American Desert came into play, a legend that was somewhat strengthened by Major John Wesley Powell's impassioned pleas to the Dakotans to adjust their laws, institutions, and economy to fit the semi-arid region in which they lived.[12]

This view called forth violent denunciation from the real estate owners, the land speculators, and the immigration bureau officials, some of whom were at that very time urging that the Sioux Reservation lands west of the Missouri River be opened to settlement. So terrified were these men that Dakota would get a bad name because of the droughts and the suffering they had caused the farming population that Governor Mellette, himself a real estate agent, followed the reprehensible policy of preventing the news of the drought of 1889 from being carried in eastern newspapers. At the same time he refused to ask for aid to the suffering farmers by appealing to eastern cities. The reason for this policy was made clear in a letter to the Governor from F. C. Buten, president of the "Jim River Valley Land and Immigration Bureau," who wrote in the fall of 1889 that he was alarmed at the news being spread about Dakota suffering. It would do "un-

---

12. "Don't let these streams get out of the possession of the people," Powell wrote. "If you fail in making a constitution in any other respect, fail not in this one. Fix it in your constitution that no corporation—no body of men—no capital can get possession and right of your waters. . . . Such a provision will prevent your great agricultural resources from falling into the hands of a few." Quoted in Nelson, *Land of the Dacotahs*, p. 139.

told injury in the Immigration line in this first year of our statehood," he warned Mellette.[13] Marvin Hughitt, president of the
Chicago and Northwestern Railroad, actually congratulated Mellette upon his refusal to solicit funds in behalf of the sufferers.
The Chicago and Northwestern, it should be added, quietly
donated a large relief fund to the hard-hit farmers of the Dakotas
in the hopes that this gift would prevent more appeals from being
made.[14]

The Farmers' Alliance furnished the first means in independent
political expression for the Scandinavian and German segments
of the Dakota population which by 1889 numbered at least one-
third of the Territory's citizens.[15] These two ethnic groups had
never questioned the wisdom of voting solidly for the Republican
party before 1885. After that year, however, the more independent
of the Scandinavians, particularly those who were second-genera-
tion Americans or who had come to understand the mysteries of
American politics, entered into the political arena as members
of the Alliance. With the practical experience of the Alliance behind them, many of them individually joined the Republican party
or formed "Scandinavian Leagues" which were designed to act
as independent minority pressure groups in politics.[16] By this
latter tactic, the Scandinavians were able to achieve a political
power disproportionate to their actual numbers. A perusal of the
names of the candidates for state office in the Dakotas since 1892
would suggest that the Scandinavians are still a dominant factor
in Dakota politics.

Just as the Alliance did not hesitate to disturb the old political
patterns by bringing the Scandinavians and Germans into active
politics, it did not fear to face the problem of reform. As a group

13. F. C. Buten to Mellette, October 22, 1889; Mellette Papers.
14. Marvin Hughitt to Mellette, September 11, 1889; Mellette Papers.
15. Dick, *Sod-House Frontier*, pp. 192–3. The immigrant was even more interested in survival than in politics during most of the territorial stage, so that the
native Americans ran the government. See Herbert E. Gaston's discussion of the
effects of this situation on North Dakota politics in *The Non-Partisan League*
(New York, 1920), pp. 11–13.
16. The Bismarck *Tribune*, July 2, 1889, reported that "The Scandinavian
Union of North Dakota" had been organized at Fargo for the purpose of fighting
for their rights and protecting themselves against discrimination.

just assuming power they could advocate thorough reforms, whereas the statehood forces, already partly in power, could not. The Alliance-dominated North Dakota State Constitutional Convention was an excellent example of their reform-mindedness, for every new constitutional wrinkle and legislative fad being discussed in the country at that time was seriously considered at the Bismarck sessions.[17]

The seventy-five delegates—twenty-nine of whom were farmers —were deeply conscious of the fact that a new age called for new measures. When Governor Mellette suggested that they write a document containing specific regulations, they carried out his advice with a vengeance.[18] In the matter of corporate control alone, which the delegates considered the most pressing problem of the day, they went so far as to forbid the blacklisting of labor by corporations.[19]

The constitution makers further included labor arbitration machinery, a prohibition clause, civil service reforms, and a child labor clause in their document. They adopted the Australian ballot, and in quite another field they passed water rights laws suggested by Major Powell, who had addressed them on this subject.[20]

In the field of legislative reform the convention seriously considered a unicameral system, as well as a plan which "amounted practically to substituting the constitutional convention for the legislature as the chief law-making body." [21] The referendum method of passing laws also came in for its share of discussion. While none of these systems were adopted, the delegates did drastically curb the powers of the legislature. They took special

17. The Bismarck *Tribune,* itself a violent advocate of the unicameral legislature, discusses many of the reforms which the convention considered. Ibid., April 28, May 10, June 22, and 30, and July 1 to August 2, 1889.

18. Crawford, *History of North Dakota, 1,* 525. Judge Thomas M. Cooley of the University of Michigan Law School warned the delegates, on the other hand, not to substitute a code of laws for a constitution. Hicks, "Constitution of the Northwest States," p. 53.

19. Hicks, p. 90; Crawford, p. 330.

20. See above, p. 279.

21. "It was proposed that every seven years the governor would submit to the qualified voters of the state the question of calling a convention, and in case the vote proved favorable, the convention should be called." Hicks, pp. 41–2.

pains to limit the appropriating power, for the territorial Assembly had spent money lavishly.[22]

Similarly, the powers of the governor were restricted and the judiciary system underwent modification in a multitude of ways.[23] Professor John D. Hicks rightly says that these curbs on the legislature, the executive, and the judiciary were enacted not because the Dakota farmer saw government as a necessary evil—he was not a Jeffersonian in this sense—but because he was trying to find a better way to govern.[24] The farmer already had the familiar precedent of a large, many-faceted government in the territorial system. He was willing to retain its size and breadth of activities if he could at the same time make it a good government. The North Dakota convention represented a coincidence, then, of a plains frontier concept of government, which played a large role in the economy, with the reform spirit and the concept of the so-called "positive state," which were sweeping the nation.

Too often the Alliance has been called a movement to cure economic ills through political action. It has been claimed that this method of procedure was either unrealistic or revolutionary; yet the active role that government, both federal and local, played in the settlement of the Dakota frontier made it inevitable that the farmer should follow the pattern of action that he did. He was not a revolutionary, nor was he seeking to return to a past golden age of agriculture which had never existed. He was willing to try new techniques and reforms, but above all he was a pragmatist, retaining a basic faith in the American political system that would not be shaken. He was more democratic than the Yankton oligarchy, and it was he who urged a more democratic concept of government in the Territory, and later in the two states. But the farmer, in the form of the Alliance, was able to democratize government only at the end of the frontier period, not at the beginning.

22. Hicks found that "Want of confidence in the judgement and integrity of public officials show conspicuously in the provisions relating to public indebtedness, revenue, and taxation. Every safeguard that could be devised was called into use in an attempt to insure the people against exploitation at the hands of the men whom they had elected to office." Ibid., p. 121; see also pp. 38–45.

23. Ibid., pp. 59–62, 63–73.

24. Ibid., pp. 74–5.

The great and important fact arising out of this entire study has been this: the exigencies of the plains environment, and the accompanying doubt that the region was of much value agriculturally, allowed a federally supported territorial government to assume a primary economic importance during the region's development. This fact in turn made the politician and the businessman synonymous persons for the first decade of settlement, so that a sort of political and economic oligarchy resulted. While this oligarchy was shot through with warring factions, they all agreed that government must play a large part in the territory's economic life; thus they built railroads with territorial bonds and adopted a peace policy toward the Indian so that the latter could continue to furnish a market for the white man's goods.

Then the boom period came, when Dakota seemed an imperial domain, criss-crossed by railroads, dotted by burgeoning towns, and exporting gold and wheat in great quantities. All the earlier doubts of the region's inhabitability, of its being able to stand alone, came to an end. Only then could the desire for self-rule, taking the form of the statehood movement, begin. But the dry-weather cycle returned, wheat and farm prices fell, and the exorbitant fees levied by the banker, the elevator owner, the railroads, and the farm machinery salesman produced profound agrarian unrest. The farmer himself now turned to the state as a source of wealth, as the beneficent economic prop, as the subsidizers of a periodically nonself-sufficient economy.

The prairie politicians and farmers, in adjusting to their environment, produced and practiced in their crude way a kind of state socialism. From their pragmatic experience sprang some of the ideas advanced by the Alliance in the 19th century and by the Non-Partisan League during the 20th century. And from the belief that agriculture needed outside support in certain periods of distress could well have come the rationale, at least, for a federally subsidized agriculture, and perhaps even some parts of that contemporary phenomenon the much-disputed welfare state.

The rich forested lands of the United States that lay east of the Mississippi River produced, it is said, the first true American. An independent, democratic, vigorous, pragmatic man, who was distrustful of any government save the most frugal. Contrast this pioneer with that of the Dakota settler. The latter was as brave and as basically democratic as the forester; he possessed the true pioneer spirit. But reared in the forest area, he was convinced, when arriving in Dakota, that he was in a new and different land, delightful to behold in many ways—with its big sky, black earth, and rich grasses—but fearsome in other ways—its lack of water and wood, its drought and cold. He came, whether businessman, lawyer, or farmer, doubting that he could survive alone in this new environment, and he welcomed a partner to aid him. This partner was government in a dozen forms, at first manipulated by the politician-businessman, later appropriated by the farmer himself.

Today the descendants of these doubting pioneers who themselves went through a period of doubt in the dust storm years of the 1930's and through a new period of federal subsidies in the form of agricultural price supports are prosperous and happy. Two huge dams have been flung across the Missouri, one at Fort Randall, South Dakota, and the other at Garrison, North Dakota. Built by the federal government, they promise power for industry and water for irrigation that can mean a new era for the Upper Missouri Plateau.

Even without the benefits of the Missouri Valley Authority, the Dakotans are as independent, as conservative, and as solid a group of true Americans as one could wish for. Yet both North and South Dakota, which are largely rural areas, have the highest percentage of their population working for government of any states in the Union.[25] Government and politics, it seems, are still the rural Dakotas' largest industry.

25. North Dakota leads the nation in the percentage of its working population employed by government: 34,000 are employees, which is approximately 15 per cent of the employed adult population. See *Statistical Abstract of the United States for 1950* (Washington, 1950), pp. 32, 359.

Bibliographical Note

Chief Sources

THERE ARE four major collections of materials which deal with the history of Dakota Territory. The most voluminous and rewarding of these is the Territorial Papers of Dakota, 1861–89, to be found in the records of the Departments of State, Justice, and the Interior in the National Archives, Washington. These Papers are all in manuscript, and although the State Department plans to publish the Territorial Papers of the United States, it will be at least another five years before those dealing with Dakota Territory are available in printed form. The Dakota Papers include thousands of manuscript letters written by local Dakota office holders, as well as official and private reports of the various federal officers to their superiors in the national capital. Since most of the Dakota Papers remain unexplored, they constitute a valuable collection of source material.

The manuscript and newspaper collections of the State Department of History in Pierre, South Dakota, are a second major source of materials. While only a few of the newspapers go back further than 1872, the territorial history could not be understood without consulting these files.

The Department of History of North Dakota, with headquarters in Bismarck, offers the researcher complete coverage of important northern Dakota newspapers for the years 1885–89. The Official Papers of the Governors of Dakota, 1861–89, are also available in Bismarck.

The fourth repository of Dakota sources may be found in the W. R. Coe Collection of Western Americana in the Yale University Library. The Collection includes many manuscript journals and diaries of persons living in or traveling through Dakota in the period covered by this book. Even more valuable are the newspaper files of the Collection and several rare printed works. In addition to the Coe Collection, the Yale University Library and the Yale Law School Library house an unusually complete set

of secondary works on Dakota territorial history which proved
to be extremely useful.

A helpful guide in locating Dakota material in the above collections and in other libraries was Albert H. Allen, ed., *Dakota Im-
prints, 1858–1889*, New York, 1947.

Manuscript Collections

The most pertinent manuscript materials concerning Dakota poli-
tics until 1873 are the Dakota Territorial Papers and the Letters
of Application and Recommendation in the Appointments Di-
vision of the Department of State records (National Archives).
A second source bearing on the entire territorial period is the
Appointment Letters and Appointment Papers for Dakota in the
Appointments Divisions of the Department of Justice (National
Archives). For the years after 1873 the Dakota Appointment
Papers of Territorial Governors and Secretaries, and the Dakota
Territorial Papers, in the Patents and Miscellaneous Division of
the Appointments Division of the Department of the Interior
(National Archives) are indispensable. The annual and special
reports of Indian agents and inspectors for the Dakota reserva-
tions are useful in establishing the relation between the Yankton
oligarchy and the Indian rings. These reports may be found in the
Chronological Files of the Office of Indian Affairs, 1861–89, of
the Department of the Interior records (National Archives).

The Official Papers of the Governors of Dakota (Bismarck,
North Dakota) contain a surprising amount of material in the
form of letters, petitions, and copies of mining codes, which political leaders had sent to Governor John L. Pennington during
the Black Hills gold rush.

The Papers and Letters of Governor Arthur C. Mellette, covering the years 1886–93, and including some 5,000 separate items,
were extremely helpful in piecing together the story of the statehood movement and in understanding the make-up of the Republican party after 1886. These extraordinary papers were
supplemented by the Statehood Papers, 1883–89, a collection of
letters and papers consisting chiefly of the correspondence of
Hugh J. Campbell, W. S. Bowen, and Augustine Davis, all active

statehood men. The Statehood Papers have been deposited at the State Department of History at Pierre, South Dakota.

The twelve-volume diary of Dr. Henry F. Livingston, one of the agents tried in the Indian ring cases at Yankton between 1878 and 1880, and Alfred Vaughan's "Upper Missouri Journal," 1855, were available in the Coe Collection, but their historical value has been greatly overrated. On the other hand, a typescript copy of the diary of General W. H. H. Beadle, covering the years 1868–72, was helpful in explaining some of the intricacies of the Burbank administration. This typescript copy is included in Barrett Lowe's "The Public Activities of General W. H. H. Beadle, 1863–1889," Master's thesis, Department of History, University of South Dakota, 1938. Lois Malvina Drake's "The Influence of the Newspapers of Dakota Territory upon the Administration of Nehemiah G. Ordway, Governor from 1880 to 1884," Master's thesis, Department of Journalism, University of Missouri, 1941, is actually an excellent account of Ordway's entire career, and it was very useful in explaining details of the capital removal issue. Ruth Elizabeth Bergman's "Printing in South Dakota during the Territorial Period," Master's thesis in Library Science, University of Illinois, 1936, was of limited use. The above three theses were made available through the kind offices of Will G. Robinson of the South Dakota State Department of History.

Official Published Documents

The *Annual Reports of the Attorney-General of the United States for the Years 1861–1889*, the *Annual Reports of the Secretary of the Interior, 1874–1889*, and the *Annual Reports of the Governor of Dakota Territory, 1861–1889* (all Government Printing Office publications, 1861–89) treat Dakota in such general terms that they are of little use. Very pertinent to this study, however, were the *House and Council Journals of the Legislative Assembly of Dakota, 1861–1889* (Yankton and Bismarck, Dakota Territory, 1861–89) and the *General Laws . . . of Dakota Territory, 1861–1889* (title and imprint vary).

For the struggle to organize Dakota the *Congressional Globe, 1858–1861* (Washington, 1858–61) provided most of the information. The *Congressional Record, 1883–1889* (Washington, 1883–89), was a necessary source for congressional views of the statehood movement and the admission controversy.

Newspapers

Although over three hundred newspapers were published in Dakota during the 1880's, most of these were devoted to the printing of land notices, so that less than a dozen papers were of any continuing importance as a public forum. Of these I have used the Yankton *Press,* 1870–71 (Coe Collection), and its successor, the powerful Yankton *Press and Dakotaian,* 1872–89 (State Department of History, Pierre), which was the most influential Republican paper in the Territory. It was a weekly paper until 1878, when it began daily publication. The *Dakota Herald,* 1872–84 (Coe Collection), was particularly valuable as a source, since it was the chief Democratic organ in Dakota. Though its comments are inevitably partisan, its views are generally less prejudiced than those of the *Press and Dakotaian.* The Bismarck *Tribune,* 1885–89 (Department of History, Bismarck), served as the administration paper of Governors Ordway, Pierce, and Church, as well as spokesman for the so-called "Bismarck ring" led by Alexander McKenzie. The *Tribune* files, therefore, were consulted at length. Other papers, the St. Paul *Pioneer Press,* 1883–85 (Library of Congress, Washington), and the Chicago *Tribune,* 1883 (Yale University Library), were useful for outside accounts of the first efforts of the Dakotans to achieve statehood.

Both the *Dakota Herald* and the *Press and Dakotaian* followed the practice of quoting editorial opinions of every other paper in Dakota, so that a convenient summary of the political views of all parts of the Territory appeared in print almost weekly. As a major source of political history these two papers were invaluable.

Moses K. Armstrong's "Scrapbook," which consists almost wholly of newspaper clippings concerning Dakota politics from 1861 to 1885, was a helpful guide in tracing Armstrong's own political career. Finally, hundreds of loose clippings from a score of small Dakota papers are available in the State Department of History at Pierre.

Secondary Works

George W. Kingsbury's *History of Dakota Territory* (2 vols. Chicago, 1915) occupies a unique position in Dakota historiography. Kingsbury, who was part owner of the Yankton *Press and Dakotaian,* had been secretary to many of the Republican territorial conventions and had attended most of the statehood meetings. As a member of the Yankton oligarchy he had a familiarity with, and access to, many materials and sources of information which are so often denied the historian. In his massive work— 1953 pages in length—he reprinted in full nearly every political document and convention resolution, and the attendance record of nearly every important political gathering, Republican, Democratic, and otherwise, that occurred in Dakota between 1861 and 1889. Some of these materials cannot be found elsewhere, so that in a sense Kingsbury's *Dakota Territory* is as much a source book as it is a history. These documents, strung together by a verbose, rambling narrative of very partisan nature, are of inestimable use in tracing the histories of the Republican and Democratic parties. The narrative portion of *Dakota Territory* openly defends the Indian rings, glorifies the statehood leaders from Yankton, praises the Republican party, and hints darkly that the Farmers' Alliance of Dakota was a combination of cranks and demagogues. Kingsbury is the H. H. Bancroft of Dakota, and with his collection of documents and his sixty or more superb photographs of the founders of Dakota government, he deserves much praise, but he has certainly presented a biased account of Dakota's beginnings.

No definitive history of Dakota Territory or of South Dakota exists, but Arthur Weston Goodspeed has edited a series of volumes on the early history of several northwestern states collectively entitled *The Province and the States,* 6 vols. Madison, 1904. Volume 6 contains a helpful, factual summary of Dakota territorial beginnings which appears to have been written by Judge Bartlett Tripp, leader of the Democratic party in southern Dakota from 1880 to 1890. Doane Robinson's *History of South Dakota* (2 vols. Yankton, 1904) and his later version, *History of*

South Dakota (2 vols. Chicago, 1930) are somewhat dated and antiquarian in tone. Moses K. Armstrong's works, *History and Resources of Dakota, Montana, and Idaho* (Yankton, 1866), *History of Southeastern Dakota* (Sioux City, Iowa, 1881), and his amusing *Early Empire Builders of the Great West* (St. Paul, 1901) are valuable for an account of the first decade of territorial history.

For specific regions of Dakota, Lewis F. Crawford, *History of North Dakota* (2 vols. New York, 1931) and C. A. Lounsberry, *Early History of North Dakota* (Washington, 1919) have a limited value for this study. No adequate study of the Black Hills exists, although Estelline Bennett's *Old Deadwood Days* (New York, 1928) and Jesse Brown's and A. M. Willard's *The Black Hills Trails* (Rapid City, South Dakota, 1924) were of some use.

For a general background, F. J. Turner, *The Frontier in American History* (New York, 1920), Walter P. Webb, *The Great Plains* (New York, 1931), and Fred A. Shannon, *The Farmer's Last Frontier* (New York, 1945) were provocative. Earl S. Pomeroy's brilliant *The Territories and the United States, 1861–1890* (Philadelphia, 1947) was indispensable. Solon J. Buck, *The Agrarian Crusade* (New Haven, 1920) largely ignores the territories. John D. Hicks, *The Populist Revolt* (Minneapolis, 1931) is still excellent. Everett Dick, *The Sod-House Frontier, 1854–1890* (New York, 1937) is good for the story of settlement, but Harold E. Briggs, *Frontiers of the Northwest* (New York, 1940) is even better. Bruce E. Nelson, *Land of the Dacotahs* (Minneapolis, 1946) is a well-written journalistic account of various significant events and themes in Dakota history. R. A. Billington, *Westward Expansion* (New York, 1948) and Henry Nash Smith, *Virgin Land* (Cambridge, 1950) were very useful for background material.

Many excellent articles, reprints of documents, biographical sketches, memoirs, and monographs were found in the following: *Collections of the State Historical Society of North Dakota* (7 vols. Bismarck, 1905–25), *Collections of the State Historical Society of South Dakota* (16 vols. Aberdeen and Pierre, 1902–32), *North Dakota Historical Quarterly* (6 vols. Bismarck, 1926–33), *Quarterly Journal of the University of North Dakota* (23 vols. Grand

Forks, 1910–33), and the *University of Nebraska Studies, 23* (1923).

Interviews

The Honorable Thomas Hall, secretary of state of North Dakota, kindly permitted an interview on August 20, 1948, in Bismarck. Mr. Hall knew Alexander McKenzie personally and provided much information on the "Bismarck ring." Russell Reid, superintendent of the State Department of History of North Dakota, Mrs. Florence H. Davis, a pioneer resident of Bismarck, and E. T. Taylor, law librarian for the North Dakota supreme court, provided much valuable information. Interviews with Mrs. Mabelle Patrick and Will G. Robinson of the State Department of History of South Dakota were rewarding and helpful.

Index

Ackerman, A. T., 133

Adams, A. W., 162

Adams, Herbert B., 154

Adams, John, 10, 16

Albright, Samuel J., 46, 48

Apportionment, as issue in the first and second Assemblies, 86, 95

Arizona, Territory of, 18, 27, 60, 67

Arkansas, Territory of, 14

Armstrong, Moses Kimball, 49, 82, 94–6, 101, 114, 130, 142, 174, 206; career of, 76 n., 81 n., 81; supports Todd, 77, 90; and capital location, 84; speaker of the second Assembly, 86; and Negro exclusion bill, 87; secretary of the Peace Commission (1867), 105; president of the Council, sixth Assembly, 112; delegate candidate (1870), 121–2; reelected, 122, 136–7; and railroads, 132–4

Arthur, Chester A.: removes Ordway, 219, 240; removes Campbell, 240

Ash, H. C., 177

Ash, Mrs. H. C., 72

Assembly. See Dakota Territory

Bachelder, George A.: appointed secretary of Dakota Territory, 118; supports Spink, 114; convenes special assembly, 132–3

Bancroft, H. H.: on extralegal government, 152, 156–7; on mining customs, 170

Barnes, A. H., 140

Bartlett, Ara, appointed to the Dakota Supreme Court, 108, 130

Beadle, William Henry Harrison, 124–5, 138; on the 1868 election, 115; appointed surveyor general, Dakota, 119; on Dakota politics and institutions, 123–4, 189–90, 196; and railroads, 134–5; and the 1872 election, 137; career, 167; organizes company, 177; elected superintendent of public in-

struction, 198; and the statehood movement, 198, 200, 230, 244; opposes Ordway, 221; at the 1883 Constitutional Convention, 230; and school lands, 231, 269

Belknap, W. W., 118, 124

Bell, A. J., 74 f., 82

Bemis, Dr., 160

Bénard, Jean Baptiste (de la Harpe), 28

Bennett, Granville G.: appointed to the Dakota Supreme Court, 163; candidate for delegate (1878), 171–3, 180; loses nomination (1880), 196

Benton, Thomas Hart, 13

Berkeley, George, 127

Betts, 87

Big Sioux County, 44

Big Sioux River, 43–4

Billington, Ray A., 148

Bingham and Livingston cases, 185 ff.

Bismarck *Tribune*, 218, 245

Black Hills: petition for cession of, 89; frontier of, 148–76; and the gold rush, 149–50; law and order in, 159 ff.; origin of settlers in, 160–1; election in, 163–5; separatist movement in, 165; effect on territorial politics, 170–1; court system in, 170–2

Blaine, James G., and the 1861 Organic Acts, 62–3

Blair, Frank P., 70

Blair, John I., 130

Bliss, Philemon: appointed to the Dakota Supreme Court, 69–70; career, 69–71; and the 1862 election, 90–2; candidate for delegate, 95–6, 108

Blount, William, governor of the Southwest Territory, 9–10

Bodmer, Carl, 31

Bonesteel, Harvey W., 174

Bon Homme *Citizen*, 206

Bon Homme (D.T.): town of, 30, penitentiary site, 77

293